Lecture Notes in Artificial Intelligence   10523

Subseries of Lecture Notes in Computer Science

More information about this series at http://www.springer.com/series/1244

Thomas Barkowsky · Heather Burte
Christoph Hölscher · Holger Schultheis (Eds.)

Spatial Cognition X

13th Biennial Conference, KogWis 2016
Bremen, Germany, September 26–30, 2016, and
10th International Conference, Spatial Cognition 2016
Philadelphia, PA, USA, August 2–5, 2016
Revised Selected Papers

 Springer

Editors
Thomas Barkowsky (iD)
University of Bremen
Bremen
Germany

Heather Burte (iD)
Tufts University
Medford, MA
USA

Christoph Hölscher
ETH Zurich
Zurich
Switzerland

Holger Schultheis (iD)
University of Bremen
Bremen
Germany

ISSN 0302-9743   ISSN 1611-3349   (electronic)
Lecture Notes in Artificial Intelligence
ISBN 978-3-319-68188-7   ISBN 978-3-319-68189-4   (eBook)
https://doi.org/10.1007/978-3-319-68189-4

Library of Congress Control Number: 2017959593

LNCS Sublibrary: SL7 – Artificial Intelligence

Printed on acid-free paper

This Springer imprint is published by Springer Nature
The registered company is Springer International Publishing AG
The registered company address is: Gewerbestrasse 11, 6330 Cham, Switzerland

Preface

This is the tenth volume of a series of books dedicated to the dissemination of basic research in the interdisciplinary field of spatial cognition. Researchers in spatial cognition investigate the foundations, representations, and processes involved in the acquisition, organization, utilization, and revision of information about spatial environments. These environments can be real or virtual spaces, and research questions and findings even apply to abstract, non-physical realms such as organization structures and formal descriptions. Moreover, both natural and technical cognitive systems are investigated and employed in the diverse subfields of spatial cognition. Thus, research in human spatial cognition often serves as an inspiration for technical solutions, as well as it is supported by the implementation of intelligent procedures in technical devices.

The present volume contains a collection of 11 selected papers that originally were presented at one of the following two conferences focused on spatial cognition research held in 2016: KogWis 2016: Space for Cognition and Spatial Cognition 2016.

KogWis 2016: Space for Cognition was the 13th biennial conference of the German Society for Cognitive Science, which was held September 26–30, 2016, in Bremen, Germany. This conference belongs to a series that in general is open to all research topics pursued in cognitive science; a special emphasis in the 2016 conference, however, was on research on spatial cognition. Three of the papers contained in this volume were originally presented at KogWis 2016.

Spatial Cognition 2016 belongs to a series of biennial international interdisciplinary conferences dedicated to all aspects of intelligent spatial information processing in humans and in technical systems. This conference series was established in 2002. In 2016, the meeting took place August 2–5, 2016, in Philadelphia, USA. Eight papers of the current volume originate from Spatial Cognition 2016.

The selection of contributions to the above conferences – both for oral and poster presentations – was based on extended abstracts submitted by the authors. For the present volume we issued a call for contributions directed to the authors of accepted presentations at one of the conferences. In response to this call we received 20 submissions, which were thoroughly peer-reviewed by three reviewers each. On the basis of the reviewers' assessments, 11 contributions were selected covering a variety of aspects of spatial abilities and skills, findings in human wayfinding and navigation, insights into structures and processes of human spatial memory, as well as technical systems that enable research in virtual environments and simulations of verbally described motion events.

Many people participated in the realization of the present volume. Thus, we would like to thank everybody involved in the organization of KogWis 2016 and Spatial Cognition 2016. We thank all authors for submitting their work to either of the two conferences, as well as for extending their contributions and submitting them for this book. We thank all the reviewers of both conferences and of this volume for their critical assessment and the numerous suggestions that helped us select the best papers and further improve the work of all submitting authors.

Finally, we would like to thank Alfred Hofmann, Anna Kramer, and their team at Springer for their continuing support of our book series.

August 2017

Thomas Barkowsky
Heather Burte
Christoph Hölscher
Holger Schultheis

Organization

KogWis 2016: Space for Cognition (Bremen, Germany)

Chair

Thomas Barkowsky   University of Bremen, Germany

Local Organizing Team

Zoe Falomir Llansola   University of Bremen, Germany
Holger Schultheis   University of Bremen, Germany
Jasper van de Ven   University of Bremen, Germany

Spatial Cognition 2016 (Philadelphia, USA)

Program Chairs

Nora S. Newcombe   Temple University, USA
Daniel R. Montello   UC Santa Barbara, USA
Christoph Hölscher   ETH Zurich, Switzerland
Mary Hegarty   UC Santa Barbara, USA

Submission Chair

Heather Burte   Tufts University, USA

Local Planning Chair

Steven M. Weisberg   University of Pennsylvania, USA

Review Committee for this Volume

Ahmed Loai Ali
Elena Andonova
Marios Avraamides
Sven Bertel
Michela Bertolotto
Stefano Borgo
Simon Büchner
Christophe Claramunt
Michel Denis
Matt Duckham
Max Egenhofer
Russell Epstein

Sara Irina Fabrikant
Zoe Falomir Llansola
Evelyn Ferstl
Paolo Fogliaroni
Christian Freksa
Antony Galton
Klaus Gramann
Stephen Hirtle
Toru Ishikawa
Georg Jahn
Peter Kiefer
Werner Kuhn

Antonio Lieto
Gérard Ligozat
Andrew Lovett
Tobias Meilinger
Daniel R. Montello
Ana-Maria Olteteanu
Eric Pederson
Marco Ragni
Terry Regier
Kai-Florian Richter
Victor Schinazi
Ute Schmid

Thomas Shipley
Holly Taylor
Thora Tenbrink
Sabine Timpf
Nico van de Weghe
Constanze C. Vorwerg
Jan Oliver Wallgrün
Frances Wang
Steven Weisberg
Stephan Winter
Stefan Woelfl
Wai Yeap

Contents

Systems and Simulations

Spatial Ability

Individual and Gender Differences in Spatial Ability and Three Forms of Engineering Self-efficacy

Meredith Minear[1]([✉]) [iD], Leonard Lutz[2] [iD], Nathan Clements[3] [iD], and Mikaela Cowen[1] [iD]

[1] Department of Psychology, University of Wyoming, Laramie, WY, USA
{mminear2,mcowen}@uwyo.edu
[2] Engineering and Applied Science, University of Wyoming, Laramie, WY, USA
len.lutz@uwyo.edu
[3] Department of Mathematics, University of Wyoming, Laramie, WY, USA
nclements@uwyo.edu

Abstract. In this study, we explored the relationship between two predictors of engineering success: spatial ability and self-efficacy. Spatial ability, especially mental rotation, has been linked to successful performance in engineering. Self-efficacy is an individual's belief in his or her ability to perform successfully [1] and has received increased attention as a predictor of persistence in STEM fields. We examined the possible relationships between mental rotation, spatial visualization, engineering self-efficacy, and self-efficacy for two subsets of skills important in engineering majors: tinkering and design. Tinkering refers to the hands-on ability to construct, take apart, modify, and repair mechanical devices while design refers to the ability to develop a system, component or set of processes to solve a specific problem. We also investigated the possible role of previous design or tinkering related experience such as certain hands-on hobbies. We found spatial ability was correlated with multiple forms of engineering self-efficacy in less experienced, but not more experienced engineering students. Tinkering and design related hobbies were not related to spatial ability, but were related to tinkering and design self-efficacy. They also predicted performance on a measure of mechanical reasoning. Gender differences in engineering students on spatial ability and general engineering self-efficacy were small. The largest and most consistent gender differences were on tinkering-related experience and tinkering self-efficacy, although the latter appeared to be mitigated by the amount of engineering experience. Individual differences in tinkering-related experience is an understudied possible source of individual and gender differences in STEM fields such as engineering.

Keywords: Spatial ability · Engineering · Self-efficacy · Tinkering

1 Introduction

The past three decades have seen strong interest in increasing undergraduate recruitment and retention in the engineering fields, especially in raising the participation of women and minority students who remain underrepresented in engineering [2]. Multiple factors affecting academic performance and retention in engineering have been identified. These

© Springer International Publishing AG 2017
T. Barkowsky et al. (Eds.): KogWis/Spatial Cognition 2016, LNAI 10523, pp. 3–18, 2017.
https://doi.org/10.1007/978-3-319-68189-4_1

range from individual differences in cognitive abilities [3], social beliefs [4], and precollege experiences [5] to larger institutional factors such as interaction with instructors, engineering culture, and a feeling of belonging [6]. In this paper, we focus on the relationship between two demonstrated correlates of engineering success, spatial ability and self-efficacy. We also examine how early certain spatial experiences previously identified as contributing to engineering readiness are predictive of both performance on spatial tasks and different forms of engineering self-efficacy.

1.1 Spatial Ability

Spatial ability generally refers to an individual's capacity to visualize, manipulate and reason about the spatial aspects of objects or environments [7]. Spatial visualization, the ability to create a mental representation and perform multistep processing of spatial information, and mental rotation, the ability to mentally rotate two and three dimensional figures, have been shown to be especially related to success in engineering courses [3, 8]. Interventions that identify engineering students weak in spatial ability and provide additional spatial training have shown considerable promise in improving course performance [9, 10] and retention [11]. Many studies have reported a gender difference in spatial performance, especially in mental rotation [12, 13]. This has been proposed as a possible source of the gender disparity seen in engineering where women only make up approximately 20% of university degrees [2]. However, it is not clear that gender differences in spatial ability translate into a gender difference in engineering course performance [14].

1.2 Self-efficacy

Self-efficacy is defined as "beliefs in one's capabilities to organize and execute the courses of action required to produce given attainments" [15]. Self-efficacy is not only the result of one's direct success or failure in a particular domain, but can also be influenced by vicarious experiences, social beliefs, and physiological states. Self-efficacy has been tied to academic and career pursuits, and those who have high self-efficacy on a particular task are more likely to persist and perform well [16]. Academic self-efficacy, a person's belief in their ability to perform an academic task, has been found to be positively related to academic performance and persistence [17, 18]. For example, math self-efficacy, an individual's belief in his or her mathematical competence, predicts students' likelihood of enrolling in STEM fields [19]. Gender differences in math self-efficacy [20–22] have been reported, and some have speculated that this difference in which females may underestimate their math ability due to negative stereotypes about female math competence could also contribute to the underrepresentation of women in STEM fields [23].

Self-efficacy has also become an important focus of research in engineering education. In the past 30 years, multiple measures of general engineering self-efficacy have been developed. These consist of a students' overall self-efficacy in engineering course performance and completion of the engineering degree [5, 24–26]. Similar to other academic fields, self-efficacy has been shown to be positively related to academic performance [27] and persistence in the engineering major [28, 29]. More recently, attention has turned to developing more specific self-efficacy measures, especially those capturing the hands-on skills required in engineering coursework and careers [30–32].

Two areas of growing importance are self-efficacy in engineering design and in tinkering. Design, in the context of engineering, refers to the ability to develop a system, component or set of processes to solve a specific problem [31]. This is often included as a professional standard for engineering programs [33]. Tinkering refers to the hands-on ability to construct, take apart, modify, and repair mechanical devices [30]. Tinkering has been rated as an important engineering characteristic by practicing engineers, although it has not been officially incorporated into the standards for engineering education in the same way design has [34]. The research on gender differences in engineering self-efficacy is mixed, with some studies finding men reporting greater self-efficacy than women [24, 35], while other studies have found no gender differences [32, 36, 37].

1.3 Spatial Experience

Spatial ability has been shown to be important in the successful pursuit of STEM careers [38, 39]. One source of individual differences in spatial ability may lie in differences in spatial activities, such as playing sports or hobbies that involve spatial processing [40, 41]. Engineering self-efficacy has also been linked to hobbies involving spatial processing as well as hands-on tinkering and design-related elements [5]. One possible source of overlap between spatial ability and engineering self-efficacy could be spatially based hobbies and experiences, especially those involving tinkering or design-like elements. As discussed above, a key contributor to the development of self-efficacy is mastery experience. However, to date there is little to no research on the relationship between spatial ability, spatial experience and engineering self-efficacy.

1.4 Study Goals

Therefore, the present research had three primary questions (1) What is the relationship between spatial ability and various forms of engineering self-efficacy? Do students with better spatial performance have higher overall self-efficacy, or is spatial ability more predictive of specific forms of self-efficacy such as design and tinkering skills? (2) Does experience in tinkering and design-related hobbies predict spatial ability as well as self-efficacy in engineering? (3) Are there gender differences in tinkering and design-based self-efficacy measures and if so, are they related to gender differences in spatial ability and tinkering/design-related experiences?

We report the results of two studies of engineering students using three measures of engineering self-efficacy, two measures of spatial ability, and retrospective reports of prior engagement in tinkering and design-related hobbies. We also included a measure of mathematical self-efficacy because of its importance in STEM fields, but also because it captures a skill set that is important for engineering, but is not engineering specific. In study one, we recruited engineering majors from all years. In study two, we focused on engineering freshmen.

2   Study One

In our first study, we tested engineering students from multiple years who were enrolled in math courses (Algebra through the Calculus sequence), using a measure of mental rotation commonly employed to assess spatial ability in engineers as well as a measure of spatial visualization involving cross-sections. We also measured students' engineering and mathematical self-efficacy and retrospective reports of tinkering/design-related hobbies.

2.1   Method

Participants.   Three hundred and ten engineering students, 252 male (mean age: 20.0, $SD = 3.8$) and 58 female (mean age: 20.3, $SD = 6.1$) from the University of Wyoming participated. 141 students (28 female) described themselves as completing 24 college credits or less (mean age: 18.2, $SD = .61$) and 169 students (30 female) who had completed more than 24 credits (mean age: 21.6, $SD = 5.4$). The majority of our participants identified themselves as majoring in either mechanical (32.9%) or petroleum engineering (20%), and the rest were distributed among architectural (3.2%), chemical (10%), civil (7.1%), computer (6.8%), electrical (7.4%), energy (4.8), and general engineering (6.1%).

Materials

The Revised Purdue Visualization of Rotations Test.   The PSVT-R is a 30-item multiple choice measure of mental rotation consisting of 13 symmetrical and 17 asymmetrical figures of 3-D objects drawn in a 2-D isometric format [42]. For each test item, participants see an object portrayed in two different orientations. A second object is shown in the first orientation, and then participants are asked to rotate this object to match the second orientation and to choose this view of the object from 5 possibilities. An example item is shown in Fig. 1a.

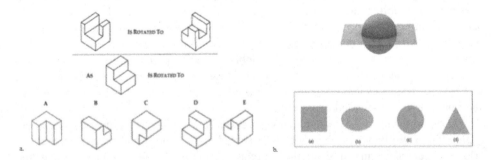

Fig. 1.   a. Example item for the PSVT-R b. Example item from the SBST

Santa Barbara Solids Test.   The SBST is a recently developed 30-item multiple choice test which measures individual differences in the ability to identify the two-dimensional cross section of a three- dimensional geometric solid [43]. An example is shown in Fig. 1b.

Engineering Self-efficacy Measures. We used three short engineering self-efficacy surveys of General Engineering, Tinkering Skills and Engineering Design self-efficacy, developed by Mamaril [44]. All three scales used a 6-point Likert scale ranging from 1 = completely uncertain to 6 = completely certain. The General Engineering measure consisted of 6 items asking students to rate their certainty in being able to do well in their engineering courses. An example item is "I can do an excellent job on engineering-related problems and tasks assigned this semester." This measure has a range from 6 to 36. Tinkering Skills self-efficacy was measured by 5 items describing the ability to build, fix and take apart devices. An example item is "I can manipulate components and devices." Scores range from 5 to 30. The Engineering Design self-efficacy survey had 4 items assessing students' certainty in their ability to recognize, evaluate and solve design problems. An example item is "I can develop design solutions." Scores range from 4 to 24.

Math Self-efficacy. We used the math self-efficacy subscale drawn from the Mathematics Self-Efficacy and Anxiety Questionnaire [45]. The MSEAQ is a 29-item measure of students' mathematical self-efficacy and anxiety. 14 items are used to measure mathematical self-efficacy, both inside and outside the classroom. Participants are asked to rate how frequently each item describes their feelings or beliefs on a 5-point Likert type scale ranging from 1 (Never) to 5 (Usually). Math self-efficacy scores can range from 14–70.

Tinkering and Design Experiences. In order to compute a Tinkering/Design Experience score, we drew 14 items from the 81-item spatial experience measure developed by Newcombe, Bandura and Taylor [42]. These items described hobbies involving design or manipulation such as building models or sketching plans. The majority of the excluded items focus on spatial processing in the context of physical activities such as sports or dance. Participants rate how often they engaged in the activity using a 6-item Likert scale with 1 indicating "never participated" to 6 "participated more than once a week". Scores ranged from 14 to 84. The specific items used are listed in the appendix.

Demographic Information. We also asked participants to complete the following demographic items: gender, age, major, number of college credits completed, parents' education, and high school GPA.

Procedure. The spatial measures and questionnaires were administered on-line as a three-part class assignment in the participants' respective mathematics or engineering course. The measures were given in the following order: the PSVT-R, the SBST, and finally the self-efficacy measures in the following order (General Engineering, Tinkering Skills, Engineering Design and the MSEAQ) and finally the tinkering and design experience questions followed by the demographics survey. At the end of the measures, students were provided with an online consent document and given the option to consent to having their responses on the assignment to be used for research purposes, or to withhold their consent with no effect on their course participation.

2.2 Results

The descriptive results for our measures are presented in Table 1.

Table 1. Descriptive statistics for all dependent measures

Measure	Mean	SD	Skew	Kurtosis	Reliability	Range
PSVT-R	21.3	5.4	−.56	−.19	.84	5–30
SBST	20.0	6.5	−.98	.14	.85	2–29
General SE	30.8	4.1	−1.3	4.8	.92	6–36
Tinkering SE	24.1	4.6	−.70	.41	.88	10–30
Design SE	18.3	4.0	−.79	.72	.95	4–24
Math SE	56.3	8.4	−.25	−.57	.92	31–70
T/D Exp.	24.9	9.2	1.2	2.0	.85	13–68

Relationships Between Spatial Ability, Self-efficacy and Experience. We initially tested the possible relationships between our spatial measures, engineering self-efficacies and tinkering/design experience using simple correlation. These data are presented in Table 2. We also tested for relationships between these measures and the demographic information we collected: mother and father's level of education, high school GPA and credits completed. We only found significant correlations between the number of college credits completed and tinkering self-efficacy, $r(305) = .12, p = .03$, design self-efficacy, $r(305) = .13, p = .02$, and tinkering/design experience $r(305) = .12, p = .04$. Although these correlations are quite small, this suggested that there might be some differences between engineering students in the early versus later states of their coursework.

Table 2. Correlations between all dependent measures utilizing the full sample (N = 310).

	PSVT-R	SBST	General SE	Tinkering SE	Design SE	Math SE
PSVT-R						
SBST	.56**					
General SE	.19**	.16**				
Tinkering SE	.13**	.15**	.35**			
Design SE	.09	.11	.32**	.69**		
Math SE	.21**	.16**	.55**	.22**	.26**	
T/D Exp.	.04	.05	.09	.49**	.38**	.17**

*p < .05, **p < .01

We chose to further investigate this possibility by creating a variable that distinguished between early engineering students who were very likely still in their first year and students who had completed their first year and beyond. To do this, we divided the students into two groups, first year engineering versus post first-year engineering students, using the self-reported course credits. The first group had 24 credits or less, while the second group had more than 24 credits. We reran the correlations reported above in each sample and found that while the correlations between the two spatial measures and between the different self-efficacies measures were the same in the two groups, the relationships between our spatial measures and the various self-efficacies were only significant in our less experienced sample (see Table 3). These relationships were not significant in students with more than a year's college experience (see Table 4). However, in each sample there was a lack of a correlation between spatial ability and tinkering/design (T/D) experience, and fairly strong relationships between T/D experience and both tinkering and design self-efficacies.

Table 3. Correlations computed using the sample consisting of only first year students (N = 141)

	PSVT-R	SBST	General SE	Tinkering SE	Design SE	Math SE
PSVT-R						
SBST	.56**					
General SE	.27**	.18*				
Tinkering SE	.21**	.23**	.38**			
Design SE	.14	.11	.35**	.68**		
Math SE	.28**	.24**	.50**	.26**	.26**	
T/D Exp.	.06	.15	.09	.46**	.36**	.13

*$p < .05$, **$p < .01$

Table 4. Correlations computed using the sample with more than 24 college credits (N = 169)

	PSVT-R	SBST	General SE	Tinkering SE	Design SE	Math SE
PSVT-R						
SBST	.56**					
General SE	.11	.15				
Tinkering SE	.07	.08	.33**			
Design SE	.05	.11	.30**	.70**		
Math SE	.13	.12	.60**	.24**	.25**	
T/D Exp.	.04	.05	.11	.51**	.40**	.24*

*$p < .05$, **$p < .01$

Gender and Engineering Experience. Given the above differences in more versus less experienced student samples, we decided to include this variable when testing for gender differences and to test for a possible gender by experience interaction with engineering experience as operationalized above as first year v. more advanced student. To do this, we used a MANOVA with our spatial, self-efficacy and tinkering/design experience measures as dependent variables and gender and engineering experience (as described above) as our independent variables. All the multivariate tests were significant, Gender $F (7, 299) = 5.5$, $p < .002$, $\eta_p^2 = .10$, Engineering Experience $F (7,$

299) $= 2.8$, $p < .01$, $\eta_p^2 = .06$ and the interaction between Gender and Engineering Experience $F\,(7, 299) = 2.2$, $p < .05$ $\eta_p^2 = .05$. Turning to the task specific ANOVAs, for Gender, significant group differences were present for the PSVT-R, $F\,(1, 305) = 4.2$, $p < .05$, $\eta_p^2 = .01$, tinkering self-efficacy, $F\,(1, 305) = 24.8$, $p < .001$, $\eta_p^2 = .08$, and tinkering/design experience, $F\,(1, 305) = 16.3$, $p < .\,001$ $\eta_p^2 = .05$. There were no significant gender differences in SBST, mathematical, general engineering or design self-efficacy. Means and standard deviations for both genders are shown in Table 5. For Engineering Experience, the only significant effects were for tinkering self-efficacy, $F\,(1, 305) = 12.2$, $p < .001$, $\eta_p^2 = .04$ and design self-efficacy, $F\,(1, 305) = 5.3$, $p < 05$, $\eta_p^2 = .02$, with increased self-efficacy for students with more experience.

Table 5. Means and standard deviations for all measures broken down by gender.

	Male mean (SD)	Female mean (SD)
PSVT-R	21.6 (5.6)	20.1 (4.6)
SBST	21.2 (6.5)	19.7 (6.5)
General SE	31.0 (4.2)	30.0 (3.8)
Tinkering SE	24.7 (4.3)	21.6 (4.8)
Design SE	18.5 (3.9)	17.5 (4.5)
Math SE	56.4 (8.5)	56.2 (8.4)
T/D Exp.	25.9 (9.4)	20.6 (6.8)

The only significant Gender × Experience interaction was seen for tinkering self-efficacy, with a large gender difference in favor of males in the first year of engineering that was greatly reduced in more experienced students, $F\,(1, 305) = 10.1$, $p < .01$, $\eta_p^2 = .03$. This was due to a significant increase in tinkering self-efficacy in female students from first year to later years, $t\,(56) = -3.7$, $p < .001$, while tinkering self-efficacy did not change for male students, $t\,(250) = -.34$, $p = .73$. These data are shown in Fig. 2.

3   Study Two

In our first study, we found spatial ability to be correlated with engineering self-efficacy in early stage engineering students. In our second study, we collected a similar set of data from students enrolled in a freshmen engineering seminar rather than basing our categorization on number of credits. This allowed us the opportunity to replicate the study one finding. We also found in study one that tinkering/design experience was unrelated to our spatial visualization measures. We wished to test whether a more applied spatial reasoning task would be related to tinkering/design experience. Therefore, we replaced the cross-sections task (SBST) used in study one with the Mechanical Reasoning Test as an engineering performance-based measure. This gave us the opportunity to test the extent to which spatial ability and tinkering/design experience can predict a measure of engineering performance.

3.1   Method

Participants. 142 Engineering freshmen (20 female) were recruited from a first year engineering seminar at the University of Wyoming. In this sample, 61.3% of our participants were in the mechanical engineering program, 17.6% in electrical engineering, 9.9% were undeclared engineering, 5.6% were in energy, 3.5% in chemical, 1.4% in petroleum and 0.7% in civil engineering. The descriptive statistics for all measures are shown in Table 6.

Table 6. Descriptive statistics for all measures

Measure	Mean	SD	Skew	Kurtosis	Reliability	Range
PSVT-R	22.1	5.7	−.94	.37	.86	4–30
MR	36.1	5.8	−1.0	.87	.84	18–44
General SE	31.0	4.8	−2.7	11.6	.95	6–36
Tinkering SE	25.0	4.7	−1.5	3.6	.92	5–30
Design SE	19.1	3.7	−1.1	1.9	.95	4–24
Math SE	56.8	8.5	−.29	−.62	.94	34–80
T/D Exp.	18.9	8.3	.97	1.0	.85	0–46

Materials and Procedure. We used the same materials and procedure as study one with the exception that we replaced the cross-sections task with the Mechanical Reasoning (MR) subtest of the Differential Aptitude Tests [46]. This test contains 45 pictorial items of various mechanical devices consisting of levers, gears and pulleys. Participants were asked to make judgments that required visualizing the effect of the

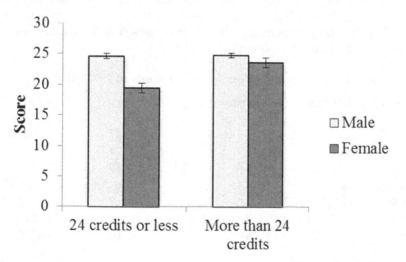

Fig. 2. The gender difference in tinkering self-efficacy for early engineering students (24 credits or less) compared to students with more university experience (more than 24 credits). Bars indicate standard error.

system in motion. Such tests are frequently used in the hiring process for a number of jobs including engineering.

3.2 Results

We examined the correlations between our dependent measures (see Table 7). The relationships between the PSVT-R and self-efficacy measures were similar to those seen in our first year sample in Study One. However, in this sample, the correlation with general engineering self-efficacy was weaker and did not reach significance, while the correlation with design self-efficacy was significant.

Table 7. Correlations between all dependent measures

	PSVT-R	MR	General SE	Tinkering SE	Design SE	Math SE
PSVT-R						
MR	.73**					
General SE	.14	.09				
Tinkering SE	.24**	.36**	.36**			
Design SE	.17*	.39**	.39**	.69**		
Math SE	.24**	.29**	.40**	.30**	.33**	
T/D Exp.	.07	.22**	−.13	.45**	.36**	.11

*$p < .05$, **$p < .01$*

Gender Differences. We did test to see if these data would produce a similar pattern of gender differences although with caution as we only had 20 female students. We did again observe significantly higher scores for male students for both tinkering self-efficacy and tinkering/design experience. There were no gender differences for any of our other measures. These data are shown in Table 8.

Table 8. The full results for gender based comparisons for all measures.

	Male mean (SD)	Female mean (SD)	t	p	95% CI
PSVT-R	22.2 (5.6)	21.5 (6.7)	.56	.57	[−1.9, 3.5]
MR	36.3 (5.8)	34.7 (5.7)	1.2	.24	[−1.1, 4.4]
General SE	30.9 (4.8)	31.1 (5.0)	−.14	.89	[−2.5, 2.1]
Tinkering SE	25.4 (4.7)	22.6 (4.4)	2.5	.01*	[.62, 5.0]
Design SE	19.2 (3.8)	18.8 (3.5)	.50	.62	[−1.3, 2.2]
Math SE	57.0 (8.5)	55.1 (8.8)	.93	.35	[−2.2, 6.0]
T/D Exp.	19.6 (8.5)	14.2 (4.6)	2.7	.007*	[1.5, 9.4]

Predicting Individual Differences in Mechanical Reasoning. Finally, we tested the extent to which mental rotation, self-efficacy and tinkering/design experience could predict individual differences in mechanical reasoning using stepwise regression. Only the PSVT-R and tinkering/design experience were significant unique predictors of mechanical reasoning performance. These results are summarized in Table 9. These results were unchanged when omitting the small number of female students in the sample. There were not enough female students to run this analysis separately.

Table 9. Summary of regression results for predicting mechanical reasoning using mental rotation and tinkering design experience.

$F(1, 139) = 146.3\, p < .001\, R^2 = .51$					$F(2, 138) = 81.2\, p < .001\, R^2 = .54$			
Variable	B	SE	95% CI	β	B	SE	95% CI	β
PSVT-R	.72	.06	[.60, .83]	.70	.70	.06	[.60, .82]	.70
T/D Exp.					.11	.04	[.04, .19]	.17

4 Discussion

We will now discuss the three major results of this work. The first was that we found spatial ability to be weakly correlated with our three different forms of engineering self-efficacy, but only in our early stage engineering student samples. When sampling students who were past their first year, these relationships were no longer significant. One possibility is that inexperienced students base their self-efficacy more on general cognitive abilities such as mental rotation, but as students continue in their engineering program, they gain more engineering related experience through course work and internships so that their self-efficacy may be based more on direct experience. Another possibility is that students' spatial abilities also change or become more developed with engineering experience although we did not observe experience related differences in our dataset. However, as the data are cross-sectional, it is also possible that selective attrition could contribute to the differences seen between early and more experienced engineering students. Students who enter the program lower in self-efficacy may be at greater risk of performing poorly and then dropping out of the program.

Our second major finding was that tinkering and design-related hobbies were not related to either mental rotation or the spatial visualization of cross-sections in our engineering samples. Instead, tinkering and design experience did predict additional variance in performance on a measure of mechanical reasoning beyond that of mental rotation. Tinkering and design experience was also consistently related to tinkering and design self-efficacy in both first year and more advanced students, but it was not related to general engineering self-efficacy.

Our third significant result was that our largest and most consistent gender differences were in tinkering self-efficacy and tinkering/design experience. The gender difference in tinkering self-efficacy was greatly reduced in our more experienced engineering sample due to increases in female self-efficacy, while male self-efficacy did not change. One possibility is that that female students with less tinkering self-efficacy are more likely to drop out of the major. However, it is also possible that the female students who come to the engineering major with lower tinkering self-efficacy than the average male student then develop greater tinkering self-efficacy in manipulating and working with devices due to their engineering course work and internship experiences. That there are persistent gender differences in the amount of self-reported tinkering/design experience may not be too surprising given that most of the activities that we chose as tinkering or design related are stereotypically male [41]. However, so is majoring in engineering. One possibility we had considered before collecting these data is that female engineering students may engage in similar levels of tinkering or design related hobbies as their male counterparts in spite of cultural gender stereotypes. This does not appear to be the case. However, these findings need to be viewed with caution given our relatively small sample of females in both studies. Another limitation is that we drew our tinkering/ design experiences from an established, but older measure of spatial activities [41]. There may be other more feminine or gender neural activities that are more likely to be experienced by female students and possibly contribute to their tinkering self-efficacy as well as persistence in the engineering major.

Multiple factors have been proposed as contributing to the lack of gender parity in fields such as engineering. Stereotype threat is an anxiety-based decrement in perform-ance resulting from the fear that poor performance will confirm a negative stereotype about a group the tester belongs to [47]. Stereotype threat has been shown to contribute to gender differences in math and spatial performance [48]. Given the strong identifi-cation of the tinkering/design with masculinity, perhaps female students underestimated their tinkering self-efficacy in line with gender stereotypes. However, we do not view this as a likely explanation for two reasons. The first is that there is evidence that females in STEM actually have weaker gender related biases than non-STEM female students [49]. There is also evidence that females such as engineering students who have chosen a gender non-conforming field can actually experience a stereotype boost or improved performance when negative gender comparisons are made [50]. Stereotype threat would also not explain the lack of significant gender differences in our spatial tasks as well as in general engineering and math self-efficacies.

The lack of a gender difference in general engineering self-efficacy is consistent with prior reports [36, 37]. However, to date, only one other study has compared male and female students' tinkering self-efficacy, and they reported no gender or year level differ-ences [44]. Future work both with larger samples of female students and longitudinal measurement will be necessary, not only to disambiguate the possible reasons for the changes seen in female levels of tinkering self-efficacy from early to later stages in the engineering major, but also to determine whether tinkering self-efficacy or changes in tinkering self-efficacy predict achievement and retention in engineering for both female and male students.

Tinkering is garnering attention in the educational community, especially in the context of what has been termed the Maker Movement, a grassroots movement to engage people in creative, hands on tinkering and design activities similar to those measured in our study [51]. After-school experiences incorporating making activities show promise in helping to get students interested in STEM fields [52]. However, some feel that tink-erers may be turned off by the highly structured nature of many STEM classrooms, and that tinkering is frequently undervalued in more formal educational settings [53]. This may help explain why Mamaril [44] found a negative relationship between tinkering self-efficacy and core engineering GPA. Our work, while preliminary, points to a skill set developed from tinkering and design based experiences that appears to be (1) separable from spatial ability, (2) an independent contributor to mechanical reasoning performance and (3) another variable in which there are possible gender differences in incoming engineering students. The potential benefits of developing tinkering skills in addition to interventions such as training spatial ability need to be more intensively examined.

Acknowledgments. This work was supported by a Faculty in Aid Grant from the University of Wyoming awarded to Drs. Minear and Clement.

Appendix

Hand or Machine Sewing Requiring Tailoring (e.g., collars, cuffs, lining), Building Model Trains or Racing Car Sets, Building Go-Carts or Soapbox Cars, Building Model Planes, Mechanical Drawing, Car Repair—complex engine work (e.g. brakes), Electrical Repairs—relay or solid-state circuitry, Making or Fixing Radios, Stereos, Writing computer code, Plumbing, Carpentry, Sketching Clothes Designs, Sketching Auto Designs, Sketching House Plans.

References

1. Bandura, A.: Self-efficacy: toward a unifying theory of behavioral change. Psychol. Rev. **84**, 191–215 (1977)
2. National Science Board: Science and Engineering Indicators 2016. National Science Foundation (NSB-2016-1), Arlington (2016)
3. Ilsi, S., Linn, M.C., Bell, J.E.: The role of spatial reasoning in engineering and the design of spatial instruction. J. Eng. Educ. **86**, 151–158 (1997)
4. Lent, R.W., Sheu, H.-B., Singley, D., Schmidt, J.A., Schmidt, L.C., Gloster, C.S.: Longitudinal relations of self-efficacy to outcome expectations, interests, and major choice goals in engineering students. J. Vocat. Behav. **73**, 328–335 (2008). https://doi.org/10.1016/j.jvb.2008.07.005
5. Fantz, T.D., Siller, T.J., DeMiranda, M.A.: Pre-collegiate factors influencing the self-efficacy of engineering students. J. Eng. Educ. **100**(3), 604–623 (2011)
6. Marra, R., Rodgers, K., Shen, D., Bogue, B.: Leaving engineering: a multi-year single institution study. J. Eng. Educ. **101**(1), 6–27 (2012)
7. Casey, B.M.: Individual and group differences in spatial ability. In: Waller, D., Nadel, L. (eds.) Handbook of Spatial Cognition, pp. 117–134. APA Books, Washington, DC (2012)
8. Hamlin, A.J., Boersma, N., Sorby, S.: Do spatial abilities impact the learning of 3-D solid modeling software? In: Proceedings of the 2006 ASEE Annual Conference and Expo, Chicago, IL (2006)
9. Baartmans, B.J., Sorby, S.A.: Introduction to 3-D Spatial Visualization. Prentice Hall, Englewood Cliffs (1996)
10. Sorby, S.A., Baartmans, B.J.: The development and assessment of a course for enhancing the 3-D spatial visualization skills of first year engineering students. J. Eng. Educ. **89**(3), 301–307 (2000)

11. Sorby, S.: Developing 3D spatial skills for engineering students. Australas. Assoc. Eng. Educ. **13**, 1–11 (2007)
12. Linn, M.C., Petersen, A.C.: Emergence and characterization of sex differences in spatial ability: a meta-analysis. Child Dev. **56**, 1479–1498 (1985)
13. Voyer, D., Voyer, S., Bryden, M.P.: Magnitude of sex differences in spatial abilities: a meta-analysis and consideration of critical variables. Psychol. Bull. **117**(2), 250 (1995)
14. Peters, M., Chisholm, P., Laeng, B.: Spatial ability, student gender, and academic performance. J. Eng. Educ. **84**, 69–73 (1995). https://doi.org/10.1002/j.2168-9830.1995.tb00148.x
15. Bandura, A.: Self-efficacy: The Exercise of Control. W.H. Freeman and Company, New York (1997)
16. Bandura, A., Barbaranelli, C., Caprara, G.V., Pastorelli, C.: Self-efficacy beliefs as shapers of children's aspirations and career trajectories. Child Dev. **72**(1), 187–206 (2001)
17. MacPhee, D., Farro, S., Canetto, S.S.: Academic self-efficacy and performance of underrepresented STEM majors: gender, ethnic, and social class patterns. Anal. Soc. Issues Public Policy **13**(1), 347–369 (2013). https://doi.org/10.1111/asap.12033
18. Correll, S.J.: Gender and the career choice process: the role of biased self-assessments. Am. J. Sociol. **106**(6), 1691–1730 (2001)
19. Sax, L.J., Kanny, M.A., Riggers-Piehl, T.A., Whang, H., Paulson, L.N.: "But I'm Not Good at Math": the changing salience of mathematical self-concept in shaping women's and men's STEM aspirations. Res. High. Educ. **56**(8), 813–842 (2015)
20. Else-Quest, N.M., Hyde, J.S., Linn, M.C.: Cross-national patterns of gender differences in mathematics: a meta-analysis. Psychol. Bull. **136**(1), 103 (2010)
21. Gwilliam, L.R., Betz, N.E.: Validity of measures of math- and science-related self-efficacy for African Americans and European Americans. J. Career Assess. **9**, 261–281 (2001)
22. Pajares, F.: Gender differences in mathematics self-efficacy beliefs. In: Gallagher, A.M., Kaufman, J.C. (eds.) Gender Differences in Mathematics: An Integrative Psychological Approach, pp. 294–315. Cambridge University Press, Boston (2005)
23. Betz, N.E., Hackett, G.: The relationship of mathematics self-efficacy expectations to the selection of science-based college majors. J. Vocat. Psychol. **23**(3), 329–345 (1983)
24. Jones, B.D., Paretti, M.C., Hein, S.F., Knott, T.W.: An analysis of motivation constructs with first-year engineering students: relationships among expectancies, values, achievement, and career plans. J. Eng. Educ. **99**, 319–336 (2010). https://doi.org/10.1002/j.2168-9830.2010.tb01066.x
25. Lent, R.W., Brown, S.D., Larkin, K.C.: Relation of self-efficacy expectations to academic achievement and persistence. J. Couns. Psychol. **31**, 356–362 (1984). https://doi.org/10.1037//0022-0167.31.3.356
26. Marra, R.M., Bogue, B.: Women engineering students' self-efficacy: a longitudinal multi-institution study. In: Proceedings of the 2006 Women in Engineering Programs and Advocates Network, Pittsburgh, Pennsylvania (2006)
27. Purzer, S.: The relationship between team discourse, self-efficacy and individual achievement: a sequential mixed-methods study. J. Eng. Educ. **100**(4), 655–679 (2011)
28. Marra, R., Bogue, B., Rodgers, K., Shen, D.: Self-efficacy of women engineering students? Three years of data at U.S. institutions. In: Proceedings of the 2007 ASEE Annual Conference and Exposition, Honolulu, HI (2007)
29. Pajares, F.: Self-efficacy beliefs in academic settings. Rev. Educ. Res. **66**(4), 543–578 (1996)
30. Baker, D., Krause, S., Purzer, S.Y.: Developing an instrument to measure tinkering and technical self-efficacy in engineering. In: 2008 ASEE Annual Conference and Exposition (2008)

31. Carberry, A.R., Lee, H.S., Ohland, M.W.: Measuring engineering design self-efficacy. J. Eng. Educ. **99**(1), 71–79 (2010)
32. Mamaril, N.A., Usher, E.L., Li, C.R., Economy, D.R., Kennedy, M.S.: Measuring undergraduate students' engineering self-efficacy: a scale validation. J. Eng. Educ. **105**, 366–395 (2016)
33. Accreditation Board for Engineering and Technology: Criteria for accrediting engineering programs, 20 October 2015. http://www.abet.org/wp-content/uploads/2015/05/E001-15-16-EAC-Criteria-03-10-15.pdf
34. Baker, D., Krause, S.: Do tinkering and technical activities connect engineering education standards with the engineering profession in today's world? In: American Society for Engineering Education Annual Conference and Exposition, Honolulu, Hawaii (2007)
35. Vogt, C.M., Hocevar, D., Hagedorn, L.S.: A social cognitive construct validation: determining women's and men's success in engineering programs. J. High. Educ. **78**, 337–364 (2007). https://doi.org/10.1353/jhe.2007.0019
36. Concannon, J.P., Barrow, L.H.: A cross-sectional study of freshmen engineering majors' self-efficacy. In: Proceedings of the American Society for Engineering Education 2008 Annual Conference and Exhibition, Pittsburgh, Pennsylvania (2008)
37. Hutchinson, M., Follman, D., Sumpter, M., Bodner, G.: Factors influencing the self-efficacy beliefs of first year engineering students. J. Eng. Educ. **95**(1), 39–47 (2006)
38. Lubinski, D.: Spatial ability and STEM: a sleeping giant for talent identification and development. Pers. Individ. Differ. **49**, 344–351 (2010)
39. Shea, D.L., Lubinski, D., Benbow, C.P.: Importance of assessing spatial ability in intellectually talented young adolescents: a 20-year longitudinal study. J. Educ. Psychol. **93**, 604–614 (2001)
40. Baenninger, M., Newcombe, N.: The role of experience in spatial test performance: a meta-analysis. Sex Roles **20**(5/6), 327–344 (1989)
41. Newcombe, N., Bandura, M.M., Taylor, D.G.: Sex differences in spatial ability and spatial activities. Sex Roles **9**, 377–386 (1983)
42. Yoon, S.Y.: Revised Purdue Spatial Visualization Test: Visualization of Rotations (Revised PSVT:R) [Psychometric Instrument] (2011)
43. Cohen, C.A., Hegarty, M.: Inferring cross sections of 3D objects: a new spatial thinking test. Learn. Individ. Diff. **22**, 868–874 (2012)
44. Mamaril, N.J.: Measuring undergraduate students engineering self-efficacy: a scale validation study. University of Kentucky (2014)
45. May, D.K.: Mathematics self-efficacy and anxiety questionnaire. Unpublished doctoral dissertation, University of Georgia, Athens, USA (2009)
46. Bennett, G.K., Seashore, H.G., Wesman, A.G.: Differential Aptitude Tests, 5th edn. Pearson Assessment & Information, San Antonio (1990)
47. Steele, C.M.: A threat in the air: how stereotypes shape intellectual identity and performance. Am. Psychol. **52**, 613–629 (1997)
48. McGlone, M.S., Aronson, J.: Stereotype threat, identity salience, and spatial reasoning. J. Appl. Dev. Psychol. **27**, 486–493 (2006)
49. Smeding, A.: Women in Science, Technology, Engineering, and Mathematics (STEM): an investigation of their implicit gender stereotypes and stereotypes' connectedness to math performance. Sex Roles **67**, 617–629 (2012)
50. Crisp, R.J., Bache, L.M., Maiter, A.T.: Dynamics of social comparison in counter-stereotypic domains: Stereotype boost, not stereotype threat, for women engineering majors. Soc. Influ. **4**(3), 171–184 (2009)

51. Martinez, S.L., Stager, G.: Invent to learn: Making, Tinkering, and Engineering in the Classroom. Constructing Modern Knowledge Press, Torrance (2013)
52. Honey, M., Kanter, D.E. (eds.): Design, Make, Play: Growing the Next Generation of STEM Innovators. Routledge, New York (2013)
53. Resnick, M., Rosenbaum, E.: Designing for tinkerability. In: Honey, M., Kanter, D. (eds.) Design, Make, Play: Growing the Next Generation of STEM Innovators, pp. 163–181. Routledge, New York (2013)

Physical Touch-Based Rotation Processes of Primary School Students

Sven Bertel[1]([⊠]), Stefanie Wetzel[1], and Steffi Zander[2]

[1] Flensburg University of Applied Sciences, Flensburg, Germany
{sven.bertel,stefanie.wetzel}@hs-flensburg.de
[2] Bauhaus-Universität Weimar, Weimar, Germany
steffi.zander@uni-weimar.de

Abstract. We present a novel method for deriving solution strategies used when solving rotation tasks. Process-based findings about physical rotation are obtained from an analysis of how angular disparity between stimuli changes over time. Data on angular disparity was gathered through a study on mental and physical rotation with 37 primary school students between the ages of 8 and 11. For controlling physical rotation, students used touch-based input on our iOS app *Rotate it!*, which also logged their interactions. Data on changes of angular disparity was used in the construction of Markov models. The models were employed to generate sets of synthetic angular disparity time courses, based on which we identified three distinct rotation-based solution strategies. Our analysis has implications for understanding processes involved in physical and mental rotation alike. It helps to lay grounds on which novel interactive diagnostic and training tools for spatial skills can be developed.

Keywords: Physical and mental rotation · Solution strategies for spatial tasks · Spatial skills · Qualitative description of rotation processes

1 Introduction

Spatial intelligence is a main part within multi-component models of intelligence [11], important for performance in many visual and spatial tasks. It is of special importance for tasks within STEM domains [43,46]. Not everyone is equally good at spatial and visual tasks, though. Among other factors, individual performance has been strongly linked to training and practice (e.g., [3,40]), which may affect the availability and use of mental strategies, or simply lead to more effective mental processing (e.g. [20]). In spite of this, the training of spatial skills is widely underrepresented in educational curricula at primary and secondary levels when compared to how verbal or mathematical skills are trained (e.g., for schools in the U.S., [5]). It has been pointed out that enriching school curricula to include an adequate training of spatial skills will likely increase students' professional participation in STEM domains [44]. More generally, investing into cognitive

T. Barkowsky et al. (Eds.): KogWis/Spatial Cognition 2016, LNAI 10523, pp. 19–37, 2017.
https://doi.org/10.1007/978-3-319-68189-4_2

skill formation has been linked to economic success in life for the individual, as well as for the society as a whole [18].

This situation opens up opportunities for educators and spatial cognition researchers alike. Aspects that need to be addressed both theoretically and practically relate to which spatial tasks should best be trained when, with whom, in which form, and at which age (cf. [35]). The crucial aspect is what precisely constitutes an "adequate training of spatial skills". A number of previous studies have focused on general issues of training, such as on how narrowly or broadly expertise in one spatial skill transfers to other spatial skills [44,50]. Population subgroups for which specific spatial ability levels have been investigated have been typically chosen based on age (mostly focusing on developmental aspects, [9,33,35]) or sex/gender [22,31]. Less research exists that puts an emphasis on individual spatial abilities and on differences in the mental strategies that are employed by different individuals (see e.g. [13,28], for recent exceptions).

As spatial abilities, skills, and strategies frequently differ inter-individually, it seems plausible to assume that the best way to practically train individual spatial abilities in a student population through spatial and visual tasks will also involve different training methods for different individuals. The general aim of this contribution is to lay suitable empirical and model-based grounds on which effective individualised training programs may subsequently be developed.

1.1 Foci of this Contribution

In this contribution, we will focus on procedural aspects of rotation tasks, which were registered through touch events on mobile devices, and will use physical rotation as a proxy for mental rotation. Our questions include: How do typical solution processes differ between correct and incorrect trials? How do they differ for different tasks? What differences can be observed between different, but similarly successful solution processes for the same task? Novel, model-based descriptions of solution processes will be employed to derive information about successful and unsuccessful strategies.

1.2 Outline

In the following section, we will establish a focus on mental rotation as one class of generally well-researched spatial tasks that, in spite of much research, still offers a number of interesting research opportunities. We developed the iOS app *Rotate it!* to present spatial tasks to users and to log their interactions while solving rotation tasks. In Sect. 3, we will describe an exploratory study with students at a primary school in which we employed *Rotate it!* to record solution processes of students' physical rotations of objects. Importantly, we will make the case that physical rotation trajectories may be used to gain novel, process-based insights also into students' general and individual mental rotation strategies. Next, we will analyse and discuss results, in large parts based on qualitative, probabilistic process models built based on the data that we gathered during the study. As a result of this modelling step, a population of synthetic trajectories will be generated that reflect frequent problem solving moves. Based on these, three distinct rotation strategies will be identified and compared on success rates and times per task. We will conclude by drawing implications for further process-based research into spatial problem solving as well as for a better description of individual spatial abilities, and will discuss ramifications for developing more effective and efficient individualised, dynamic training programs for spatial skills.

2   Mental and Physical Rotation

Tasks that have been frequently employed to study various factors of spatial intelligence include, among many others, mental transformations of perceived or imagined objects (e.g., mental rotation, [38,45]) and mental transformations of perceived or imagined scenes (e.g., mental orientation or perspective taking, [30]). While underlying mental skills for both groups of tasks seem related and performance is usually found to be significantly correlated, there is nevertheless evidence to assume a fundamental dissociation of faculties [30].

The two most frequently used mental rotation test paradigms employ 2D visualisations of 3D objects made by joining cubes side by side (cf. Fig. 1). An individual task either consists of two object visualisations (following [38]) or five (following [45]). In the former case, participants need to decide whether the two visualisations do, or do not, show the same object. In the latter, they need to compare the first visualisation to the four other ones and decide which two of the four show the same object as the first.

We define physical rotation tasks as tasks during which the problem solver has an option to physically rotate object representations before deciding whether same or different objects are shown. This definition of physical rotation is similar to how the term was recently employed by Gardony et al. [12].

2.1   Similarities, Commonalities, and Analogies

There is robust evidence to assume that, in many cases and for most participants, mental rotation solution processes will involve some form of visual mental imagery (for exceptions, see e.g. [32]). The processes are thought to be similar to those active during the physical rotation of objects. Support for this assumption comes, first, from behavioural studies: For pairs of visualisations that show the same object, correct response times are linearly proportional to the angular offset between the two object visualisations (angular disparity effect; [6,38]). The existence of the angular disparity effect has been often interpreted as a sign that, procedurally, mental rotation is analogous to physically rotating an object. In this sense, mental rotation can be seen as a kind of mental simulation that is comparable to a physical rotation process and during which the two visualisations become gradually aligned.

Further support for such interpretation comes from dual-task studies, during which participants generate additional physical, rotary movements with their arms or hands. When the direction of the physical rotation corresponds to the direction of the mental rotation, mental rotation response times are decreased; when the directions do not correspond, response times are increased [47,49]. Enacting (congruent) physical gestures has been found to improve performance in spatial visualisation tasks, such as during mental rotation, especially in people who have difficulties at such tasks [4]. Explanations for the beneficial effect of gesturing do not just point at an offloading of mental spatial representations, but to a general improvement of mental spatial transformations through using gestures [4]. In a recent comparison between mental and physical rotation tasks (the latter being controlled through rotating a ball in hand), Gardony et al. [12] have found comparable angular disparity effects for both mental and manual rotation.

Secondly, support for common (or, at least, overlapping) mental processes in mental and physical rotation comes from developmental perspectives (cf. [35]). Mental rotation task performance in children at the age of 5 to 6 years correlates with individual motor control (for rotation) [23], to the extent that children with impaired motor control have also shown reduced mental rotation performance (e.g., for overweight children [24]).

Thirdly, there is a body of neuroanatomical evidence for common or overlapping functions in mental and physical rotation, or for a mental simulation of a physical process during mental rotation. For example, areas within the primary motor cortex have been found to be active also during mental rotation [7,10]. Finding M1 activation was dependent on whether participants had been instructed to imagine that it was them who were rotating an object (activation) or that the object was being rotated by some exogenous force (no activation; [29]).

2.2   The Training of Mental and Physical Rotation

We have discussed in the introduction that, for spatial and visuo-spatial tasks in general, performance is strongly related to practice and training. More specifically, this statement also holds for mental rotation tasks (e.g., [20,48]), for which effects of training can last up to several months [40]. Importantly, mental rotation skills can also be trained by manual rotation, while the converse is not true: manual rotation skills are not significantly improved by mental rotation training alone [1]. Effects of practice seem to be process-based, rather than instance-based, and there is evidence that mental rotation skills can transfer to other spatial tasks, such as to paper folding [50].

Various studies have investigated mental rotation abilities in infants, preschoolers, and students at primary and secondary schools [9,21]. Mental rotation of some sorts can be reliably performed around the age of 4 to 5 years [33], while mentally rotating 3D objects is still difficult at an age of 8 to 10 [25]. Neurologically, structures involved in spatial thinking are fully functional already at a very early age, so that, again neurologically speaking, early practice seems important, if not essential, for developing high spatial thinking skills later on [15].

Spatial task performance of both males and females benefits from practice and training. Training may in fact reduce, or even fully level, existing gender differences [8,42]. While older research (including meta-analyses) consistently reported gender differences for paper-and-pencil-based mental rotation tasks to the advantage of males [31], more recent studies have failed to detect a gender difference for all types of mental rotation tasks. Notably, no difference was found for stimuli that employ 3D cube figures, while stable differences were found for stimuli based on 2D polygonal objects [22]. Using human figures as test stimuli decreased gender differences in mental rotation scores compared to using 3D cube figures [2]. For test participants around the age of 7 to 12, the extent of an existing male benefit in mental rotation varies strongly with the selected stimulus type [37].

2.3   Strategies, Theories, Models, and Research Methods

Early, defining procedure-oriented insights into mental rotation were provided by Shepard and Metzler [38], and Cooper and Shepard [6] through describing the angular disparity effect: Response times increase in a linear fashion with the angular disparity between the object visualisations. In an eye tracking study (and based on previous, conceptual suggestions by Metzler and Shepard [34]), Just and Carpenter [26] identified three major, idealised phases of mental rotation: (1) *search*, during which pairs of superficially corresponding object segments are identified; (2) a series of *transform-and-compare* operations. During each operation, two corresponding segments are first rotated in stepwise fashion such that they gradually become more aligned. After each transformation, a check for sufficient congruence is performed; and (3) *confirmation*, during which an additional check is performed whether the transformation of the matching segments has also brought the objects as a whole into sufficient congruence. According to Just and Carpenter [26], individual transformations in phase 2 are in 50° increments and a 25°-offset constitutes a suitable level of congruence between two objects to stop repeating the phase.

Khooshabeh et al. [28] examined individual differences in mental rotation strategies. In particular, they focused on whether participants employed piecemeal rotation strategies similar to the three-phase strategy described above, or holistic strategies in which the entire object is mentally rotated. Strategy choice was found to depend on individual working memory capacity, such that lower capacity was associated with using piecemeal strategies. In terms of adults' strategy use for rotating 2D polygons, holistic strategies have more frequently been found with males and piecemeal strategies with females [19]. It is important to keep in mind that rotation-based strategies, whether piecemeal or holistic, are not the only type of strategy for effectively solving mental rotation tasks. Other existing strategies may be more analytical and, for example, rely on comparing cube counts between roughly corresponding object segments. Logie et al. [32] reports on individuals who employed such analytic strategies in an fMRI study. It should be clear, that, when analytical strategies are used for solving mental rotation tasks, the mental processes involved are likely to be very different from mental processes involved in solving physical rotation tasks. Furthermore, people who mentally rotate stimuli (*rotators*) have been associated with using holistic strategies, while *nonrotators* use analytic strategies [14].

Recent studies replicated the angular disparity effect as an increase of response time with angular disparity, though the found relationships were not always perfectly linear (see e.g., [12,17]). Naturally, an angular disparity effect as defined by Shepard and Metzler [38], and Cooper and Shepard [6] and used by Just and Carpenter [26] only exists for *same* stimuli, that is, when both object visualisations show the same object (cf. results of Gardony et al. [12], and Jansen and Heil [22]). For *different* stimuli, there likely exist multiple ways of trying to match visualisations without succeeding, while there usually exists only one perfect match between *same* stimuli.

It is interesting to note that very few approaches in the mental rotation literature have attempted to map involved mental processes to the degree attempted by Just and Carpenter [26]. While more recent contributions such as Khooshabeh et al. [28] shed light onto use of overall strategies, although on an individual problem-solver's basis, there is little detailed information provided as how to the solution processes progress over time. For example, how does the angular disparity change during the course of solving a mental rotation problem? How well does the model suggested by Just and Carpenter [26] really match stepwise mental rotations? The lack of research on this point is not surprising, as tracking a (hypothesised) mental process (e.g., of a changing angular disparity) over time is not easy. Likely, no current method based on fMRI or EEG will permit the tracking of transformations of mental representations with adequate temporal or spatial precision, nor does a suitable experimental methodology seem to exist for such an endeavour. However, the various similarities between mental and physical rotations discussed above may provide us with a window onto some of the inner workings of mental rotation.

In recent research, Gardony et al. [12] first opened up this window by contrasting mental and physical rotation tasks (inputs to the latter were through turning a ball held in hand). Stimulus objects were 3D cube figures taken from Peters and Battista [36]. Based on the tracking of angular offsets between stimuli over the course of solving a physical rotation task, Gardony et al. [12] established that, for successfully solved *same* tasks, participants on average rotated until a characteristic offset of around 30° was reached. This mark is surprisingly similar to the 25°-mark postulated by Just and Carpenter [26] as the final offset for transformations in mental rotation. In terms of method, the present contribution draws inspiration from Gardony et al. [12], though our analysis of time courses of angular offsets goes significantly beyond that. In addition, differences exist in the method of rotational input and in the targeted group of participants.

3   Our Study

Tablets are widely available in educational contexts today and allow for touch-based inputs. We decided to use a tablet-based app to present visuo-spatial training tasks to school students and to track their problem solving actions.

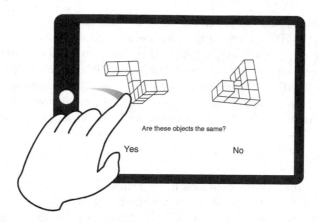

Are these objects the same?

Yes   No

Fig. 1. A sample rotation task as presented in the *Rotate it!* app.

To this end, we developed the iPad app *Rotate it!* and employed it to track students' 2D touch gestures used for rotational control during the physical rotation of stimuli. *Rotate it!* displays a sequence of rotation tasks with two object visualisations each and permits rotating the left-hand figure using an Arcball interaction metaphor ([39]; see Fig. 1). We chose the Arcball, as it is easy to understand and does not require much familiarisation. All touch-based interactions (e.g., finger positions or object rotations over time) as well as response times and given answers are automatically logged.

The school curriculum at primary schools in the German state of Thuringia includes at least simple spatial tasks, such as the mental folding of cube nets [27,41]. We teamed up with a local primary school to conduct a pilot study that was aimed, first, at testing the *Rotate it!* app and, secondly, at gathering data about how students at the school solved rotation tasks. Mental and physical rotation tasks were administered in a within-subject design. Written parental and school approval for the study and for gathering data was sought and obtained.

During the study, students were presented with series of cube figure pairs (in the style used by Shepard and Metzler [38]) and had to decide for each pair whether the shown figures were identical, or not (see Fig. 1, for an illustration). In order to better compare our results with those of past research, we chose to employ the pairwise figure comparisons from the Vandenberg and Kuse Mental Rotation Test [45]. Reconstructed figures were used and, based on the 20 1-to-4 comparisons of the original instrument, we constructed 80 1-to-1 comparisons, which were grouped into two sets of 40 comparisons each. Each set contained 20 tasks with identical stimulus pairs (*same*, with initial angular disparities between 0° and 180°) and 20 tasks with *different* stimulus pairs. For the *physical* condition, tasks were presented via *Rotate it!* to allow us to log all actions that students produced. For the *mental* condition, we used a static paper-based version of the tasks, again with the intention of staying close to formats of original paper-based mental rotation test instruments. Stimulus size was kept constant between conditions, and sheets in the *mental* condition had the same size and aspect ratio as the iPad screen in the *physical* condition. The order in which the two conditions were presented was balanced across all students to compensate for potential learning effects. Consequently, students either started with the iPad-based *physical* condition, followed by the paper-based *mental* condition, or vice versa. For the *mental* condition, time was only measured over all tasks due to practical constraints within the classrooms, and not for single tasks.

4 Results

We gathered complete data from 37 students (m = 19 / f = 18; age: 8–11, mean: 9.08 years). In a first step of analysis, we used a mixed within- and between-subjects design to compare data on mental effort, motivation and performance data between conditions. We found descriptive (though non-significant) differences in means for success (*mental*: 66.04%; *physical*: 71.13%), time per task (*mental*: 12.61 s; *physical*: 9.13 s), and mental efficiency (computed as a ratio of mental effort over time, with self-assessed ratings of mental effort; *mental*: 10.94; *physical*: 14.54). The overall success rate of 68.59% indicates that our tasks were suitable for our sample of students, as they were of medium to high task difficulty. For a detailed analysis and discussion of success rates, response times, and different efficiency measures, as well as of condition order, we refer to Zander et al. [51]. For the present context, we will focus on an analysis of changes of angular offsets gathered over the courses of physical rotation tasks.

Courses of Angular Offsets. For an initial analysis of rotational offsets, we pooled all the data that we had gathered through *Rotate it!*. We first wanted to see if our study qualitatively replicated the final angular disparity patterns for physical rotation found by Gardony et al. [12, p. 610]. This was of particular interest, as our input of rotational control differed from that in Gardony et al. [12] (touch and Arcball vs. rotating a ball in hand). As Fig. 2 shows, this was indeed the case: For *same* correct answers, we found an overall decrease towards low final angular disparities, which was larger for larger initial angular disparities. The final median angular disparity was 29° (N = 416). For *same* incorrect trials, the median angular disparity was 121° (N = 118). The difference to correct trials was significant (Z = −11.29, p < 0.001, r = 0.49). We focused our present analysis on *same* trials, as, in a first step, we are chiefly interested in characteristics and variation of successful problem solving strategies. Also, one has to note that the *different* trials derived from the Vandenberg and Kuse instrument [45] do not differ systematically (e.g., are mirror images, as in Gardony et al. [12]), but in many different ways. Consequently, data from *different* Vandenberg and Kuse pairwise comparisons cannot be easily aggregated across tasks.

Angular Disparity Effect. We were further interested in whether our data showed a linear angular disparity effect, similar to the one reported in the literature [6,38]. For *physical* rotation, initial angular disparity in *same* trials was

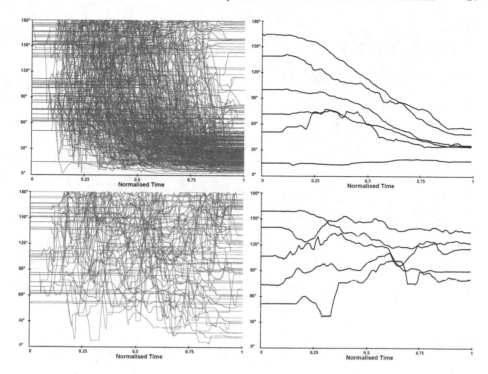

Fig. 2. Angular disparities for *same* tasks over time (I). Normalised time-on-task on abscissa and angular offsets (0–180°) on ordinate. *Upper row: correct, lower row: incorrect* answers. *Left column:* Observed trajectories of angular disparities over time. *Right column:* plots of average angular disparities over time for tasks grouped by 30° initial angular disparity bands.

indeed positively linearly associated with time-per-task ($p < 0.05$, $r = 0.124$). As times-per-task could not be gathered for *mental* rotation, no corresponding coefficient could be computed.

5 Modelling Physical Rotation

The differences in the final angular disparities between *correct* and *incorrect* *same* trials indicate that being able to get to final angular disparities of around 30° may be an important factor for task success. Additional comparisons revealed that *correct* trials included fewer distinct rotations, as well as more angular disparity-reducing and fewer angular disparity-increasing rotations. It thus seems quite likely that *correct* and *incorrect* trials can also be differentiated based on formal descriptions and models of the observed angular disparity changes.

It is important to note that our models are not based on data produces by students' arm or finger movements on the touch screen. Instead the models address the underlying problem solving processes. For a scheme-based modelling of the angular disparity trajectories, we concentrated on qualitative changes in

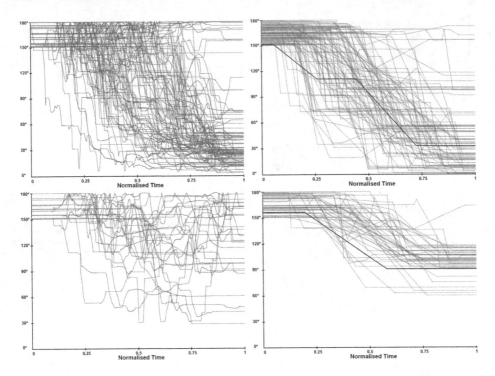

Fig. 3. Angular disparities for *same* tasks over time (II). For increased readability, only tasks with initial angular disparities of 150–180° are shown. *Upper row: correct, lower row: incorrect* answers. *Left column:* observed trajectories. *Right column:* synthetic trajectories generated from observed trajectories. Centroids in black, exemplifying *correct/incorrect* answer trajectories.

the trajectory, as we assume that these changes will often correspond to transitions between problem solving stages. The coding scheme was the following: each angular disparity change was coded for general direction (up, neutral, down), duration (short, medium, long), and resulting angular disparity band (one of the six 30°-bands). We then described each course as a sequence of qualitative changes, with each change represented through a tuple of values for these three variables. All courses with less than 10° accumulated rotation throughout the task (29.4% for all trials) were deemed as showing non-rotating strategies and were consequently excluded from our analysis of rotations. We assume that, for these trials, participants either employed purely analytical strategies or only employed mental rotation.

5.1   Generating Synthetic Trajectories

For *correct* and *incorrect same* trials, we respectively computed relative frequencies of all change-to-change transitions across all students. These relative frequencies were then used as probabilities in the construction of two Markov models of angular disparity trajectories, one each for *correct* and *incorrect* trials. The idea was to employ the models to generate large populations of synthetic trajectories, which would be similar to the trajectories that we observed in our study. As the models are based on observed relative frequencies of change-to-change transitions, trajectories that include high frequency transitions, and are thus highly typical, could be generated most frequently. Less typical trajectories were also generated, but at suitably lower frequencies. The result was a population of synthetic trajectories that included variation while reflecting typicality. As a second advantage of our approach, we could increase the size of the set of trajectories available for subsequent steps of analysis (more synthetic trajectories than observed ones).

By analysing these large trajectory populations, prototypical trajectories could be extracted. Analysing the prototypes would then not only help us to get to the most typical rotation strategies, but hopefully also increase contrast between rotation trajectories leading to *correct* and to *incorrect* answers. In a sense, the synthetic trajectories represent minimal sets of angular disparity changes needed to describe how students typically solved tasks correctly and incorrectly.

For each of the two models, we generated 1,000 synthetic trajectories per 30° initial angular disparity band. For an illustration of these synthetic trajectories, we will largely focus on the upper-most initial angular disparity band, which includes task with initial angular disparities between 150° and 180°. Figure 3 shows these trajectories for *correct* and *incorrect* answers for *same* trials. The two graphs on the right-hand side also each include a centroid as the most typical trajectory. As we had already noted based on the observed trajectories, most of the synthetic trajectories for the correctly solved tasks show a fast decrease of angular disparity, resulting in a final angular disparity between 0° and 60°. In contrast, the decrease of angular disparity for incorrectly solved tasks is less and stops at higher final angular disparities (between 90° and 120°).

Prototypes of Synthetic Trajectories. To find the most typical synthetic trajectories, k-means clustering was applied. We computed pairwise distances between synthetic trajectories based on their qualitative descriptions (i.e., the sequences of changes) and by means of a weighted Levenshtein distance. Setting $k = 1$ produced markedly different prototypes for correct and incorrect *same* answers (shown as centroids in bold in the right column of Fig. 3). As Markov models are probabilistic, it is important to note that trajectory prototypes may vary between model runs and that the two prototypes shown in Fig. 3 are examples which may not be representative of model variability.

5.2   Populations of Prototypes

To address this issue, we ran each model 100 times. For the present context, we again focus on the upper-most initial angular disparity band. In each model iteration, k prototypes were extracted, as before by k-means clustering. Figure 4

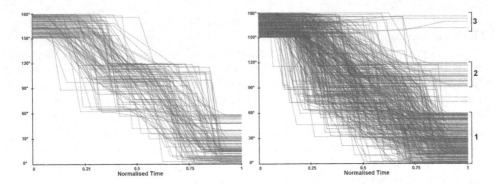

Fig. 4. Prototypes for *same correct* synthetic trajectories with initial angular disparities between 150° and 180°, based on 100 model runs and based on k-means clustering. *Left:* With ($k = 1$), *Right:* with ($k = 3$). Three distinct patterns are marked with numbers 1, 2 and 3, representing different successful rotation strategies in order of decreasing relative prominence.

shows the result of these iterations with $k = 1$ (left) and $k = 3$ (right) for *same correct* synthetic trajectories. While the left graph includes 100 prototypes (one per iteration), the right graph includes 300 prototypes (three per iteration).

For $k = 1$, only one group of typical courses can be seen, indicating the existence of one dominant rotation strategy. It involves a fast decrease of initial angular disparity until a final angular disparity between 0° and 60° is reached.

Increasing k beyond 1 leads us to include also trajectories representative of secondary, tertiary, etc. strategies. For $k = 3$, three distinct groups of prototypes can be observed which differ in their relative prominence. The most dominant pattern (*strategy 1*; includes 89% of all prototypes) is the same pattern that we already observed with $k = 1$. A second pattern shows a smaller decrease of angular disparity and ends within a range of 90° to 120° (*strategy 2*; includes 9% of all prototypes). A third pattern includes prototypes with only slight changes of angular disparity, resulting in high final angular disparities between 150° and 180° (*strategy 3*; includes 2% of all prototypes). When we compare these groups of synthetic prototypes to the original trajectories that the students had produced for trials starting between 150° and 180°, we find that 72% of the original trajectories correspond to *strategy 1*, 16% to *strategy 2*, and 9% to *strategy 3*. As expected, the degree of dominance that dominant strategies possess within our population of prototypes is increased compared to their degree of dominance within the original, observed trajectories. Increasing k to values above 3 did not reveal additional distinct patterns.

Table 1 shows mean values per task for all three strategies for time, accumulated distance covered during rotation (in degrees), and number of touch-based drag events during rotation. When assuming an average initial angular disparity of 165° for trials starting in the 150–180° band, *strategy 1* should on average involve a net change of angular disparity of 135° (reaching 30°, as the central value of the 0–60° band). *Strategy 2* should involve an average net change of

Table 1. Means per task for time, accumulated angular distance, and number of drag events during rotations for the original, observed angular disparity trajectories. The association to one of the three strategies extracted from the model is based on final angular disparity. Data is for tasks starting in the 150–180° band.

	Time per task	Acc. way	# of drags
Strategy 1	11.25 s	227°	12.6
Strategy 2	10.88 s	183°	10.51
Strategy 3	11.83 s	179°	13.53

60° (reaching 105°) and *strategy 3* one of 0°. The respective ratio between these values and the angular distances that were actually accumulated on average during rotation with the strategies provides us with an efficiency measure that tells us how goal-directed rotations were. For *strategy 1*, this ratio is 0.59 and for *strategy 2*, it is 0.33. For *strategy 3*, it is 0, of course, as initial and final angular disparities did not differ. In comparison, *strategy 1* is more efficient than *strategy 2*, meaning that solving a physical rotation problem with *strategy 2* involved moving through relatively more angular distance per angular distance gained in the end. Data on the number of drag events confirms that rotations with *strategy 1* were more goal-directed than with *strategy 2*, as one drag respectively covered 10.7° and 5.7° on average. Reducing angular disparity with *strategy 2* thus occurred in smaller steps than with *strategy 1*. Mean times per task were comparable between strategies.

As a last point, how strongly associated was using one of the three strategies with task success? Based on an analysis of final angular disparities, *same* trials that follow *strategy 1* were solved correctly with a probability of 96%. In contrast, only 56% of all *same* trials following *strategy 2* and 40% of all *same* trials following *strategy 3* were solved correctly.

6   Discussion

For the purposes of the present context, we analysed physical rotation trajectories that were captured by our app during the solving of physical rotation tasks. We were able to reproduce the angular disparity effect for *same physical* trials that were previously described by Just and Carpenter [26], and Gardony et al. [12]. This replication is important as it provides evidence for concluding that finding an angular disparity effect for 3D physical rotation tasks is likely unrelated to the choice of physical rotation control. Whereas participants in Gardony et al. [12] held a ball in hand, participants in our study used touch-based input to rotate an Arcball on an iPad display. Also, participants' age is likely not much of a factor for finding an angular disparity effect, at least between the ages of 9 and 19 (mean age in our study: 9.08 years; [12]: 19.47 years). Insofar as a general comparison of mental and physical rotation is concerned, existence of the effect in our study provides further support for assuming common or overlapping mental processes, at least for problem solvers who are *rotators* (cf. [14]). This is useful on a methodological level, since we employ physical rotation as a proxy for and a window onto mental rotation.

We also were able to replicate the overall time courses of angular disparity for *same correct* trials that were reported by Gardony et al. [12]. Such replication again points to small or no effects of the specific physical rotation control on the involved problem solving processes.

To analyse rotation trajectories in more detail, we conducted a three-step analysis starting with a comparison of the final angular disparities between *correct* and *incorrect same* trials. We found that correctly solved *same* trials ended with a significantly lower median final angular disparity than incorrectly solved *same* trials (around 30° compared to around 120°). Achieving a final angular disparity between 0° and 60° increases the probability of correctly solving the task. With a low angular disparity, the stimuli are visually similar, which likely facilitates a visual comparison without further mental transformation.

In the second step of our analysis, we developed a qualitative description of rotation trajectories to make them more easily comparable. We coded trajectories as sequences of states, each consisting of information on direction and duration of change, as well as on final angular disparity range. Two distinct Markov models were constructed for *same correct* and *same incorrect* trials and were used to generate synthetic trajectories. A subsequent cluster analysis revealed the k most typical trajectories per model run, representing the most frequently used solution strategies. As we were especially interested in successful solution strategies and the distribution of typical trajectories, we further analysed prototypical *same correct* synthetic trajectories created across 100 model runs. This analysis revealed, first, the single dominant pattern of synthetic trajectories; this represents the most frequently used successful solution strategy (*strategy 1*). We then increased k step-wise to detect further distinct patterns. Using $k = 3$, we found two additional, although less frequent, successful patterns, which represent secondary and tertiary rotation strategies (*strategies 2* and *3*). Of these, *strategy 1* is the most efficient and goal-directed, based on an analysis of observed angular disparity change.

When we compare these three strategies to those reported in the literature, *strategy 1* seems to match a holistic or piecemeal mental rotation strategy where the whole object or parts thereof are mentally rotated until an angular disparity of below 25° is reached. Data on performance shows that this rotation strategy is also the most successful one. A differentiation of whether users of *strategy 1* employ holistic or piecemeal strategies does not seem possible based on an analysis of time courses of angular disparities alone. We expect that including data from additional channels (for instance, on gaze during physical rotation tasks) can help clarify on a trial-by-trial basis whether holistic or piecemeal rotation strategies are employed.

Strategy 3 that we derived from the Markov model consists of trajectories for which initial and final angular disparities are not much different. Data on accumulated rotations shows that this does not mean that users of *strategy 3* did not rotate. On the contrary, their rotational trajectories covered about as much overall angular distance as we observed for users of *strategy 2*. Consequently, we assume *strategy 3* to really be an example of a rotating strategy, instead of being non-rotating (e.g., analytic). We further assume that analytic strategies are to be found among those observed trajectories which we had excluded from the analysis of rotations because they hardly showed any (less than 10° accumulated throughout a trial). Performance data reveals that, compared to the other two derived strategies, *strategy 3* is least likely to lead to task success.

Interpreting *strategy 2* seems somewhat less straightforward. It involves about the same amount of overall rotation as *strategy 3*, while being directed at the final angular disparity range around 105°. *Strategy 2* is less efficient than *strategy 1* and also proceeds in smaller rotation steps. It is possible that *strategy 2* constitutes a collection of attempts at *strategy 1* that, for some reason, were not carried out to the end. Furthermore, the observation that *strategy 2*'s success rate is at chance level does suggest that terminating at higher angular disparities was unintentional. If this is so, *strategy 2* may offer potential for training-based intervention based on nudging users towards a more effective strategy.

One might ask whether some of the students' successes with the tasks were not just lucky guesses. We assume that some indeed were. However, it seems unlikely that such guesses will have had any strong influence on the process that led to extracting the three strategies. The reason for this is that there exist many ways in which a lucky guess may occur, leading to a variety of angular disparity courses. Put differently, any two lucky guesses will likely differ somewhat from one another, while any two instances of the same strategy will likely be quite similar. The consequence of lucky guessing is thus just an increase of noise surrounding the typical signatures of the three strategies.

One point still remains unclear: Did the students in our study solve tasks correctly because they achieved low final angular disparities or was successfully solving a task dependent on the process of getting there? This is a difference between an outcome- and a process-oriented view. According to Chu and Kita's view [4], it is really through the link between motor and mental rotation processes that internal computations are improved. Based on our data, we can say that trials with low final angular disparities were often solved correctly. However, we currently cannot say whether such relationship is causal or purely correlational. Assuming for the moment that it is really the process that is important for task success: Does this process need to be self-initiated to be effective, or would piloting a student to low angular disparities do the trick just as well? It seems that answering this questions will certainly be important for an interactive training of mental rotation skills. Goldin-Meadow et al. [16] compared the performance of children who were themselves gesturing during mental transformation tasks to that of children who saw someone else gesturing. They found that actually performing the gestures enhanced learning more. Whether the situation is similar with physical rotation tasks remains to be seen.

7   Conclusion

We presented a more detailed analysis of processes involved in solving rotation tasks than was previously available. Our method is based on time courses of angular disparity and involves qualitative descriptions of disparity changes to make the processes more easily comparable and to permit constructing generating models that spawn synthetic, but representative rotation trajectories. Based on the models that we constructed from data obtained in our study with 37 primary school students, we identified three distinct rotation-based strategies for tasks that involve high initial angular disparities. The strategies were then compared to how students rotated stimuli in our study. We expect that our general method is similarly applicable to other spatial task types. A transfer should, in particular, be easy for those types that involve sequences of mental spatial transformations, such as perspective taking or paper folding.

Our study involves two important shortcomings, which we share with other research that employed stimuli from the Vandenberg and Kuse mental rotation test: First, the initial angular disparities of the tasks were not equally distributed throughout the range of 0–180°. As can be easily seen in Fig. 2, gaps exist particularly around 120° and 30°. As a result, we focused our analysis on upper initial angular disparity bands, for which comparably many tasks exist. Secondly, *different* tasks include stimuli pairs that differ in many ways (e.g., are either mirror images or entirely different). This makes systematic cross-task comparisons of solution processes hard, if not impossible. We consequently focused on *same* tasks for the present. In an analysis of the constituent tasks of the Vandenberg and Kuse test, Geiser et al. [14] found that, for some tasks, comparisons can be easily made analytically and without mental rotation. A solution to both shortcomings lies in using different, more methodically generated stimuli sets in the future.

So far, the three strategies extracted from our *same* model have to be regarded as globally available. At this stage of analysis and with the used stimulus set, we did and could not sufficiently consider how strategy use was distributed among students (e.g., does each student have a dominant strategy?) and within each student (e.g., do individuals switch between strategies, and when?). Inter- and intra-individual differences in the use of rotation-based strategies will thus have to be addressed further in future work.

It seems important to keep in mind that time course data on stimulus rotations only shows one aspect of the problem solving process. We have already discussed that, based on our data, we could not say whether users of *strategy 1* employed mental strategies that were holistic or piecemeal in nature. Future analyses should thus include additional data for the modelling of mental and physical rotation processes, such as finger positions on the iPad or eye movements.

Last, although the Markov models were successful in increasing the contrast between high- and low-frequency rotation trajectories, the strategies that they generate are essentially local. The models are history-less insofar as they only consider probabilities of change-to-change transitions, but do not look back (or forward) beyond each transition. In cases where problem solvers employ more global solution strategies, models should also be able to reflect more global properties of the corresponding rotation processes. Adapting our models accordingly will be among our next steps.

References

1. Adams, D.M., Stull, A.T., Hegarty, M.: Effects of using mental and manual rotation training on mental and manual rotation performance. Spat. Cognit. Comput. **14**, 169–198 (2014)
2. Alexander, G.M., Evardone, M.: Blocks and bodies: sex differences in a novel version of the mental rotations test. Horm. Behav. **53**(1), 177–184 (2008)
3. Baenninger, M., Newcombe, N.: The role of experience in spatial test performance: a meta-analysis. Sex Roles **20**(5–6), 327–344 (1989)
4. Chu, M., Kita, S.: The nature of gestures' beneficial role in spatial problem solving. J. Exp. Psychol. Gen. **140**(1), 102–116 (2011)
5. Colangelo, N., Assouline, S.G., Gross, M.U.M.: A Nation Deceived: How Schools Hold Back America's Brightest Students, vol. 38 (2004)
6. Cooper, L.A., Shepard, R.N.: Chronometric studies of the rotation of mental images. In: Visual Information Processing, pp. 15–20 (1973)
7. Eisenegger, C., Herwig, U., Jäncke, L.: The involvement of primary motor cortex in mental rotation revealed by transcranial magnetic stimulation. Eur. J. Neurosci. **25**(4), 1240–1244 (2007)
8. Feng, J., Spence, I., Pratt, J.: Playing an action video game reduces gender differences in spatial cognition. Psychol. Sci. **18**(10), 850–855 (2007)
9. Frick, A., Wang, S.H.: Mental spatial transformations in 14- and 16-month-old infants: effects of action and observational experience. Child Dev. **85**(1), 278–293 (2014)
10. Ganis, G., Keenan, J.P., Kosslyn, S.M., Pascual-Leone, A.: Transcranial magnetic stimulation of primary motor cortex affects mental rotation. Cereb. Cortex **10**(2), 175–180 (2000)
11. Gardner, H.: Frames of Mind: The Theory of Multiple Intelligences. Basic Books, New York (2011)
12. Gardony, A.L., Taylor, H.A., Brunyé, T.T.: What does physical rotation reveal about mental rotation? Psychol. Sci. **25**(2), 605–612 (2014)
13. Gardony, A.L., Taylor, H.A., Brunyé, T.T., Wolford, G.L.: To rotate or not to rotate: strategy differences in mental rotation. In: Proceedings of the 55th Annual Meeting of the Psychonomic Society, Long Beach, CA, USA (2014)
14. Geiser, C., Lehmann, W., Eid, M.: Separating "rotators" from "nonrotators" in the mental rotations test: a multigroup latent class analysis. Multivar. Behav. Res. **41**(3), 261–293 (2006)
15. Gersmehl, P.J., Gersmehl, C.A.: Spatial thinking by young children: neurologic evidence for early development and "educability". J. Geogr. **106**(5), 181–191 (2007)
16. Goldin-Meadow, S., Levine, S.C., Zinchenko, E., Yip, T.K.Y., Hemani, N., Factor, L.: Doing gesture promotes learning a mental transformation task better than seeing gesture. Dev. Sci. **15**(6), 876–884 (2012)
17. Hamrick, J.B., Griffiths, T.L.: What to simulate? inferring the right direction for mental rotation. In: Annual Conference of the Cognitive Science Society, pp. 577–582 (2014)

18. Heckman, J.J.: Skill formation and the economics of investing in disadvantaged children. Science **312**(5782), 1900–1902 (2006)
19. Heil, M., Jansen-Osmann, P.: Sex differences in mental rotation with polygons of different complexity: do men utilize holistic processes whereas women prefer piecemeal ones? Q. J. Exp. Psychol. **61**(5), 683–689 (2008)
20. Heil, M., Rösler, F., Link, M., Bajric, J.: What is improved if a mental rotation task is repeated-the efficiency of memory access, or the speed of a transformation routine? Psychol. Res. **61**(2), 99–106 (1998)
21. Huttenlocher, J., Newcombe, N., Vasilyeva, M.: Spatial scaling in young children. Psychol. Sci. **10**(5), 393–398 (1999)
22. Jansen, P., Heil, M.: Suitable stimuli to obtain (no) gender differences in the speed of cognitive processes involved in mental rotation. Brain Cognit. **64**(3), 217–227 (2007)
23. Jansen, P., Heil, M.: The relation between motor development and mental rotation ability in 5-to 6-year-old children. Int. J. Dev. Sci. **4**(1), 67–75 (2010)
24. Jansen, P., Schmelter, A., Kasten, L., Heil, M.: Impaired mental rotation performance in overweight children. Appetite **56**(3), 766–769 (2011)
25. Jansen, P., Schmelter, A., Quaiser-Pohl, C., Neuburger, S., Heil, M.: Mental rotation performance in primary school age children: are there gender differences in chronometric tests? Cognit. Dev. **28**(1), 51–62 (2013)
26. Just, M.A., Carpenter, P.A.: Eye fixations and cognitive processes. Cognit. Psychol. **8**(4), 441–480 (1976)
27. Kelnberger, M.: Fit für den Übertritt - Bildungsstandards Mathematik: Tests zur Leistungsfeststellung (2008)
28. Khooshabeh, P., Hegarty, M., Shipley, T.F.: Individual differences in mental rotation: piecemeal versus holistic processing. Exp. Psychol. **60**(3), 164 (2012)
29. Kosslyn, S.M., Thompson, W.L., Wraga, M., Alpert, N.M.: Imagining rotation by endogenous versus exogenous forces: distinct neural mechanisms. NeuroReport **12**(11), 2519–2525 (2001)
30. Kozhevnikov, M., Hegarty, M.: A dissociation between object manipulation spatial ability and spatial orientation ability. Mem. Cognit. **29**(5), 745–756 (2001)
31. Linn, M.C., Petersen, A.C.: Emergence and characterization of sex differences in spatial ability: a meta-analysis. Child Dev. **56**(6), 1479–1498 (1985)
32. Logie, R.H., Pernet, C.R., Buonocore, A., Sala, S.D.: Low and high imagers activate networks differentially in mental rotation. Neuropsychologia **49**(11), 3071–3077 (2011)
33. Marmor, G.S.: Development of kinetic images: when does the child first represent movement in mental images? Cognit. Psychol. **7**, 548–559 (1975)
34. Metzler, J., Shepard, R.N.: Transformational studies of the internal representation of three-dimensional objects. In: Solso, R.L. (ed.) Theories of Cognitive Psychology: The Loyola Symposium. Lawrence Erlbaum, Potomac (1974)
35. Newcombe, N.S., Frick, A.: Early education for spatial intelligence: why, what, and how? Mind Brain Educ. **4**(3), 102–111 (2010)
36. Peters, M., Battista, C.: Applications of mental rotation figures of the Shepard and Metzler type and description of a mental rotation stimulus library. Brain Cognit. **66**(3), 260–264 (2008)
37. Quaiser-Pohl, C., Neuburger, S., Heil, M., Jansen, P., Schmelter, A.: Is the male advantage in mental-rotation performance task independent? on the usability of chronometric tests and paper-and-pencil tests in children. Int. J. Test. **14**(2), 122–142 (2014)

38. Shepard, R.N., Metzler, J.: Mental rotation of three-dimensional objects. Science **171**, 701–703 (1971)
39. Shoemake, K.: Arcball: a user interface for specifying three-dimensional orientation using a mouse. Graph. Interface **92**, 151–156 (1992)
40. Terlecki, M.S., Newcombe, N.S., Little, M.: Durable and generalized effects of spatial experience on mental rotation: gender differences in growth patterns. Appl. Cognit. Psychol. **22**(7), 996–1013 (2008)
41. Thüringer Ministerium für Bildung, Wissenschaft und Kultur: Lehrplan für die Grundschule und für die Förderschule mit dem Bildungsgang Grundschule - Mathematik (2010)
42. Tzuriel, D., Egozi, G.: Gender differences in spatial ability of young children: the effects of training and processing strategies. Child Dev. **81**(5), 1417–1430 (2010)
43. Uttal, D.H., Cohen, C.A.: Spatial thinking and STEM education: when, why and how? Psychol. Learn. Motiv. **57**(2), 147–181 (2012)
44. Uttal, D.H., Meadow, N.G., Tipton, E., Hand, L.L., Alden, A.R., Warren, C., Newcombe, N.S.: The malleability of spatial skills: a meta-analysis of training studies. Psychol. Bull. **139**(2), 352 (2013)
45. Vandenberg, S.G., Kuse, A.R.: Mental rotations, a group test of three-dimensional spatial visualization. Percept. Motor Skills **47**(2), 599–604 (1978)
46. Wai, J., Lubinski, D., Benbow, C.P.: Spatial ability for stem domains: aligning over 50 years of cumulative psychological knowledge solidifies its importance. J. Educ. Psychol. **101**(4), 817 (2009)
47. Wexler, M., Kosslyn, S.M., Berthoz, A.: Motor processes in mental rotation. Cognition **68**(1), 77–94 (1998)
48. Wiedenbauer, G., Jansen-Osmann, P.: Manual training of mental rotation in children. Learn. Instr. **18**(1), 30–41 (2008)
49. Wohlschläger, A., Wohlschläger, A.: Mental and manual rotation. J. Exp. Psychol. Hum. Percept. Perform. **24**(2), 397–412 (1998)
50. Wright, R., Thompson, W.L., Ganis, G., Newcombe, N.S., Kosslyn, S.M.: Training generalized spatial skills. Psychon. Bull. Rev. **15**(4), 763–771 (2008)
51. Zander, S., Wetzel, S., Bertel, S.: Rotate it! - effects of touch-based gestures on elementary school students' solving of mental rotation tasks. Comput. Educ. **103**, 158–169 (2016)

Can You Follow Your Own Route Directions: How Familiarity and Spatial Abilities Influence Spatial Performance and Sketch Maps

Rui Li[1,2]([✉]), Vanessa Joy A. Anacta[3], and Angela Schwering[3]

[1] Department of Geography and Planning, State University of New York at Albany, Albany, NY, USA
rli4@albany.edu
[2] Design Academy, Sichuan Fine Arts Institute, Chongqing, China
[3] Institute for Geoinformatics, University of Muenster, Muenster, Germany
{v_anac02, Schwering}@uni-muenster.de

Abstract. Verbal route descriptions are common in our daily lives that give us wayfinding directions. They also are important in cognitive research as they lend insight on processes associated with wayfinding. This paper reports a study that investigates the influence of familiarity and spatial abilities on acquiring spatial knowledge from verbal route directions. The familiarity of the participant was removed by replacing all names of spatial entities in the route instructions given by the same person. Specifically, the types of acquired spatial knowledge addressed are direction, distance, and configurational aspects of sketched maps. Results show that familiarity plays a crucial role on acquisition of spatial knowledge at the survey level. In particular, familiarity leads to fewer errors in directional estimation, but overestimation of distance. Spatial abilities further influence one's knowledge of distance such that higher spatial abilities lead to more accurate distance estimation in new environments. With that said, lower spatial abilities do not contribute to distance estimation in both familiar and new environments. Furthermore, measures on sketch maps show that familiarity does not lead to dramatically different sketch maps while variation exist. These results also point out the necessity of follow-up studies to address the orientation specificity in familiar and unfamiliar environment.

Keywords: Route descriptions · Familiarity · Sketch maps · Spatial abilities · Orientation

1   Introduction

When a person navigates in a new environment, asking someone for directions seems like the most convenient way of finding one's path from point A to point B. Sometimes, this is even more convenient than using one's mobile device. Verbal route directions have served as important sources for researchers to understand the planning, cognitive processing, and spatial knowledge acquisition associated with wayfinding [1, 2]. Earlier studies [3, 4] assessed the elements that would contribute

© Springer International Publishing AG 2017
T. Barkowsky et al. (Eds.): KogWis/Spatial Cognition 2016, LNAI 10523, pp. 38–52, 2017.
https://doi.org/10.1007/978-3-319-68189-4_3

to good route directions. We all have likely had the experience of receiving verbal descriptions from someone else where these descriptions may not be easy to follow due to their style and navigational preference being different from our own. Researchers have questioned the effectiveness of given verbal descriptions on accuracy or other performances of wayfinding and examined the factors that would influence the composition of route directions [5]. Furthermore, verbal descriptions can be categorized based on their intended purposes. It is pointed out that depending on the intended addresses (direction givers or receivers) significantly impact the ways that route directions were given. It is easy to assume that when a person uses his or her own given route directions, the embedded structure and characteristics are familiar to him or her. While a person has to use the direction given by others, the effectiveness of those given directions is in question. On the other hand, verbal descriptions can also be differentiated based on the type of spatial information included. For example, A study [6] assesses the differences in acquired spatial knowledge based on types of spatial information included in verbal descriptions. Route directions containing spatial information based on landmarks, skeletal descriptions (see [7]), or metric distance would lead to different spatial knowledge acquisition. Results from this study show that various types of spatial information can lead to different forms of sketch maps, as well as, contrasting types of spatial knowledge.

Motivated by these findings on verbal route directions associated with different purposes or included spatial information, we are interested to investigate if personal factors such as familiarity and spatial abilities would play a role on acquiring spatial knowledge. If so, how do they influence spatial performance that utilizes acquired spatial knowledge? In order to address these questions, we carry out this study aiming to investigate the effects of familiarity and spatial abilities on spatial performance that requires acquired spatial knowledge involving direction and distance. This report is organized as follows: Sect. 2 introduces the related work that is keen to the background and influential factors that we investigate in this study. The methods section (Sect. 3) elaborates the design of our study. In particular, we introduce the design of verbal descriptions for both familiar and unfamiliar scenarios controlled with the same style, syntax, and amount of information specific to each participant. The following sections report the results, discussions, and a summary to conclude current study.

2   Related Work

2.1   Verbal Descriptions

Analyzing verbal descriptions to find an effective way for communicating wayfinding instructions has drawn researchers' attention from different fields. Denis and Zimmer [8] investigate the importance of verbal instructions for constructing cognitive maps. Their study shows that people are capable of transforming linguistic descriptions involving configurations into mental representations, both in text and other information. They also highlight that a person is able to construct a good visuospatial representation of the environment based on the verbal descriptions. To further understand the cognitive aspects behind the construction of spatial descriptions, Denis [9] collects several route descriptions that result in the development of skeletal descriptions. Skeletal descriptions consist of a minimal set of informative route instructions with particular importance to landmarks at decision points. Such descriptions have been tested in several wayfinding studies (see [10, 11]). On the one hand, these results show the effectiveness of skeletal descriptions as good verbal descriptions. On the other hand, other researchers analyze the contextual aspects of route instructions based on different modes of transportation and a traveler's perspective [12]. This is because people may vary their route descriptions based on several factors. Klippel and colleagues [13] emphasize the importance that such directions are cognitively adequate which could be easily comprehended by persons in need. These studies indicate that several factors would influence the generation of verbal descriptions for various people. A set of verbal descriptions that is sufficient for one person may not be helpful for another due to different cognitive capacity or information sufficiency. They also point out the importance of constructing verbal descriptions in experiments that is cognitively sufficient and efficient for an individual person. We further introduce our design of constructing verbal descriptions in the section regarding methods.

2.2 Familiarity

Familiarity is an influential factor in wayfinding and the acquisition of spatial knowledge. It indicates the level of previously acquired knowledge about an environment. Therefore, it is not only positively correlated with a person's development of cognitive maps [14], but also positively correlated with a person's wayfinding performance [15, 16]. Weisman (1981) suggests differentiating between three aspects of familiarity: the frequency, recency, and context of spatial knowledge that contribute to the familiarity of an environment. Gale and colleagues [17] suggest four different aspects: locational knowledge, visual recognition, name identification, and interaction frequency which contribute to the familiarity of an environment. Instead of considering familiarity at different levels, the purpose of this study is to investigate familiarity as a single factor that contributes to the acquisition of spatial knowledge: the estimation of direction, the estimation of distance, and the configurational change of sketch maps. As the first step in assessing the role of familiarity, we only consider two different classes of familiarity: very familiar and not familiar at all, in this study.

2.3 Spatial Orientation

Spatial orientation is an important cognitive process, especially when a person is planning routes or performing actual wayfinding. It is a vital mechanism that directly relates to the correct execution of the planned routes based on the spatial knowledge of the environment that a person acquires. A person uses reference systems to estimate his/her location and specify relationships between the current location and other places [18]. The use of reference systems differentiates spatial orientation into two types. Hart and Moore [19] classify these references systems as egocentric and geocentric. Egocentric reference systems use a wayfinder's position and heading (line of sight) to assign spatial predicates such as left or right to objects in relation to the wayfinder. It is similar to the concept of piloting introduced by Sholl and colleagues [20]. The use of egocentric reference systems involves using a wayfinder's velocity and acceleration information about self-movement [21]. In contrast, the use of geocentric (absolute) reference systems is in how a person relates to the features of an environment and determines the relative locations of a feature to other features in the environment. Sholl and colleagues [20] define spatial orientation as a process of orienting to landmarks that are hidden from view using visible landmarks and a cognitive map. In this definition, the outcome of cognitive mapping, the cognitive map, is used. It is similar to the type of spatial orientation that uses an egocentric reference system as introduced above. It can occur in both familiar and unfamiliar environments in which landmarks provide wayfinders information on their location and confirmation while executing routes [22]. In this study, we use the errors of direction and distance estimation as ways to reflect one's performance related to spatial orientation.

2.4 Cognitive Maps

When an environment is so large that one needs to travel in order to learn the space through multiple vantage points, cognitive maps or mental representations are the outcome of a process called cognitive mapping. The developed cognitive maps integrate spatial knowledge of the large environment with configurational knowledge. Regarding the acquired spatial knowledge in cognitive maps, researchers such as Downs and Stea [23] suggest that knowledge in cognitive maps includes the relative locations and attributes of phenomena in one's every day spatial environment that a person can acquire, store, recall, and decode. Levine and colleagues [24] also suggest that cognitive maps are mental copies of the environment including not only sequentially experienced landmarks but also the metric information of landmarks. In short, cognitive maps are mental models where acquired spatial knowledge is stored. In the context of wayfinding, people are able to access cognitive maps to support decision making such as which direction one should head or the spatial relationship between a location and others. Using externalized representations such as sketched maps [25, 26] is one of the common methods to assess one's cognitive map. This is evident in many studies that participants are asked to sketch a route they are familiar with [27, 28] or after following a task in an unfamiliar environment [29, 30]. Analysis of sketch maps include either qualitative [31, 32] or quantitative [33–35]. As the results of qualitative evaluation suggest, sketch maps yield high accuracy in depicting topological relationship. Therefore, in this study we adapt quantitative measures on sketch maps to assess if familiarity would affect aspects associated with configuration such as distortion, scaling, and rotation.

3   Methods

To evaluate the role of familiarity and spatial abilities of a participant on their spatial knowledge and mental representations, we design our experiment to control participants' familiarity and to assess their spatial abilities. The following sections detail the information of participants, experimental materials and procedure employed in this study.

3.1 Participants

Participants were recruited through a campus wide listserv administrated by the student association. Students who received our flyer and were interested in this study contacted the experimenter to sign up. The only requirement was that a participant should have lived in the city for more a year. In total 26 students (15 male and 11 female) participated in this study. The mean age of participants is 24.58 ($SD = 1.40$). Participants received monetary reimbursement for their participation in this study.

3.2 Materials

As one of the most important aspects in this study, creating comparable verbal descriptions for familiar and unfamiliar environments was the first task. When a participant confirmed to take part in this experiment, he or she was asked to provide verbal descriptions from the *central train station* to the *student cafeteria* in the city of Muenster. All participants were given the same scenario that someone was coming to the city for their first time and wanted to go to the student cafeteria from the central train station. Each participant should provide verbal descriptions to help this person get from the central train station to the student cafeteria easily. These provided descriptions were the basis for the authors to create instructions in the unfamiliar scenario. In particular, when a participant contacted the experimenter to schedule an experiment, the confirmation email with experiment time and location also included a task requesting the participant to give verbal descriptions from the central train station to the student cafeteria in the aforementioned scenario. Each participant's experiment took place at least a few days after signing up. During this period, we altered each participant's provided instructions to create verbal descriptions for the unfamiliar scenario. To do so, we first identified all mentioned entities in the original descriptions and replaced them with foreign street names. For the start and ending point, the *central train station* was changed to *theatre*, the *student cafeteria* was changed to *library*. The street names were replaced by the most frequently used street names in the United States [36] in order to create an unfamiliar scenario for this participant. In this way, only the spatial entities' names were changed, but the syntax, style, or information sufficiency remained the same to each participant based on their provided verbal descriptions.

In addition to familiarity, participant's spatial abilities was the other factor we investigated in this study. To do so, we selected one psychometric test mental rotation task (MRT) and the self-rated spatial strategies scale [37]. The MRT was adapted from Vandenberg's test [38] that participants had to find two out of four 3D rotated objects that was identical to a given object. Only correctly selecting both two matching objects would qualify for earning one point. Partial or non correct selection resulted in zero points. Participants' scores in this task were further adjusted for chance of random guess by deducting 25% of the number of incorrectly answered questions. The self-rated questionnaire for assessing spatial strategies consisted of 19 statements addressing egocentric strategies, cardinal strategies, and general confidence and sense of direction. Participants could rate on 7 scales from strongly disagree (1) to strongly agree (7). Participant's scores were normalized and later mean split in order to create two groups of spatial abilities: high and low in later analysis.

3.3 Procedure

When a participant contacted the experimenter expressing interest in joining this experiment through email, the experimenter provided available timeslots and asked the participant to choose his/her preferred slot, which would take place a few days later. In the email sent to a participant confirming the time and location of the experiment, the participant was also asked to provide directions in the form of verbal descriptions to help someone who is new to the city to get from the central train station to the student's cafeteria (Fig. 1). These instructions were written and sent to the experimenter. During the days before each participant's scheduled experiment, the experimenter then replaced all names of mentioned spatial entities to create the verbal descriptions in the unfamiliar scenario.

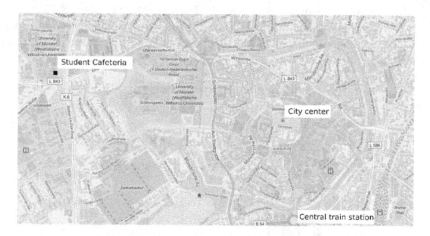

Fig. 1. Selected starting and ending locations in Muenster (NRW), Germany.

Days later the participants came to the scheduled experiment where he or she started working on the remaining tasks. All participants were not reminded that days ago they provided the verbal descriptions of getting from central train station to the student cafeteria. Instead, they were told to draw a sketch map to show the directions for someone new to the city to get from the central train station to the student cafeteria. In addition, they were asked to estimate the distance and direction to the cafeteria, while imagining they were standing at the front of the train station facing north. After that, each participant received a set of verbal descriptions that was altered based on his or her original directions. They were asked to assume that they arrived in a city they had never been to and received the directions from some locals to get from the theatre to the library. They were told to read the directions carefully and then complete a map sketching task and the estimation tasks of direction and distance. During this task, there were two participants who thought the instructions were similar to what they wrote a while ago. The experimenters then stated that it might be due to coincidence as the instructions were given for an American city, in order to distract the participant to relate this instructions with their written ones, This session ended with participant's completion of the psychometric tests including MRT and the self-rated spatial strategies scale.

4   Results

The errors of each estimation task were used as the dependent variables in a mixed design. Participants were categorized into two groups using a mean split of scores of their MRT and self-rated scores. The spatial abilities group was entered in a repeated ANOVA as a between-subject variable while familiarity was entered as a within-subject variable. Regarding direction estimation, participant's absolute errors between $0°$ and $180°$ were used as the dependent variable. Familiarity was found to be a significant factor that participants made fewer errors in the familiar condition ($M = 60.42$, $SD = 55.60$) than in the unfamiliar condition ($M = 88.08$, $SD = 50.53$), $F(1, 24) = 8.15$, $p < .01$, partial $\eta2 = .25$). Spatial abilities and the interaction between familiarity and spatial abilities were not found significant factors ($p = .58$ and $p = .38$, respectively). The results are shown in Fig. 2.

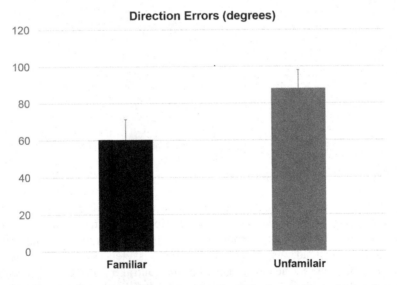

Fig. 2.   Absolute errors of direction estimation in both experimental scenarios.

Regarding the distance estimation, we did not use the absolute errors in this measure as the positive and negative errors could provide us valuable information about the influence of familiarity and spatial abilities on distance overestimation or underestimation. Using the same mixed design in which familiarity was entered as a within-subject variable while spatial abilities group based on mean split was entered as a between-subject variable, results showed that the familiarity had main effect on the distance estimation errors ($F(1, 24) = 8.32$, $p < .01$, partial $\eta 2 = .26$) while the interaction of familiarity and spatial abilities also contributed to the influence significantly ($F(1, 24) = 6.50$, $p < .05$, partial $\eta 2 = .21$). The spatial abilities were not found a significant factor of distance estimation errors ($p = .67$). In particular, familiarity seems non influential to participants in the low spatial abilities group, as their estimation in both familiar and unfamiliar scenarios are similar ($M = 1.69$, $SD = 3.28$; $M = 1.56$, $SD = 3.14$, respectively). Spatial abilities seem non influential on participants in the familiar scenario as well ($p = .68$). Familiarity, however, plays a significant role influencing participants in the high spatial abilities group, as their estimation errors in the familiar scenario is higher ($M = 2.21$, $SD = 2.93$) than those in the unfamiliar scenario ($M = .11$, $SD = 1.90$). Figure 3, below, shows these results in details. We further discuss participants' distance estimation in Sect. 5.2.

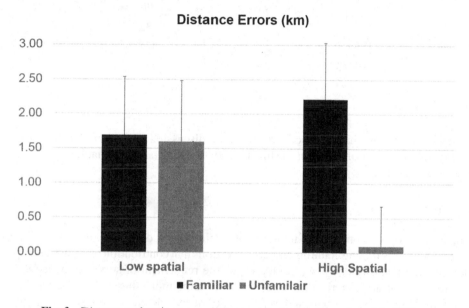

Fig. 3. Distance estimation errors influenced by familiarity and spatial abilities.

Due to the fact that participants were asked to draw the sketch map showing direction from the central train station (theatre) to the student cafeteria (library) without the requirement of including the same landmarks, the sketch maps provided by participants include various types and numbers of landmarks. This diversity made the comparison between each participant's sketch maps with a cartographic map less informative. Therefore, we only applied the spatial abilities as the between-subject factor to compare participants' sketch maps between the two spatial abilities groups. To do so, we used Gardony Map Drawing Analyzer [39] to quantify all drawn sketch maps. Once a coordinate file was created based on the first sketch map and landmarks (drawn in the familiar scenario), the second sketch map (drawn in the unfamiliar scenario) was imported to measure several aspects including configurational accuracy (r), scaling (ϕ), and rotation

(θ). The reason for choosing these measures is because they provide valuable information about configurational changes of sketch maps between familiar and unfamiliar scenarios. Each aspect of these measures was entered in a one-way ANOVA. Results showed that spatial abilities did not significantly differentiate sketch maps' configurational distortion, size, or rotation ($p = .88; p = .98; p = .42$, *respectively*). However, the results from these bi-dimensional measures provide valuable information for us to understand the change of sketch maps drawn by each participant from familiar scenario to unfamiliar scenario. In particular, the descriptive statistics of configuration accuracy, scaling, and rotation of participants in both spatial abilities groups are shown in Table 1. We further address these measures in our discussion on sketch maps in Sect. 5.3.

Table 1. Descriptive statistics of participants' sketch map measures

Participants	Configurational accuracy (r)	Scaling (ϕ)	Rotation (θ)
Low spatial	.85	.78	13.56°
High spatial	.84	.78	45.64°
Average	.85	.78	27.13°

5   Discussion

Based on the results that we described above, the discussion is structured as following three sections: errors of directional estimation, errors of distance estimation, and measures of sketch maps.

5.1   Directional Estimation

The first important notion is the influence of familiarity on directional estimation. Not surprisingly, this finding confirms earlier suggestions that contribution of verbal description to survey knowledge is weak [40, 41] as the refinement of survey knowledge is sensitive to time and experience of a person [42]. Furthermore, this study further reveals that familiarity to an environment has a more dominant role on refining survey knowledge. This finding further supplements the suggestion of a previous study that development of spatial orientation which helps one to estimate direction in one environment is mostly associated with the person's familiarity [43, 44]. These previous studies suggest that the influence of familiarity on spatial orientation is more dominant than that of the environment. Although this study does not address the role of the environment, it is worthwhile in future studies to clarify the roles between environment and spatial abilities while counting the major influence of familiarity. It is likely that familiarity helps a person embed a planned route in a larger context, which contributes to globally orienting the route in an environment. Therefore, when a person has no familiarity of larger context in the environment, he or she is likely to be less spatially oriented.

It is also important to note the large errors of estimation by participants in both familiar and unfamiliar scenarios. Even in the familiar scenario, participants' estimation had errors over 60°. The error is greater when the instructions were altered to appear as an unfamiliar environment to participants. This further indicates that the refinement of spatial knowledge is a lengthy process, especially if one does not acquire spatial knowledge of the environment through representation such as maps.

5.2 Distance Estimation

Participants' estimation of distance in this study shows large variation. In general, the influence of familiarity and spatial abilities seems more intricate. It is easy to note that familiarity seems non influential on participants with lower spatial abilities, as their errors of distance estimation are very similar between the familiar and the unfamiliar scenario. It is interesting to find that in the unfamiliar scenario, participants with high spatial abilities are benefited the most. Their estimation of distance based on the altered route descriptions yield very small errors. Furthermore, if only considering the main effect of familiarity, all participants overestimate the distance in the familiar scenario rather than in the unfamiliar scenario. The findings here are parallel to the suggestion from a few previous studies. For example, Sadalla and Magel [45] suggested that a higher number of turns in an environment leads to overestimation of distance. This suggestion explains our findings in this study as well. When participants were estimating the distance from the central train station to the student cafeteria, they mentally walk through the route in order to estimate the distance. The mentally walked route involved small turns or slight changes of direction, which were not exactly represented in their verbal descriptions or sketch maps. Those provided verbal descriptions and sketch maps show the route in a simpler fashion to make the directions easier for a person to follow. Therefore, when they were given the altered verbal descriptions, the number of turns is directly controlled by the information provided in those directions, which leads to less number of turns, hence less overestimation. This finding was later verified and replicated using a virtual environment (see [46]). Furthermore, an early study by Cohen and colleagues [47] discussed the roles of task demand and familiarity on estimation of distance that showed estimation of distance is more accurate in an unfamiliar environment than in a familiar environment. A recent study by Jackson and colleagues [48] also demonstrated that spatial experience such as time spent in an environment does not lead to improvement of estimation but overestimation. The factor that contributes the refinement of distance estimation is not time in an environment but the evolutionary navigation costs. These theories also explained participants' performance of distance estimation in this study. When participants are given altered directions, they have to actively engage and process the provided information during the experiment to estimate. While during their daily activities in the city, their acquisition of spatial knowledge and learning of the environment could be subconscious and not so purpose oriented.

5.3 Sketch Map Measures

Results of sketch map measures further confirm that the influence of spatial abilities on configuration of sketch maps is not dominant. Based on our measures of the configurational aspects of sketch maps, including distortion and scaling, participants in both spatial abilities group have almost the same ratio indicating that the distortion of sketch map configuration is not affected by spatial abilities. Looking at the configurational accuracy, sketch maps drawn based on altered verbal descriptions only have about 15% distortion. Similarly, the scaling indicates how much a sketch map is resized when participants draw them based on altered verbal descriptions. Participants in both spatial abilities groups tend to draw sketch maps 22% smaller than the ones drawn based on their own spatial knowledge. This could be an indicator that familiarity may have played a role influencing the size of sketched maps. When participants are familiar with an environment, they are likely to think of more details. According to our earlier discussion on the overestimation of distance, they tend to draw longer lines and more segments of street. They can both lead to a larger configuration of a sketch map. When participants read through the altered verbal descriptions which provides the only available spatial information, their estimation of distance seems less, hence the drawn segments of streets would be shorter.

The third aspect of sketch map measures on rotation, worth further exploration. As the rotation is related to participant's orientation, our findings in directional estimation are also associated with this aspect. We introduced earlier that due to the familiarity of a person, the participant can orient the planned route within a global context of environment, which can be orientation specific. Depending on the position of the participant when taking this task, participants could rotate the page to draw their orientation-specific sketch maps. When processing the altered verbal descriptions, participants no longer have an orientation-specific context to embed the route, so most of them tend to draw a sketch map align their map north with the upright orientation of the given sheet. It is necessary to point out that the accurate angle between the start-end locations and north is $-68°$ ($68°$ anti-clockwise). All participants tend to rotate their orientation-specific sketch maps clockwise towards a north-upright alignment in the unfamiliar scenario. In particular, higher spatial abilities participants rotate sketch maps $45.64°$ clockwise and lower spatial abilities participants rotate sketch maps $13.56°$. Because we did not specify the sitting position of each participant, it is unknown if their facing direction during the sketching task would influence this sketch map measure. We plan to carry out a follow-up study, in particular, to address the influences of familiarity, spatial abilities, and actual sitting position on the configurational rotation of sketch maps.

6   Conclusion

Verbal descriptions are common in our daily lives helping one get from one location to another in a new environment. We acknowledge the large individual variation among people's given directions, creating only one version may not meet the need of individual's information sufficiency and style. To avoid this bias, we design to create the familiar and unfamiliar conditions based on ones' own given directions. We only replace the names of entities such as street names and landmarks in the directions and keep the syntax and amount of information the same. Therefore, each individual would be acquainted with the style that verbal descriptions are given. Besides the familiarity as a considered factor, we employ psychometric tests and self-rated spatial strategies to place participants into two groups: high spatial abilities and low spatial abilities. Participants' performance such as estimation of direction and distance and measures on sketch maps were used as dependent variables, while these introduced factors were entered as independent variables in our analyses to investigate the different roles that they play. However, it is important for use to acknowledge that we have only asked each participant to estimate only once in each condition regarding direction and distance. The estimations may have not fully represented a participant's full scale of spatial knowledge but mainly the survey-level knowledge of direction and distance, Further studies are needed to investigate more comprehensively about one's spatial knowledge.

It is important to summarize the impact of familiarity on spatial performance together with spatial abilities. The most important finding of this study is that it shows different impacts that familiarity and spatial abilities have on various aspects of spatial performance. Familiarity plays a dominant role on spatial orientation that involves direction regardless of spatial abilities. Regarding spatial knowledge associated with distance, familiarity tends to have a negative role on accuracy of distance estimation. This is because of the mentally navigated route in an familiar environments involves more details and small turns which are normally eliminated when expressing routes for others for navigation purpose, these details and higher number of turns lead to overestimation of distance. However, when given descriptions of an unfamiliar environment, participants with higher spatial abilities seem to benefit the most. Their higher spatial abilities lead to more accurate estimation of distance when they actively engage and process the provided descriptions. Participants with lower spatial abilities estimate almost the same in both familiar and unfamiliar scenarios. The measure of participant's sketch maps confirm the findings in estimation of direction and distance. Like the estimation of distance, familiarity tends to lead one person to draw a slightly less distorted and larger sketch map. The orientation of sketch maps seems to be perspective specific when one is familiar with an environment. In unfamiliar environments, the sketch map seems to be orientation free that north of the map is aligned with the upright direction of page. The information may provide some more evidence to characteristics regarding cognitive maps developed in familiar and novel environments. These results provide useful information regarding the design of navigation systems that can contribute to one's spatial orientation compared to the poor contribution of existing navigation systems regarding this aspect (see example in [49]).

It is also important to acknowledge the limits of this study. First of all, due to its relatively small sample size, our results show necessity for further investigation on the roles of familiarity and spatial abilities on acquiring spatial knowledge with more participants. Second, we instruct participants to perform free sketching task without requiring them to include identical spatial entities in their verbal descriptions and sketch maps, which provides difficulty when comparing each participant's two maps with a cartographic map. In order to clarify the role of familiarity on sketch maps, we aim to design an experiment that controls the number of landmarks to be sketched in order to provide a comparable basis. In this way, sketch maps will be further compared with metric maps for more qualitative assessments. Third, our finding of the orientation specific and orientation free trend in drawn sketch maps of familiar and unfamiliar environments motivates us to further investigate if the siting position and facing direction would play a role on the orientation specificity of sketched maps. To do so, we will conduct an experiment with a siting condition factor, together with the factors of familiarity and spatial abilities to shed light on their impacts.

References

1. Denis, M., Pazzaglia, F., Cornoldi, C., Bertolo, L.: Spatial discourse and navigation: an analysis of route directions in the city of Venice. Appl. Cogn. Psychol. **13**, 145–174 (1999)
2. Giudice, N.A., Bakdash, J.Z., Legge, G.E.: Wayfinding with words: spatial learning and navigation using dynamically updated verbal descriptions. Psychol. Res. **71**, 347–358 (2006)
3. Allen, G.L.: Principles and practices for communicating route knowledge. Appl. Cogn. Psychol. **14**, 333–359 (2000)
4. Lovelace, K.L., Hegarty, M., Montello, D.R.: Elements of Good Route Directions in Familiar and Unfamiliar Environments. In: Freksa, C., Mark, D.M. (eds.) COSIT 1999. LNCS, vol. 1661, pp. 65–82. Springer, Heidelberg (1999). https://doi.org/10.1007/3-540-48384-5_5
5. Hölscher, C., Tenbrink, T., Wiener, J.M.: Would you follow your own route description? Cognitive strategies in urban route planning. Cognition **121**, 228–247 (2011)
6. Li, R., Fuest, S., Schwering, A.: The effects of different verbal route instructions on spatial orientation. In: The 17th AGILE Conference on Geographic Information Science, Castellon, Spain (2014)
7. Tom, A., Denis, M.: Language and spatial cognition: comparing the roles of landmarks and street names in route instructions. Appl. Cogn. Psychol. **18**, 1213–1230 (2004)
8. Denis, M., Zimmere, M.: Analog properties of cognitive maps constructed from verbal descriptions. Psychol. Res. **54**, 286–298 (1992)
9. Denis, M.: The description of routes: a cognitive approach to the production of spatial discourse. Cahiers de psychologie cognitive **16**, 409–458 (1997)
10. Daniel, M.P., Tom, A., Manghi, E., Denis, M.: Testing the value of route directions through navigational performance. Spat. Cogn. Comput. **3**, 269–289 (2003)
11. Michon, P.-E., Denis, M.: When and why are visual landmarks used in giving directions? In: Montello, D.R. (ed.) COSIT 2001. LNCS, vol. 2205, pp. 292–305. Springer, Heidelberg (2001). https://doi.org/10.1007/3-540-45424-1_20
12. Timpf, S.: Ontologies of wayfinding: a traveler's perspective. Netw. Spat. Econ. **2**, 9–33 (2002)
13. Klippel, A., Winter, S.: Structural salience of landmarks for route directions. In: Cohn, A.G., Mark, D.M. (eds.) COSIT 2005. LNCS, vol. 3693, pp. 347–362. Springer, Heidelberg (2005). https://doi.org/10.1007/11556114_22
14. Gale, N., Golledge, R.G., Pellegrino, J.W., Doherty, S.: The acquisition and integration of route knowledge in an unfamiliar neighborhood. J. Environ. Psychol. **10**, 3–25 (1990)
15. Weisman, J.: Evaluating architectural legibility: way-finding in the built environment. Environ. Behav. **13**, 189–204 (1981)
16. Prestopnik, J.L., Roskos-Ewoldsen, B.: The relations among wayfinding strategy use, sense of direction, sex, familiarity, and wayfinding ability. J. Environ. Psychol. **20**, 177–191 (2000)
17. Gale, N., Golledge, R.G., Halperin, W.C., Couclelis, H.: Exploring spatial familiarity. Prof. Geogr. **42**, 299–313 (1990)
18. Montello, D.R.: Navigation. In: Shah, P., Miyake, A. (eds.) Cambridge Handbook of Visuospatial Thinking, pp. 257–294. Cambridge University Press, Cambridge, England (2005)

19. Hart, R.A., Moore, G.T.: The development of spatial cognition: A review. In: Downs, R., Stea, D. (eds.) Image and Environment: Cognitive Mapping and Spatial Behavior, pp. 124–288. Aldine Publishing, Chicago (1973)
20. Sholl, M.J., Acacio, J.C., Markar, R.O., Leon, C.: The relation of sex and sense of direction to spatial orientation in an unfamiliar environment. J. Environ. Psychol. **20**, 17–28 (2000)
21. Loomis, J.M., Blascovich, J.J., Beall, A.C.: Immersive virtual environment technology as a basic research tool in psychology. Behav. Res. Methods **31**, 557–564 (1999)
22. Allen, G.L.: Spatial abilities, cognitive maps, and wayfinding: bases for individual differences in spatial cognition and behavior. In: Golledge, R.G. (ed.) Wayfinding Behavior: Cognitive Mapping And Other Spatial Processes, Baltimore, pp. 46–80 (1999)
23. Downs, R.M., Stea, D.: Cognitive maps and spatial behavior: Process and products. In: Downs, R.M., Stea, D. (eds.) Image and Environment. Aldine, Chicago (1973)
24. Levine, M.: You-are-here maps psychological considerations. Environ. Behav. **14**, 221–237 (1982)
25. Billinghurst, M., Weghorst, S.: The use of sketch maps to measure cognitive maps of virtual environments. In: Virtual Reality Annual International Symposium, pp. 40–47. IEEE (1995)
26. Li, R., Bell, S.: Performance of directional estimation and route sketching: What differentiates and what predicts? In: Proceedings of Workshop of an Interdisciplinary Approach to Understanding and Proceeding Sketch Maps in conjunction with COSIT 2011, vol. 42, pp. 33–44. IFGI Prints, Belfast, ME (2011), ISSN 2191-5237
27. Wang, J., Li, R.: An empirical study on pertinent aspects of sketch maps for navigation. Int. J. Cogn. Inf. Natural Intell. (IJCINI) **7**, 26–43 (2013)
28. Schwering, A., Wang, J., Chipofya, M., Jan, S., Li, R., Broelemann, K.: SketchMapia: Qualitative Representations for the Alignment of Sketch and Metric Maps. Spatial Cogn. Comput. **14**, 220–254 (2014)
29. Rovine, M.J., Weisman, G.D.: Sketch-map variables as predictors of way-finding performance. J. Environ. Psychol. **9**, 217–232 (1989)
30. Münzer, S., Zimmer, H.D., Baus, J.: A trade-off between wayfinding support and configural learning support. J. Exp. Psychol. Appl. **18**, 18–37 (2012)
31. Kettunen, P., Irvankoski, K., Krause, C.M., Sarjakoski, L.T.: Landmarks in nature to support wayfinding: the effects of seasons and experimental methods. Cogn. Process. **14**, 245–253 (2013)
32. Chipofya, M., Wang, J., Schwering, A.: Towards cognitively plausible spatial representations for sketch map alignment. In: Egenhofer, M., Giudice, N., Moratz, R., Worboys, M. (eds.) COSIT 2011. LNCS, vol. 6899, pp. 20–39. Springer, Heidelberg (2011). https://doi.org/10.1007/978-3-642-23196-4_2
33. Okamoto, K., Okunuki, K.-i., Takai, T.: Sketch map analysis using gis buffer operation. In: Freksa, C., Knauff, M., Krieg-Brückner, B., Nebel, B., Barkowsky, T. (eds.) Spatial Cognition 2004. LNCS, vol. 3343, pp. 227–244. Springer, Heidelberg (2005). https://doi.org/10.1007/978-3-540-32255-9_14
34. Friedman, A., Kohler, B.: Bidimensional Regression: Assessing the configural similarity and accuracy of cognitive maps and other two-dimensional data sets. Psychol. Methods **8**, 468–491 (2003)
35. Gardony, A.L., Taylor, H.A., Brunyé, T.T.: Gardony Map Drawing Analyzer: Software for quantitative analysis of sketch maps. Behav. Res. Methods **48**, 151–177 (2016)
36. National League of Cities: Most Common U.S. Street Names (2016). http://www.nlc.org/most-common-us-street-names. Accessed 10 Jan 2017

37. Münzer, S., Christensen, A.E., Liben, L.: Finding your way around the environment: Differences and similarities across countries in self-reports. In: Rapp, D. (ed.) Poster Proceedings of International Conference on Spatial Cognition 2010, Mt. Hood, Oregon, p. 66 (2010)

38. Vandenberg, S.G., Kuse, A.R.: Mental rotations, a group test of three-dimensional spatial visualization. Percept. Mot. Skills **47**, 599–604 (1978)

39. Gardony, A.L., Taylor, H.A., Brunyé, T.T.: Gardony map drawing analyzer: software for quantitative analysis of sketch maps. Behav. Res. Methods **48**, 151–177 (2016). https://doi.org/10.3758/s13428-014-0556-x

40. Taylor, H.A., Tversky, B.: Spatial mental models derived from survey and route descriptions. J. Mem. Lang. **31**, 261–282 (1992)

41. Tversky, B., Lee, P.U.: Pictorial and verbal tools for conveying routes. In: Freksa, C., Mark, D.M. (eds.) COSIT 1999. LNCS, vol. 1661, pp. 51–64. Springer, Heidelberg (1999). https://doi.org/10.1007/3-540-48384-5_4

42. Ishikawa, T., Montello, D.: Spatial knowledge acquisition from direct experience in the environment: Individual differences in the development of metric knowledge and the integration of separately learned places. Cogn. Psychol. **52**, 93–129 (2005)

43. Li, R., Klippel, A.: Wayfinding Behaviors in Complex Buildings: the Impact of Environmental Legibility and Familiarity. Environ. Behav. **48**, 482–510 (2016)

44. O'Neill, M.J.: Effects of familiarity and plan complexity on wayfinding in simulated buildings. J. Environ. Psychol. **12**, 319–327 (1992)

45. Magel, S.G., Sadalla, E.K.: The Perception of Traversed Distance. Environ. Behav. **12**, 65–79 (1980)

46. Jansen-Osmann, P., Berendt, B.: Investigating Distance Knowledge Using Virtual Environments. Environ. Behav. **34**, 178–193 (2002)

47. Cohen, R., Weatherford, D.L., Byrd, D.: Distance estimates of children as a function of acquisition and response activities. J. Exp. Child Psychol. **30**, 464–472 (1980)

48. Jackson, R.E., Willey, C.R., Cormack, L.K.: Learning and exposure affect environmental perception less than evolutionary navigation costs. PLoS ONE **8**, e59690 (2013)

49. Parush, A., Ahuvia, S., Erev, I.: Degradation in spatial knowledge acquisition when using automatic navigation systems. In: Winter, S., Duckham, M., Kulik, L., Kuipers, B. (eds.) COSIT 2007. LNCS, vol. 4736, pp. 238–254. Springer, Heidelberg (2007). https://doi.org/10.1007/978-3-540-74788-8_15

Wayfinding and Navigation

Are Wayfinding Self-efficacy and Pleasure in Exploring Related to Shortcut Finding? A Study in a Virtual Environment

Francesca Pazzaglia[1](✉), Chiara Meneghetti[1], Enia Labate[1], and Lucia Ronconi[2]

[1] Department of General Psychology, University of Padova, Padua, Italy
francesca.pazzaglia@unipd.it
[2] Department of Philosophy, Sociology, Pedagogy, and Applied Psychology,
University of Padova, Padua, Italy

Abstract. The analysis of individual factors supporting wayfinding ability is attracting increasing interest in the spatial cognition domain. The present study aimed to investigate whether two variables, wayfinding self-efficacy and pleasure in exploring, relate to shortcut-finding performance. A group of 124 university students were led along a route through one of two virtual environments that differed only in that one contained landmarks, while the other did not. Then they were asked to find a shortcut from the start to the end of the route they had learned. Two questionnaires were also administered to assess their wayfinding self-efficacy and pleasure in exploring. The results showed a better performance in the shortcut task for the environment containing landmarks. Individual differences correlated with shortcut-finding ability, but their predictive power was stronger in the without- than in the with-landmarks condition. The authors concluded that individual variables, such as wayfinding self-efficacy and a positive attitude to exploring, interact with environmental features (landmark availability) and relate to wayfinding performance.

Keywords: Wayfinding · Shortcut finding · Landmarks · Virtual environment · Wayfinding self-efficacy · Pleasure in exploring

1 Introduction

1.1 Wayfinding: A Multifaceted Ability

Wayfinding (WF) is generally defined as the ability to move around efficiently, and to find a route from a starting point to a destination [36]. It is an important component of everyday life and can even be vital in some circumstances, in adverse weather conditions or emergencies, for example [16]. It is generally acknowledged that WF is a multifaceted skill that requires a broad range of mental processes, cognitive functions, and strategies [14, 52]. It is also susceptible to wide individual differences [58]: some people find WF easy [8], while others have serious difficulties right from their childhood [18, 45], with all the gradations in between.

© Springer International Publishing AG 2017
T. Barkowsky et al. (Eds.): KogWis/Spatial Cognition 2016, LNAI 10523, pp. 55–68, 2017.
https://doi.org/10.1007/978-3-319-68189-4_4

Studying individual differences has helped to shed light on the neural substrates [54] and cognitive mechanisms implicated in WF ability [58], showing that optic flow [22], working memory [24, 31, 32, 56], attention and planning [8] functions are involved in WF tasks. Personal traits are not the only components affecting WF, however. Some studies have underscored that environmental features and the type of task at hand can strongly affect navigation [4]. What emerges is a complex pattern of individual and environmental features interacting in influencing performance in WF tasks, which can also vary considerably, from visual landmark recognition to retracing a route, estimating direction and distance, and finding a shortcut. Different tasks are assumed to demand different spatial representation strategies, with distinct implications for perception, attention, and memory [57].

1.2 Shortcut Finding

A psychologically relevant distinction exists between WF tasks that involve retracing an already-learned route and those in which a novel, hitherto unknown path has to be found. Examples of the latter are shortcut-finding tasks, which involve identifying the shortest route to reach a destination. Finding a shortcut involves using a configurational representation obtained by integrating information acquired during navigation [12].

A paradigm frequently used to test people's ability to integrate environmental information gleaned from navigation is triangle completion, in which participants are led along two sides of a given triangle-shaped configuration and have to find the shortest way back to the starting point [28]. Typically, performance in triangle completion is more accurate in the presence of landmarks than in their absence [13, 43]: participants integrate their information and find a shortcut more easily in relation to the landmarks, whereas without them they are only able to retrace their steps [9, 10].

The presence of landmarks does not always guarantee that environmental information will be integrated to form a configured representation, however. There is evidence of individual differences - in terms of working memory [24], visuo-spatial abilities [43], strategies [9, 47], and also subjective measures of Sense of Direction (SOD) [15, 21] - all contributing to explaining the variability in people's shortcut-finding abilities.

1.3 Subjective Measures and Wayfinding

People's subjective measures regarding their spatial preferences and attitudes, such as spatial anxiety, spatial strategies, and SOD, have been studied intensively in terms of how they relate to WF ability. Self-assessed SOD (an individual's estimation of their ability to locate and orient themselves in an environmental space) is perhaps the most often studied subjective index since Kozwlosky and Bryant [23] identified significant relationships between SOD and performance in pointing tasks after learning spatial information.

More recently, Janzen and colleagues [21] found that individuals scoring higher for SOD on the Santa Barbara Sense of Direction Scale (SBSOD) [15] consolidated landmark information better (with more activity in the hippocampus) than those reporting a weaker SOD. In the work of Labate and colleagues [24], higher SBSOD scores again coincided with better shortcut-finding skills in a real environment previously learned from navigation. Spatial strategies have also been found related to WF, and susceptible to gender-related differences, females being more likely to adopt route strategies, while males show a stronger preference for configurational strategies and survey representations [25, 26].

Several instruments have been devised to assess individual differences in a variety of subjective measures: spatial anxiety [25], strategies [25], preference for spatial representation [40], and SOD [15]. The last of these seems to be related to memory consolidation for navigationally relevant objects [20], and to WF in real [24] and virtual [42] environments. Interestingly, the strength of the relationship between subjective measures and environment learning tasks depends on the demands of the tasks and their difficulty: the relationship is stronger for spatial than for visual tasks, and for difficult than for simple tasks [55].

1.4 Emotions, Motivation, and Socio-cognitive Factors in the Spatial Domain

So far, research on WF has devoted little attention to the role of emotions, motivation, and socio-cognitive factors, although these variables have proved important in the performance of other spatial tasks. There is consistent evidence, for instance, that socio-cognitive factors such as stereotype threat (which refers to the risk of individuals seeing confirmed in themselves a negative stereotype applied to their social group) [29, 51], and gender identification [59] have a role in determining performance in mental rotation tasks. Young women performed less well in the Mental Rotations Test (MRT) when under stereotype threat than in a control, non-stereotyped condition [35]. It seems that personality factors should be taken into account too in explaining MRT performance, since gender identification interacts with stereotype threat in worsening MRT performance [39].

There are also studies supporting the link between emotions and WF. Schmitz [48] found that spatial anxiety (the degree of anxiety experienced when performing environment tasks) influenced WF speed in a virtual environment (VE). Lawton [25] showed that females experienced more spatial anxiety than males, and this factor correlated with route WF strategies. More recently, a number of studies have further demonstrated that anxiety interferes with WF performance [17, 53], particularly in difficult tasks [50]. On the other hand, no studies have so far investigated the role of positive emotions (such as pleasure in exploring) in sustaining WF despite a growing body of evidence of positive emotions enhancing performance in a variety of cognitive tasks [11]. The present paper aims to start filling this gap.

1.5 Wayfinding Self-efficacy

Over the years, an impressive amount of evidence has shown that motivational factors can sustain (or hinder) cognitive performance and goal-directed behavior. In this domain, one of the most often studied constructs is that of self-efficacy [2], described as a person's belief about his or her ability to accomplish a task. Perceived self-efficacy has been proved to influence numerous domains, including cognitive development [1], self-regulated learning and academic motivation [49], sport performance [37]. One of the goals of the present study was to explore whether perceived self-efficacy in spatial tasks can predict WF performance.

1.6   The Present Study

The aim of this study was to explore the role of a positive attitude (pleasure in exploring) and perceived self-efficacy in spatial tasks in relation to WF perform-ance in a VE. A VE was used because previous studies had shown that people are able to acquire spatial knowledge from VEs in the same way as they do in the real world (e.g. [46]). The use of VEs also enables variables of interest (such as the pres-ence of landmarks) to be controlled, and is a useful way to objectively assess indi-vidual differences in WF [14, 55].

As mentioned in the above review, positive emotions have a distinct role in enhancing cognitive performance, and a number of studies have demonstrated the influ-ence of socio-cognitive and personality factors on spatial learning. We feel that this line of investigation should be extended to WF ability, exploring its relationship with emotions, motivation, and personality factors.

In our study, participants completed two questionnaires, one designed to assess their WF self-efficacy, the other to assess their attitude to spatial tasks. They were then conducted along a path through an urban VE that they were asked to memorize. Imme-diately afterwards, they were returned to the starting point and asked to find a shortcut to the destination. In order to do so, the information they had acquired from an egocentric perspective while navigating needed to be integrated in an allocentric representation and a completely new route had to be identified. Our expectation was that WF self-efficacy and attitude to spatial tasks would relate to shortcut-finding performance.

Participants were assigned to one of two groups: one group learned a VE that contained numerous elements that might be used as landmarks: buildings, a fountain, a traffic light, trees, etc. They are all items typically found in an urban environment. The other learned the same VE, but without any of these potential landmarks: only the layout of the streets was displayed. We expected WF self-efficacy and attitude to spatial tasks to be more strongly associated with WF performance in the no-landmark condition, based on past studies suggesting that personal features – such as anxiety [50] and SOD [38, 55] - were more predictive of performance in difficult spatial tasks than in easier ones. Muehl and Sholl [38] showed that SOD predicted participants' ability to path-integrate over longer routes with more turns in a VE, but not over shorter routes. In the same vein, Weisberg et al. [55] found that SOD explained a significant portion of the variance for between-route pointing trials, but was not a significant predictor for within-route pointing trials.

2 Method

2.1 Participants

A total of 124 undergraduates (63 females) took part in the study (age M = 23.6, SD = 2.11). They were randomly assigned to one of two groups: 59 participants (29 females) learned a route through a virtual environment with landmarks (Landmark) and 65 (34 females) learned the same route but without any landmarks (No Landmark).

2.2 Materials

Individual differences measures

Attitude to spatial exploration questionnaire (Attitude), revised from [41]. This is designed to assess attitude towards orientation tasks and pleasure in exploring. It comprises 8 statements that describe feelings, attitudes, and preferences in situations involving environmental orientation (e.g. "I love exploring different places that I still don't know well, and finding new ways to get to places"; "I would like to play a sport like orienteering, where people have to move very fast in unknown places"). For each statement, respondents indicate their agreement on a 5-point scale from 1 (not at all) to 5 (very much), and the total score is obtained from the sum of each item rating. Internal consistency (a measure of a test's reliability based on correlations between items) was good (Cronbach's α = .83, calculated on the current sample).

Wayfinding self-efficacy questionnaire (Efficacy), revised from [34]. This investigates how confident individuals feel about their ability to perform typical WF tasks. It consists of 8 items that describe precise tasks (e.g. "Finding the car in a large parking lot"; "Visiting friends who live in an unfamiliar neighborhood"), scored on a 6-point scale from 1 (not at all) to 6 (very much) in response to the prompt: "Indicate how well you think you would cope in the situations described", and the total score is given by the sum of each item rating. Internal consistency was good (α = .85, calculated on the current sample).

Learning phase

A virtual environment prepared with Superscape 5.61 software, adapted from [42]. Two versions of the same outdoor urban VE were used, one with and the other without landmarks (Landmark and No Landmark, respectively), with a path some 300 m long that consisted of 12 segments between two adjacent nodes, which included 2 roundabouts and 9 turns (4 to the right and 5 to the left). In the Landmark version the environment contained buildings, a fountain, a monument, trees, a traffic light, flower beds, and other elements typically found in an urban environment that can serve as navigation aids (Fig. 1, panels a and c). The environment without landmarks was identical except for the absence of any buildings or other elements of the urban landscape. Only the layout of the streets was displayed (Fig. 1, panels b and d). Another VE was used for practice.

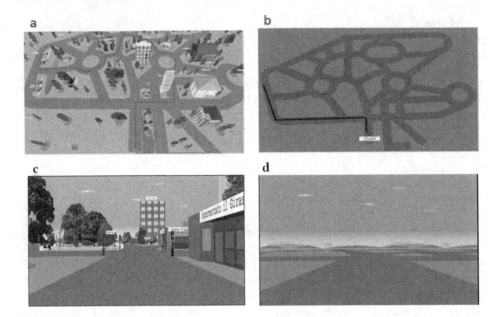

Fig. 1. The path through the VE with (panel a) and without landmarks (panel b). The best shortcut is shown on panel b. Panels c and d show the starting point from a participant's perspective (for the Landmark and No landmark conditions, respectively).

The virtual navigation (learning) phase was conducted on a desktop PC running Window 7 Professional 64 bit (SP1); processor: CPU intel i7, 3.33 GHz, Ram 12,0 GB; graphic board: NVIDIA QUADRO FX 3800, refresh rate 60 Hz; resolution: 1280 × 1024, Screen BENQ: FP93VW. The VE was presented on a 17-inch screen placed 50 cm away from the participant.

2.3 Procedure

Participants were tested individually during a single session lasting about 45 min. First they completed the Attitude and Efficacy questionnaires (in addition to other questionnaires that were not considered in the current study).

Then the route learning phase started. Participants were told that their task was to memorize a path through a VE and afterwards to perform a number of spatial tasks. They were familiarized with the use of the joystick (using the Logitech cordless Freedom R 2.4) and the desktop virtual reality apparatus in a sample VE for 3 min before starting the experimental task. Participants watched an avatar walk for about 3 min from the start to the end of a path through the Landmark or No Landmark VE. Immediately afterwards, they were returned to the starting point and asked to find a shortcut to the destination, using the joystick.

The task was complete when they reached the end point. The dependent variable was the error in the length of their shortcut, calculated by subtracting the length of the best shortcut (128 m) from the length of the shortcut identified by participants.

3 Results

3.1 Landmarks and Shortcut-Finding Performance

A univariate analysis of variance was run on the shortcut error (length of the shortcut identified by participants minus 128, which was the length of the best shortcut), inserting Environment (Landmark vs No Landmark) as a factor. The results showed a main effect of Environment, $F(1, 122) = 24.84$, $p < .001$, $\eta^2 p = .17$, with better performance in the Landmark ($M = 60.85$, SD $= 94.21$) than in the No Landmark condition ($M = 236.88$, SD $= 255.96$).

3.2 Attitude to Spatial Tasks, WF Self-efficacy, and Shortcut-Finding Performance

Correlations. Table 1 shows the correlations between Attitude, Efficacy and shortcut error. Given the high correlation between Attitude and Efficacy, we averaged the z-scores of the questionnaires in a single individual differences variable (Att-Eff). The correlations between Att-Eff and shortcut error were $r = -.23$, $p = .09$, and $r = -.33$, $p = .008$, in the Landmark and No Landmark conditions, respectively, with (as expected) a significant correlation only in the former condition.

Table 1. Correlations between attitude, efficacy and shortcut error.

	1	2
1. Attitude	–	
2. Efficacy	.67***	–
3. Shortcut error	−.26**	−.21*

Note. * p ≤ .05; ** p ≤ .01; *** p ≤ .001

Regression models. A hierarchical multiple regression analysis was run using a block-wise method, and considering Environment, Att-Eff, and their interaction as predictors, and shortcut error as the dependent variable. Environment (a dichotomous variable, i.e., 1 for Landmark and 0 for No Landmark) was input in step 1, and the Att-Eff scores on a continuous level were input in step 2; then the Environment x Att-Eff interaction was considered in step 3. The gender variable was taken into account in a preliminary Step 0, given the gender-related differences in visuo-spatial strategies and tasks (e.g. Lawton [25]), but its effect was not significant (F < 1) and the final regression model only considered Steps 1, 2, and 3.

The results of final regression models (shown in Table 2), revealed at step 1 the effect of Environment ($R^2 = .17$, $F(1, 121) = 24.72$, $p \leq .001$) and at step 2 the effect of Att-Eff ($R^2 = .05$, $F(1, 120) = 8.25$, $p < .01$), accounting together for 22% of variance.

Step 3 showed a significant Environment x Att-Eff interaction, $F(1, 119) = 4.87$, $p < .05$, explained by the fact that individual differences influenced shortcut-finding performance more in the No Landmark than in the Landmark condition (see Fig. 2).

Table 2. Hierarchical multiple regression model on shortcut error.

Predictors	ΔR^2	β
Step 1: Environment[a]	.17***	−.39***
Step 2: Eff-Att[b]	.05**	−.44**
Step 3: Environment x Eff-Att	.03*	.28*
Total R^2	.25	

Note. N = 124; [a] Environment: 0 = without landmark, 1 = with landmark; [b] mean score for Efficacy and Attitude z scores; *p < .05, **p < .01, ***p < .001.

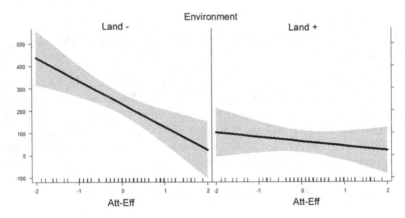

Fig. 2. Interaction between shortcut-finding performance (shortcut error) in relation to Att-Eff (individual factor, z score) by environment with landmarks (Land+) and without landmarks (Land−).

In other words, participants with a more positive attitude to spatial tasks and a higher WF self-efficacy rating found shorter shortcuts in the environment without landmarks; while these factors were less influential in the learning condition with landmarks.

4   Discussion

Previous studies found that environmental and individual features interact in contributing to WF performance [4, 14]. In the realm of general cognitive abilities and figural spatial tasks (e.g. MRT), numerous studies have pointed to the importance of socio-cognitive (e.g. stereotype threat), affective (emotions) and motivational (self-efficacy) factors in sustaining cognitive performance. The present study is the first to have explored how attitude to spatial tasks (pleasure in exploring) and WF self-efficacy interact with environmental features and relate to shortcut-finding performance.

Participants were asked to learn a path as they navigated through a VE with or without landmarks, and then to find a shortcut from their previous starting point to their destination. Their WF self-efficacy and pleasure in exploring were measured by means of two questionnaires.

As expected, the Landmark group performed better in shortcut-finding, confirming the findings of other studies that pointed to the informative value of landmarks for navigation [e.g. 3, 7, 19, 27].

Further, it newly emerged that the presence of landmarks and an aggregate measure of WF self-efficacy and pleasure in exploring accounted together for 22% of the variance in shortcut task performance. Notably, a significant interaction between environmental and individual difference factors showed that the latter were more predictive of performance in the more difficult condition (in a VE with no landmarks), whereas WF self-efficacy and pleasure in exploring were less influential in the easier condition (a VE with landmarks). Indeed, it is in the more demanding situations that personal factors intervene in coping with difficulties and finding appropriate strategies and solutions.

5 Conclusions

The multicomponent nature of WF abilities means that many variables relating to the environment, the task in hand, and individual factors, alone and in combination, need to be considered in order to account for its complexity. So far, cognitive processes (attention, memory, planning) and self-report measures of SOD and spatial anxiety have been the most often studied of the individual variables, [24, 32], whereas less attention has been paid to the potential enhancing value of a positive attitude to spatial tasks and WF self-efficacy, although an impressive amount of research has demonstrated the relevance of self-efficacy [1] and positive attitudes [5] in a variety of tasks and behavior.

The present study demonstrates that pleasure in exploring and WF self-efficacy relate to WF performance. This is a novel result, which can be explained by people's daily experiences. From childhood to old age, people frequently engage in orientation tasks - WF, planning routes, estimating direction and distance – more or less successfully (finding a destination or getting lost) and with variously positive (satisfaction, pride, relief), or negative (frustration, anger, sense of insecurity, fear of getting lost) associated emotions. It is plausible that past and present experiences contribute to building cognitive-affective units [33] relating to spatial orientation that, in turn, mediate future feelings and behavior, prompting fear and avoidance or pleasure and high self-efficacy when it comes to engaging in spatial tasks.

A limitation of this study lies in the small portion of variance (5%) explained by Att-Eff. This could depend on the instruments used and/or on the task. To measure WF self-efficacy we used a questionnaire in which the items describe spatial situations commonly found in everyday life. Bandura [1, 2] made the point, however, that the predictive power of perceived efficacy is stronger when it is assessed just before engaging in a specifically related task. It might therefore be useful to investigate the predictive power of self-efficacy by asking participants to assess it immediately before they perform a specifically related task. In addition, if WF self-efficacy derives partly from previous experience in spatial orientation tasks [1, 2], it may be that it is more predictive in previously experimented situations, i.e. in real-life tasks rather than in VEs. In future studies, it might also be interesting to test whether WF self-efficacy actually increases after spatial training and whether it can contribute to boosting any positive effects of training.

As for pleasure in exploring, this is a hitherto little analyzed construct and ours should be seen as a pilot study. Our participants were presented with relatively few items exploring their attitude to a variety of environment tasks. A broader range of situations, and the related positive emotions (satisfaction, pride, desire, fun, challenge) warrants more thorough investigation.

Finally, the specific contribution of WF self-efficacy and attitude to spatial tasks, also vis-à-vis spatial anxiety and subjective SOD, should be further analyzed in future. The existence of a strong correlation between the two variables raises questions about their actual distinctiveness and the direction of the relationship. Concerning the first point, it is worth noting that WF self-efficacy is a motivational variable likely to support performance through task-orientation and strategic behavior, whereas attitude to spatial tasks is mainly an affective component that pertains to the valence of emotions that anticipate and accompany the completion of a wayfinding task.

Motivational theories typically emphasize the close relationship between motivation and emotional states, but still consider them as two distinct components, both likely to favor goal achievement [2]. Interestingly, the affective component may be seen as a direct consequence of self-efficacy, based on the assumption that a high self-efficacy in relation to a specific task enhances positive emotions and strategic behavior, which in turn positively affect performance. A future study on a large sample should clarify this question, comparing two alternative predictive models: one where spatial self-efficacy and attitude give independent contributions to WF task performance; the other where attitude acts as a variable mediating between self-efficacy and WF task performance. In the present study, we averaged the instruments to obtain a single Att-Eff score in order to emphasize their predictive power, but the use of richer and more diversified measures might enable us to better distinguish between different variables and clarify how they relate to specific environment learning tasks.

Nevertheless, our results are innovative and should inspire further research on these topics: other non-cognitive aspects (e.g. personality traits) could be explored in relation to emotions, self-efficacy, and exploring, as recently suggested by Condon et al. [6]. Further research could also investigate the relationship between WF behavior and children's autonomy and freedom to explore their neighborhood [30, 44]. Taken together, these studies could open up new scenarios in the study of wayfinding behavior.

References

1. Bandura, A.: Perceived self-efficacy in cognitive development and functioning. Educ. Psychol. **28**, 117–148 (1993). https://doi.org/10.1207/s15326985ep2802_3
2. Bandura, A.: Self-Efficacy: the Exercise of Control. Freeman, New York (1997)
3. Caduff, D., Timpf, S.: On the assessment of landmark salience for human navigation. Cogn. Process. **9**, 249–267 (2008). https://doi.org/10.1007/s10339-007-0199-2
4. Carlson, L.A., Hölscher, C., Shipley, T.F., Dalton, R.C.: Getting lost in buildings. Curr. Dir. Psychol. Sci. **19**, 284–289 (2010). https://doi.org/10.1177/0963721410383243
5. Catalino, L.I., Algoe, S.B., Fredrickson, B.L.: Prioritizing positivity: An effective approach to pursuing happiness? Emotion **6**, 1155–1161 (2014). https://doi.org/10.1037/a0038029

6. Condon, D.M., Wilt, J., Cohen, C.A., Revelle, W., Hegarty, M., Uttal, D.H.: Sense of direction: General factor saturation and associations with the Big-Five traits. Pers. Individ. Differ. **86**, 38–43 (2015). https://doi.org/10.1016/j.paid.2015.05.023

7. Denis, M., Mores, C., Gras, D., Gyselinck, V., Daniel, M.-P.: Is memory for routes enhanced by an environment's richness in visual landmarks? Spat. Cogn. Comput. **14**, 284–305 (2014). https://doi.org/10.1080/13875868.2014.945586

8. Eccles, D.W., Walsh, S.E., Ingledew, D.K.: A grounded theory of expert cognition in orienteering. J. Sport Exerc. Psychol. **24**, 68–88 (2002)

9. Foo, P., Duchon, A., Warren, W.H., Tarr, M.J.: Humans do not switch between path knowledge and landmarks when learning a new environment. Psychol. Res. **71**, 240–251 (2007). https://doi.org/10.1007/s00426-006-0080-4

10. Foo, P., Warren, W.H., Duchon, A., Tarr, M.J.: Do humans integrate routes into a cognitive map? Map- vs. landmark-based navigation of novel shortcuts. J. Exp. Psychol. Hum. Mem. Learn. **31**, 195–215 (2005). https://doi.org/10.1037/0278-7393.31.2.195

11. Garland, E.L., Fredrickson, B., Kring, A.M., Johnson, D.P., Meyer, P.S., Penn, D.L.: Upward spirals of positive emotions counter downward spirals of negativity: Insights from the broaden-and-build theory and affective neuroscience on the treatment of emotion dysfunctions and deficits in psychopathology. Clin. Psychol. Rev. **30**, 849–864 (2010). https://doi.org/10.1016/j.cpr.2010.03.002

12. Golledge, R.G.: Human wayfinding and cognitive maps. In: Golledge, R.G. (ed.) Wayfinding Behavior: Cognitive Mapping and Other Spatial Processes, pp. 5–45. Johns Hopkins University Press, Baltimore (1999)

13. Harris, M.A., Wolbers, T.: Ageing effects on path integration and landmark navigation. Hippocampus **22**, 1770–1780 (2012). https://doi.org/10.1002/hipo.22011

14. Hegarty, M., Montello, D.R., Richardson, A.E., Ishikawa, T., Lovelace, T.: Spatial abilities at different scales: Individual differences in aptitude-test performance and spatial-layout learning. Intelligence **34**, 151–176 (2006). https://doi.org/10.1016/j.intell.2005.09.005

15. Hegarty, M., Richardson, A.E., Montello, D.R., Lovelace, K., Subbiah, I.: Development of a self-report measure of environmental spatial ability. Intelligence **30**, 425–447 (2002). https://doi.org/10.1016/S0160-2896(02)00116-2

16. Hill, K.A.: Wayfinding and spatial reorientation by Nova Scotia deer hunters. Environ. Behav. **45**, 267–282 (2013). https://doi.org/10.1177/0013916511420421

17. Hund, A.M., Minarik, J.L.: Getting from here to there: Spatial anxiety, wayfinding strategies, direction type, and wayfinding efficiency. Spat. Cogn. Comput. **6**, 179–201 (2006). https://doi.org/10.1207/s15427633scc0603_1

18. Iaria, G., Burles, F.: Developmental topographical disorientation. Trends Cogn. Sci. **20**, 720–722 (2016). https://doi.org/10.1016/j.tics.2016.07.004

19. Jansen-Osmann, P., Fuchs, P.: Wayfinding behavior and spatial knowledge of adults and children in a virtual environment: The role of landmarks. Exp. Psychol. **53**, 171–181 (2006). https://doi.org/10.1027/1618-3169.53.3.171

20. Janzen, G., Jansen, C., van Turennout, M.: Memory consolidation of landmarks in good navigators. Hippocampus **18**, 40–47 (2008). https://doi.org/10.1002/hipo.20364

21. Janzen, G., Wagensveld, B., van Turennout, M.: Neural representation of navigational relevance is rapidly induced and long lasting. Cereb. Cortex **17**, 975–981 (2007). https://doi.org/10.1093/cercor/bhl008

22. Kearns, M.J., Warren, W.H., Duchon, A.P., Tarr, M.J.: Path integration from optic flow and body senses in a homing task. Perception **31**, 349–374 (2002). https://doi.org/10.1068/p3311

23. Kozlowski, L.T., Bryant, K.J.: Sense-of-direction, spatial orientation, and cognitive maps. J. Exp. Psychol. Hum. Percept. Perform. **3**, 590–598 (1977). https://doi.org/10.1037/0096-1523.3.4.590

24. Labate, E., Pazzaglia, F., Hegarty, M.: What working memory subcomponents are needed in the acquisition of survey knowledge? Evidence from direction estimation and shortcut tasks. J. Environ. Psychol. **37**, 73–79 (2014). https://doi.org/10.1016/j.jenvp.2013.11.007

25. Lawton, C.A.: Gender differences in way-finding strategies: Relationship to spatial ability and spatial anxiety. Sex Roles **30**, 765–779 (1994). https://doi.org/10.1007/BF01544230

26. Lawton, C.A., Chrisler, J.C., McCreary, D.R.: Gender, spatial abilities, and wayfinding. In: Chrisler, J.C., McCreary, D.R. (eds.) Handbook of Gender Research in Psychology, pp. 317–341. Springer, New York (2010). https://doi.org/10.1007/978-1-4419-1465-1_16

27. Lingwood, J., Blades, M., Farran, E.K., Courbois, Y., Matthews, D.: The development of wayfinding abilities in children: Learning routes with and without landmarks. J. Environ. Psychol. **41**, 74–80 (2015). https://doi.org/10.3389/fpsyg.2015.00174

28. Loomis, J.M., Klatzky, R.L., Golledge, R.G., Philbeck, J.W.: Human navigation by path integration. In: Golledge, R.G. (ed.) Wayfinding Behavior: Cognitive Mapping and Other Spatial Processes, pp. 125–151. Johns Hopkins University Press, Baltimore (1999)

29. Maass, A., Cadinu, M.: Stereotype threat: When minority members underperform. In: Stroebe, W., Hewstone, M., Stroebe, W., Hewstone, M. (eds.) European Review of Social Psychology, vol. 14, pp. 243–275. Psychology Press/Taylor & Francis Hove, England (2003)

30. Malucelli, E., Maass, A.: The development of spatial abilities: Growing up with or without cars. Bull. People-Environ. Stud. **18**, 6–11 (2001)

31. Meilinger, T., Knauff, M., Bulthoff, H.H.: Working memory in wayfinding: A dual task experiment in a virtual city. Cogn. Sci. **32**, 755–770 (2008). https://doi.org/10.1080/03640210802067004

32. Meneghetti, C., Zancada-Menéndez, C., Lopez, L., Sampedro-Piquero, P., Martinelli, M., Ronconi, L., Rossi, B.: Navigation and individual differences: The role of visuo-spatial abilities and working memory. Learn. Individ. Differ. **49**, 314–322 (2016). https://doi.org/10.1016/j.lindif.2016.07.002

33. Mischel, W., Shoda, Y.: A cognitive-affective system theory of personality: Reconceptualizing situations, dispositions, dynamics, and invariance in personality structure. Psychol. Rev. **102**, 246–268 (1995). https://doi.org/10.1037/0033-295X.102.2.246

34. Mitolo, M., Gardini, S., Caffarra, P., Ronconi, L., Venneri, A., Pazzaglia, F.: Relationship between spatial ability, visuospatial working memory and self-assessed spatial orientation ability: A study in older adults. Cogn. Process. **16**, 165–176 (2015). https://doi.org/10.1007/s10339-015-0647-3

35. Moè, A., Pazzaglia, F.: Following the instructions! Effects of gender beliefs in mental rotation. Learn. Individ. Differ. **16**, 369–377 (2006). https://doi.org/10.1016/j.lindif.2007.01.002

36. Montello, D.R.: Navigation. In: Shah, P., Miyake, A. (eds.) The Cambridge Handbook of Visuo-Spatial Thinking, pp. 257–294. Cambridge University Press, Cambridge (2005)

37. Moritz, S.E., Feltz, D.L., Fahrbach, K.R., Mack, D.E.: The relation of self-efficacy measures to sport performance: a meta-analytic review. Res. Q. Exer. Sport **71**, 280–294 (2000). https://doi.org/10.1080/02701367.2000.10608908

38. Muehl, K.A., Sholl, M.J.: The acquisition of vector knowledge and its relation to self-rated direction sense. J. Exp. Psychol. Learn. Mem. Cogn. **30**, 129–141 (2004). https://doi.org/10.1037/0278-7393.30.1.129

39. Nori, R., Mercuri, N., Giusberti, F., Bensi, L., Gambetti, E.: Influences of gender role socialization and anxiety on spatial cognitive style. Am. J. Psychol. **122**, 497–505 (2009)

40. Pazzaglia, F., De Beni, R.: Strategies of processing spatial information in survey and landmark-centred individuals. Eur. J. Cogn. Psychol. **13**, 493–508 (2001). https://doi.org/10.1080/09541440042000124

41. Pazzaglia, F., Poli, M., De Beni, R.: Orientamento e rappresentazione dello spazio. Orientation and representation of the space. Erickson, Trento (2004)
42. Pazzaglia, F., Taylor, H.A.: Perspective, instruction, and cognitive style in spatial representation of a virtual environment. Spat. Cogn. Comput. **7**, 349–364 (2007). https://doi.org/10.1080/13875860701663223
43. Riecke, B.E., Van, Veen H.A.H.C., Bülthoff, H.H.: Visual homing is possible without landmarks: A path integration study in virtual reality. Presence: Teleoperators Virtual Environ. **11**, 443–473 (2002). https://doi.org/10.1162/105474602320935810
44. Rissotto, A., Giuliani, M.V.: Learning neighbourhood environments: The loss of experience in a modern world. In: Spencer, C., Blades, M. (eds.) Children and their environments: Learning, using and designing spaces, pp. 75–90. Cambridge University Press, New York (2006). https://doi.org/10.1017/CBO9780511521232.006
45. Roth, J.H.: Hōkō onchi: Wayfinding and the emergence of "directional tone-deafness" in Japan. Ethos **43**, 402–422 (2015). https://doi.org/10.1111/etho.12098
46. Ruddle, R.A., Payne, S.J., Jones, D.M.: Navigating buildings in 'desk-top' virtual environments: Experimental investigations using extended navigational experience. J. Exper. Psychol. Appl. **3**, 143–159 (1997). https://doi.org/10.1037/1076-898X.3.2.143
47. Sameer, A., Bhushan, B.: Route memory in an unfamiliar homogeneous environment: a comparison of two strategies. Cogn. Process. **16**, 149–152 (2015). https://doi.org/10.1007/s10339-015-0677-x
48. Schmitz, S.: Gender differences in aquisition of environmental knowledge related to wayfinding behavior, spatial anxiety and self-estimated environmental competencies. Sex Roles **41**, 71–93 (1999). https://doi.org/10.1023/A:1018837808724
49. Schunk, D.H., Di Benedetto, M.K.: Academic self-efficacy. In: Furlong, M.J., Gilman, R., Huebner, E.S., Furlong, M.J., Gilman, R., Huebner, E.S. (eds.) Handbook of Positive Psychology in Schools, pp. 115–130. Routledge/Taylor & Francis Group, New York (2014)
50. Srinivas, S.: Influence of motivation on wayfinding. Dissertation Abs. Inter. Sect. A **71**, 2689 (2011)
51. Steele, C.M., Aronson, J.: A threat in the air: How stereotypes shape the intellectual identities and performance of women and African Americans. J. Pers. Soc. Psychol. **69**, 797–811 (1995)
52. Vandenberg, A.E.: Human wayfinding: Integration of mind and body. In: Hunter, R.H., Anderson, L.A. (eds.) Community Wayfinding: Pathways to Understanding, pp. 17–32. Springer International Publishing, Switzerland (2016). https://doi.org/10.1007/978-3-319-31072-5_2
53. Walkowiak, S., Foulsham, T., Eardley, A.F.: Individual differences and personality correlates of navigational performance in the virtual route learning task. Comput. Hum. Behav. **45**, 402–410 (2015). https://doi.org/10.1016/j.chb.2014.12.041
54. Wegman, J., Fonteijn, H.M., van Ekert, J., Tyborowska, A., Jansen, C., Janzen, G.: Gray and white matter correlates of navigational ability in humans. Hum. Brain Mapp. **35**, 2561–2572 (2014). https://doi.org/10.1002/hbm.22349
55. Weisberg, S.M., Schinazi, V.R., Newcombe, N.S., Shipley, T.F., Epstein, R.A.: Variations in cognitive maps: Understanding individual differences in navigation. Journal of Experimental Psychology. Learn. Mem. Cogn. **40**, 669–682 (2014). https://doi.org/10.1037/a0035261
56. Wen, W., Ishikawa, T., Sato, T.: Working memory in spatial knowledge acquisition: Differences in encoding processes and sense of direction. Appl. Cogn. Psychol. **25**, 654–662 (2011). https://doi.org/10.1002/acp.1737
57. Wiener, J.M., Büchner, S.J., Hölscher, C.: Taxonomy of human wayfinding tasks: A knowledge-based approach. Spat. Cogn. Comput. **9**, 152–165 (2009). https://doi.org/10.1080/13875860902906496

58. Wolbers, T., Hegarty, M.: What determines our navigational abilities? Trends Cogn. Sci. **14**, 138–146 (2010). https://doi.org/10.1016/j.tics.2010.01.001
59. Yang, Y., Merrill, E.C.: Cognitive and personality characteristics of masculinity and femininity predict wayfinding competence and strategies of men and women. Sex Roles. https://doi.org/10.1007/s11199-016-0626-x. (in press)

Evaluating Age-Related Cognitive Map Decay Using a Novel Time-Delayed Testing Paradigm

Christopher R. Bennett[1,2(✉)] and Nicholas A. Giudice[1,3]

[1] Virtual Environments and Multimodal Interaction (VEMI) Laboratory,
The University of Maine, Orono, ME, USA
christopher_bennett@meei.harvard.edu
[2] The Laboratory for Visual Neuroplasticity, Department of Ophthalmology,
Massachusetts Eye and Ear Infirmary, Harvard Medical School, Boston, USA
[3] Spatial Informatics Program, School of Computing and Information Science,
The University of Maine, Orono, ME, USA

Abstract. A critical component of effective navigation is the ability to form and maintain accurate cognitive maps. Proper cognitive map maintenance can become difficult for older adults as many of the constituent memory structures exhibit degradation with age. The present study employed a novel testing paradigm where younger adult participants (20 to 40 years) and older adult participants (60 to 80 years) learned a virtual environment through free exploration using an immersive driving simulator. After the learning phase, participants immediately sketched a map of the course. As forming an accurate baseline cognitive map was critical to this methodological procedure, they were provided additional learning time if placement of landmarks and roads were not within a given accuracy tolerance. Upon meeting criterion, participants completed egocentric and allocentric pointing tasks. Following this lab-based testing, participants were given 2 packets containing the exact same map sketching and pointing tasks to complete one-day and one-week after the study. Results showed clear age group differences, with older adult map sketching and pointing performance being significantly worse than their younger counterparts. There was also a clear numeric trend showing declines in performance for the older adults at the delayed-testing time intervals as compared to the in-lab testing. These findings suggest that the stored cognitive maps of older adults may exhibit greater decay over time as compared to younger adults. Future studies using this new methodological paradigm will be helpful in further elucidating the processes underlying spatial knowledge decay in older adults.

Keywords: Spatial cognition · Driving · Aging · Virtual reality · Navigation

1 Introduction

As humans move through and learn about the environment, we develop mental representations of surrounding space that may aid subsequent navigation. These long-term memory structures are known as cognitive maps, which are spatial representations formed in the hippocampus that contain information such as routes, landmarks, and the

© Springer International Publishing AG 2017
T. Barkowsky et al. (Eds.): KogWis/Spatial Cognition 2016, LNAI 10523, pp. 69–85, 2017.
https://doi.org/10.1007/978-3-319-68189-4_5

allocentric relations between them [1–3]. Development and maintenance of accurate cognitive maps is critical to everyday navigation. Previous research has found that while older adults frequently show preservation of certain spatial abilities, e.g. egocentric tasks, they also often exhibit decline in others, including cognitive map formation and access (for review, see [4, 5]). In addition, little is known about changes (or decay) in spatial knowledge representations over time once the information is no longer being reinforced through explicit learning or direct perception, especially for older adult populations.

The goal of this work was to investigate the decay function of the cognitive map and characterize how the aging process influences this decay. The present study focuses on normal transformations of spatial processes rather than more extreme fluctuations experienced as a result of disease or impairment; thus highlighting a healthy and natural aging process. The current work also defines and evaluates a new methodological paradigm, which was designed to provide a rigorous experimental approach for characterizing changes in spatial memory at key times over the most susceptible interval of temporal decay. The knowledge gained from the current work is important for (1) improving our understanding of changes in spatial abilities that occur across the life span, (2) guiding innovative research aimed at further characterization of the decay of spatial knowledge for older adults, and (3) Providing guidelines for the development of assistive technologies aimed at supporting the maintenance of spatial knowledge found to be most susceptible to age-related decay.

After a cognitive map is formed, the navigator must maintain the integrity of this mental representation in order to perform subsequent spatial operations during navigation. The present work investigated whether learned environmental information decays more over time for older adults than younger adults, even when both groups have formed equivalent baseline cognitive maps, as assessed by meeting criterion on a map recreation task. This approach addresses the underlying mechanics of creation and maintenance of mental representations of space over time. It is postulated here that cognitive map decay occurs as a normal and natural process when an individual is no longer re-enforcing the spatial knowledge from direct experience/perception of the learned environment. Given that humans rely on a myriad of spatial knowledge for supporting navigation, it is not surprising that access to inaccurate cognitive maps can result in error-prone and unsuccessful navigation behaviors. Previous work has demonstrated that older adults have significant difficulties in the process of forming cognitive maps due to the combination of age-related change and degradation of spatial abilities [6–8]. This knowledge motivated the current paradigm used to assess decay after forming an accurate baseline, which is meant to circumvent any formation difficulties that may otherwise have arisen. Age-related losses have also been identified in general memory structures [9–11] further impacting the storage and maintenance of spatial information. The storage of cognitive map information may also undergo losses in accuracy due to limitations of spatial memory associated with aging [12]. Considering this prior research in aggregate, a key prediction of the present work is that spatial memory decay will occur at a greater magnitude for older adults as compared to their younger counterparts, due to age-related difficulties in maintaining and accessing cognitive maps, in conjunction with known memory storage limitations.

The typical spatial cognition approach for studying cognitive maps follows a procedure where participants learn an environment and are only tested once, immediately after learning, without any intervening delay. A problem with this approach is that it only measures a 'snapshot' in time, when the representation is least likely to be contaminated by any other intervening factors. As a result, this one-time, immediate testing paradigm cannot speak to what happens to the cognitive map (or any spatial knowledge representation) with multiple testing probes performed over time. While there is a dearth of extant literature investigating the decay functions of learned spatial knowledge between younger and older adult populations, there is an abundance of research investigating memory decay (retention/forgetting functions) with other types of memory based on college-aged populations. For instance, a comprehensive review by Rubin and Wenzel (1996), compiled, transformed, and analyzed retention functions for word recognition and free recall from 210 published data sets representing a large body of literature over many years [13]. In their work, they fit each data set to over 100 different mathematical functions. In most cases, the best fit was determined by the time scale. For example, linear trends tended to be more significant in extremely short time intervals (seconds to minutes of delay). By contrast, logarithmic trends were consistently well fit for most time intervals and were the preferred trend of the authors. Logarithmic trends also showed some of the highest significance values for the time intervals over days and weeks, which is the time interval emphasized in the current research. While effects of age were not fully examined in the Rubin and Wenzel 1996 review, memory impairment was discussed briefly. The conclusions were that the presence of memory impairment affected the overall magnitude of forgetting, but loss functions were still the same as with non-impairment. It is possible that older adults, with memory impairment due to age related changes, could demonstrate similar logarithmic trends of memory decay.

In order to characterize the decay process, the present study employed a methodological paradigm which tested peoples spatial knowledge at delayed (1-day and 1-week) time intervals. Critical to this approach, all participants formed accurate baseline cognitive maps from the onset. Thus, results from the time-delayed testing measures only represent the decline of that information over time while factoring out possible interference introduced from age-related inaccuracies in cognitive map formation. Performance comparisons were made between each of the testing intervals for map sketching and pointing trials. An important parameter of the methodological design used here was to provide the opportunity for equivalent baseline spatial knowledge in order to avoid individual differences due to differential spatial learning and cognitive map development abilities. Unlike traditional longitudinal research which focuses on months or years of time, this methodological paradigm emphasizes spatial memory over shorter, more susceptible intervals in the days and weeks after the spatial information is formed [13].

This work employed immersive virtual reality (VR) driving simulation in order to facilitate large-scale outdoor navigation. The use of virtual reality with older adult populations is far less prevalent than with younger adults. Additionally, VR research involving elder populations frequently does not use head-mounted displays and immersive virtual reality, as is done here. Instead, research with aging typically makes use of more readily available and easier to use desktop monitors. The use of a more modern VR solution affords advantages over these simpler approaches, including greater realism and improved immersion, while allowing for increased integration with various hardware (such as a realistic driving simulator as is used here). Previous work by our group has evaluated the efficacy and usability of the immersive VR driving simulator used in this research, with both younger and older adults [14]. That work found performance in the virtual simulation to match real-world data for known 'problem areas' of older adult drivers, such as correctly yielding at intersections, accurate speed maintenance, and degraded braking reaction times.

2 Method

Participants. Twenty participants completed the study, evenly split between two age groups. The older adult age group consisted of ten people (6 female), ages 60–80 (M = 70.3, SD = 7.6). The younger adult age group included ten people (5 female), ages 18–36 (M = 22.1, SD = 4.7). Due to the sample size, the power to detect small effects is limited. Educational experience was closely matched between age groups, averaging just under 16 years for both groups (with 16 representing an undergraduate degree). Prior to starting the experiment, the older adult group completed the Montreal Cognitive Assessment, a common instrument in aging research for assessing cognitive impairment (all participants scored equal to or greater than 26, indicating no abnormal cognitive impairment) [15]. This research was approved by the University of Maine's local ethics committee and written informed consent was obtained from all participants.

Apparatus. This study employs a novel use of VR as a research tool for evaluating spatial behaviors of older adult populations. VR motion sickness is a concern for younger adults and is further exacerbated with age [16]; thus, this system was designed to help alleviate simulation sickness through careful matching of real and virtual visual expectations, choice of textures/models, and superior clarity/refresh rate of the display (further details on, and evaluation of, the driving simulator can be found in [14]). The HMD used for this study was an nVisor SX111, from NVis inc. The SX111 has a 111° field of view, providing a wide area for the driver to see in their peripheral vision. The SX111 also provides two individually driven stereoscopic displays, with separate graphics processing for each eye, rendering images at a display resolution of 1280 × 1024 per eye. The physics software was delivered by the Unreal Engine programming environment. In order to achieve greater immersion and provide a complete residential environment, 3D models of homes, businesses, landmarks, etc., were created in-lab using the Maya 3D modeling software, a product of the Autodesk Company. The driving simulator was constructed in-house using the driver's seat from a Ford Crown Victoria and the steering wheel and pedals from a disassembled Playseat racing seat. The height of the base platform and roll-cage style stabilization bars were designed in-house to maximize safety, given the intended use of the driving simulator with an older adult population. Figure 1 below shows the driving simulator used for this research.

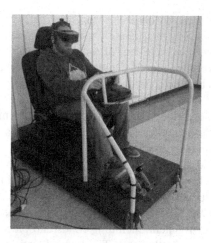

Fig. 1. Picture of the driving simulator.

The main driving course for this experiment was based on a two box grid system in the form of a figure eight. Participants learned four major landmarks within this map (playground, gas station, water tower, and corner store). An additional home location (house designated as the starting location) was placed in the environment, and each participant began their learning phase from this home location. See Fig. 2 below for a top down view of the road network and placement of landmarks.

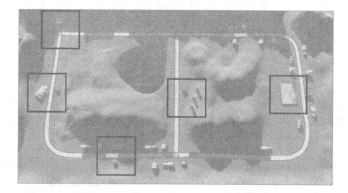

Fig. 2. Top-down view of the road grid and landmark placement. Yellow outlines represent the roads and the red squares indicate landmark locations. (Color figure online)

Design and Procedure. Participants began the experiment with a 5-minute practice phase. During this period, they practiced on a simplified course where they could adjust to the driving simulator apparatus as well as the immersive virtual reality experience. Upon completion of practice, a criterion test was given to ensure that participants were both comfortable and accurate in using the system. For this test, they had to maintain a speed between 10 and 15 mph while weaving back and forth between 6 cones, which were placed a fixed distance apart in the middle of the virtual road. After negotiating the cones, they then had to correctly observe a stop sign. This criterion test was designed to assess the participant's ability to accurately use/operate the driving simulator while managing acceleration, speed, vehicle control, and breaking behaviors, as these were all factors of interest that were subsequently evaluated in the experimental trials. No participants failed this criterion test (no cones were hit and all participants stopped before the sign).

Once participants met criterion in the practice course, they moved on to the experimental driving course. During the learning period, participants were allowed free and unlimited exploration of the environment. They were notified once they had explored the entire environment at least once, but were encouraged to continue their exploration until they self-assessed as having a comfortable level of spatial knowledge of the environment as a whole, including the position of all landmarks. After completing free exploration and removing the head mounted display, participants were required to draw a top-down map of the environment, including roads and placement of the four landmarks in the proper locations on the map. The home location (i.e., the starting point during the free exploration phase) was provided as a reference, see Fig. 3 for an image of the sheet used for map recreation.

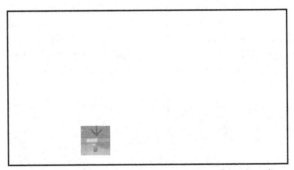

Please sketch the map including roads and landmarks.

Fig. 3. Map sketching sheet given to participants for re-creation of the learned environment. The home location (starting point) was given as a reference.

If participants were unable to correctly re-create the learned environment, they returned to the driving simulator for an additional learning phase. Participants repeated this cycle of learning followed by sketch map completion testing until they had created an accurate map of the learning environment. The map recreation criterion was determined by comparing the drawn maps to that of the correct physical map of the space being learned (landmark and road layout placement). Specifications for this criterion were based on placement within a 10% threshold of the overall map-sketching space. Accurate landmark placement and road layouts would thus need to have been within a 0.6×1.0 in. rectangular region centered on the correct landmark location or road intersection/turning point for the 6×10 in. drawing space of the sheet given (shown in Fig. 3). This sketch map served as a reflection of the accuracy of participants' internal representation, i.e. their cognitive map. The amount of repetitions of learning phases needed to complete an accurate sketch map was also collected for each participant.

Once a correct map was created, participants performed several pointing tasks. These tasks were done on paper, using a blank version of the sketch map sheet where only the boundaries of the learned space and starting landmark were provided (no internal connectivity or landmark locations were given). The first pointing task involved egocentric pointing, where participants were asked to imagine that they were at the home location facing their starting direction and to draw a line to the angle of each landmark. Egocentric pointing was done using separate sheets for each landmark. The reasoning for using separate sheets for this task was to discourage further inter-landmark learning and to mimic as closely as possible the procedure for the subsequent time-delayed take-home testing. Next, participants performed an allocentric pointing task, which is a spatial task that is known to be difficult for older adults [17]. In this task, each participant was given judgments of relative direction (JRDs) whereby they had to point to a landmark while imagining facing another landmark. For example, a participant may first be instructed to imagine that they are standing at the home location and facing the gas station. Now that they have this imagined position and facing direction in mind, they would then be requested to point to the store. JRD trials covered all combinations of pointing pairs between landmarks in aggregate. The in-lab map sketching, egocentric pointing, and allocentric pointing tasks served as a baseline for comparison to the time delayed testing that was subsequently performed one day and one week later.

Upon completing the learning and testing phases, each participant was given two packets to take home with them. Each packet contained a set of materials that matched the same tasks they did immediately upon completing the learning phase. The packet included the same mostly blank pages, as used for in-lab testing, for sketching their map, egocentric pointing, and allocentric pointing trials. Participants were then instructed to wait until approximately the same time on the following day to complete the first packet and one week from then at approximately the same time to complete the second packet. At those designated times, they were requested to open the packet and to complete all of the tasks it contained, thereby following the same procedure as was done in the lab. Each packet also included a stamped and self-addressed envelope in which all materials were placed and mailed back to the lab upon completion. The testing packets were labeled with the participant numbers and designated dates for completion. Participants were instructed to complete the packets on the specific dates, but asked to report if there were any deviations from the scheduled times/dates. All packets were completed on schedule as self-reported by the participants.

Once received, sketch maps and pointing trials were analyzed for each time interval. The sketch maps were analyzed by comparing the participant's creation of the road layout and landmark placement (representing specific x-y coordinate points on the map) against the correct map. The analysis was accomplished by using a sketch map analyzing software named the *Gardony Map Drawing Analyzer* [18] developed based on bi-dimensional regression analysis [19, 20]. This process uses the sketch map road layout and landmark points to form polygons that are then compared for translation, rotation, and scaling differences through a least squares method. Several variables are created from the output of this process, including: (1) Scale: a measure of size differences between response polygons and the ideal polygon, (2) Theta: rotational differences between the response and ideal polygon, and (3) Distortion Index (DI): a variable that represents the overall accuracy of the polygons taken from the participants' sketch maps and irrespective of translation, rotation, and scale [12]. The distortion index values are within a possible range from 0 to 100, with 0 representing a perfect placement of layout or landmark points. To score the egocentric and allocentric data, responses for each trial were physically measured on the pages using a protractor. These values were then directly compared to the correct values for each trial in order to calculate signed error and absolute error. Signed error represents directional bias of responses and absolute error indicates the overall magnitude of the response errors. Learning times and learning counts, the number of learning phases it required a participant to form an accurate baseline sketch map, were determined from the driving logs collected during the experiment. Bi-dimensional regression variables, all pointing trials, and all learning data were analyzed using a mixed model ANOVA with age group as a between subject factor and time interval as a within subject factor.

3   Results

Elimination of Outliers. Outliers were identified based on data points that were 2.5 standard deviations above the mean for each given time interval and age group combination. This resulted in 3.6% of the data being replaced by the respective mean from the condition where the outlier was calculated.

Learning Data. Data collected from the learning phases included learning times and a count of how many learning phases were required for a participant to meet criterion, assessed by the ability to create an accurate baseline sketch map (suggesting development of an accurate underlying cognitive map). Older adult learning times averaged about 12.3 min (M = 735.0 s, SD = 241.5 s) and younger adults took about 5.5 min to learn the environment (M = 329.5 s, SD = 62.7 s). An independent samples T-test comparing the learning times between the two age groups showed significant differences $t(18) = 4.392, p = 0.001$. This finding indicates that older adults took consistently longer to learn the environments; approximately twice as much time as younger adults. At most, it took participants two learning phases to form accurate baseline sketch maps. There was no difference between age groups for this measure, as both groups averaged 1.3 learning phases per person.

Sketch Map Analysis: Landmarks. Each of the participants' sketch maps contained the locations of the 5 landmarks learned during the in-lab driving session (Home, Gas Station, CVS, Water Tower, and Playground). The polygon formed between these points was run through the bi-dimensional regression analysis to calculate the differences in scale, theta (rotation), and overall distortion (DI). Distortion index value means for both age groups are shown in Fig. 4 below.

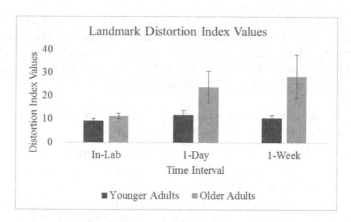

Fig. 4. Mean distortion index values for younger and older adult landmark placement with standard error shown.

Distortion Index values are perhaps the best measure of sketch map accuracy as they represent the overall error between user response and the ideal landmark placement. The results for the ANOVA on distortion index values revealed significant age group differences [$F(1,18) = 7.30, p = 0.009$, *partial* $\eta^2 = 0.119$]. Reflecting that the older adult sketch maps are less accurate than those of the younger adults. Testing time interval was not significant for older adults [$F(2,9) = 1.75, p = 0.192$, *partial* $\eta^2 = 0.115$] or for younger adults [$F(2,9) = 0.83, p = 0.449$, *partial* $\eta^2 = 0.064$]. No significant interaction was observed, $p > 0.250$. Older adults' landmark placements were consistently worse than younger adults. There were numerical differences between the distortion index values at the two delayed time intervals (1-day and 1-week) compared to the immediate in-lab testing period; however, these differences did not reach significance.

All age group and time interval means and standard deviations for scale and theta can be found in Table 1. ANOVA results for the scale measure did not reach significance for age group [$F(1,18) = 3.95, p = 0.053$, *partial* $\eta^2 = 0.076$]. Time interval for the older adults [$F(2,9) = 2.89, p = 0.075$, *partial* $\eta^2 = 0.194$] and younger adults [$F(2,9) = 0.72, p = 0.498$, *partial* $\eta^2 = 0.056$] were also not found to be significant. The interaction between age group and time interval was not significant, $p > 0.150$. As can be seen from the omnibus F-tests, the age group and time interval differences for older adults were very close to significance, indicating a clear numeric trend for differences between the sketch maps of older adults and younger adults as well as decline in scale accuracy of the cognitive maps of older adults over time. ANOVA results for the theta variable revealed significant age group differences [$F(1,18) = 9.09, p = 0.004$, *partial* $\eta^2 = 0.159$], time interval effect for older adults [$F(2,9) = 6.73, p = 0.005$, *partial* $\eta^2 = 0.359$], and the interaction between age group and time interval [$F(3,18) = 6.78, p = 0.003$, *partial* $\eta^2 = 0.220$]. These results show that older adults exhibit consistently more rotational offset within their sketch maps than younger adults and that this rotational error increased as a function of testing time, i.e. the interval from initial testing after meeting the criterion baseline to the subsequent testing at 1-day and 1-week delays. By contrast, time interval was not found to be significant for younger adults [$F(2,9) = 0.13, p = 0.877$, *partial*

$\eta^2 = 0.011$]. The lack of significance of time interval for the younger adults, indicates that this demographic did not experience any statistically measurable accruement of angular error within their sketch maps over time. The rotational error within the sketch maps ranged from 2° to 20° for older adults, and only from about 3° to 4° for younger adults (See Table 1 for all means and standard deviations).

Table 1. Displays the scale and theta averages and standard deviations for younger and older adults across the three time intervals for landmark placement.

Time	Scale		Theta (degrees)	
	Older	Younger	Older	Younger
In-lab	0.96 (0.13)	0.95 (0.11)	2.4 (1.8)	3.4 (2.3)
1-day	0.72 (0.31)	0.91 (0.06)	20.5 (19.9)	4.5 (4.0)
1-week	0.87 (0.27)	0.93 (0.04)	10.0 (12.7)	4.0 (2.7)

Sketch Map Analysis: Road Layout. Key points, including road intersections and road turn/corner placements, were used to form the road layout polygon. The layout errors of participant sketch maps were analyzed using the same bi-dimensional regression method as was used with the landmark placement. Distortion index value means for both age groups can be found in Fig. 5 below.

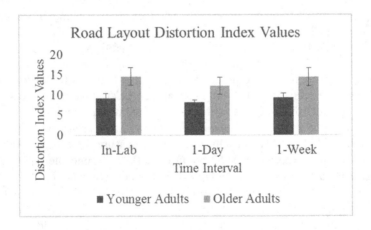

Fig. 5. Mean distortion index values for younger and older adult road layout recreation, with standard error bars depicted.

Distortion index values for the road layout were entered into the same omnibus ANOVA as was done with the landmark distortion values. Results showed a significant difference between the two age groups [$F(1,18) = 13.64, p = 0.001, partial\ \eta^2 = 0.221$]. Time interval effects were not significant for the older adults [$F(2,9) = 0.26, p = 0.777, partial\ \eta^2 = 0.021$] or younger adults [$F(2,9) = 0.42, p = 0.661, partial\ \eta^2 = 0.034$]. Likewise, the age group by time interval interaction was not significant, $p > 0.300$. These results indicate that road layout creation by older adults was reliably worse than those created by younger adults but that accuracy did not further decline over the temporal duration of testing. We interpret this age group difference as reflecting a general age effect for sketch map accuracy. Overall however, road layout was extremely accurate for both groups. This outcome indicates that the layout information (represented by the road network) was a component of the cognitive map that is stable over time, albeit slightly degraded as a general function of spatial abilities affected by the aging process.

Means and standard deviations for scale and theta of the road layouts are shown in Table 2 below. Results from the ANOVA on the scale variable were not significant for age group [$F(1,18) = 0.47$, $p = 0.496$, partial $\eta^2 = 0.010$], older adult time interval [$F(2,9) = 0.64$, $p = 0.535$, partial $\eta^2 = 0.051$], or younger adult time interval [$F(2,9) = 0.08$, $p = 0.928$, partial $\eta^2 = 0.006$]. In addition, no significant age by time interval interaction was found, $p > 0.150$. These findings suggest that there were no consistent differences in scale accuracy between older and younger adult sketch maps across the testing times used in this study. ANOVA results for the theta variable did reveal a significant effect of age group [$F(1,18) = 6.10$, $p = 0.017$, partial $\eta^2 = 0.113$], but no significance of time interval as a function of age, older adults [$F(2,9) = 1.38$, $p = 0.270$, partial $\eta^2 = 0.103$] and younger adults [$F(2,9) = 0.43$, $p = 0.656$, partial $\eta^2 = 0.035$]. The interaction between age group and time interval was not significant, $p > 0.300$. This outcome indicates that there was reliably more rotation of sketch maps for older adults than that of their younger counterparts. Overall however, scale of the re-created layout and rotational errors (theta) were very low. This outcome was most likely due to the simple layout employed to allow for an environment that older adults could readily learn.

Table 2. Displays the scale and theta averages and standard deviations for younger and older adults across the three time intervals for road layout.

Time	Scale		Theta (degrees)	
	Older	Younger	Older	Younger
In-lab	0.88 (0.12)	0.86 (0.07)	1.0 (0.6)	0.4 (0.4)
1-day	0.87 (0.16)	0.87 (0.04)	1.9 (3.0)	0.6 (0.5)
1-week	0.94 (0.19)	0.87 (0.04)	1.5 (1.5)	0.6 (0.6)

Pointing Trials: Egocentric. Participants completed egocentric pointing trials to each of the landmarks learned. Egocentric pointing reflects the accuracy of the underlying cognitive map as relates to the maintenance of self-object relations. The difference between the response angle and the actual angle was calculated to evaluate bias (signed error of pointing) and the absolute value of those values was used to determine error magnitude. Directional bias within the egocentric pointing task was analyzed using the same ANOVA model as was used with the previous measures. No significance was found for any of the measures and overall there was no left/right bias in the pointing judgments. The calculated absolute angle error averages and standard errors for both age groups across the three time intervals are shown in Fig. 6. ANOVA results for egocentric pointing revealed significant differences between the two age groups [$F(1,18) = 18.24$, $p < 0.001$, partial $\eta^2 = 0.072$]. No significant effect for egocentric pointing accuracy was found as a function of testing time interval: older adults [$F(1,9) = 1.35$, $p = 0.264$, partial $\eta^2 = 0.024$] and younger adults [$F(2,9) = 0.49$,

$p = 0.614$, *partial* $\eta^2 = 0.009$]. No significant age group by time interval interaction was observed, $p > 0.150$. These findings indicate that older adults show greater error in egocentric pointing judgments than younger adults, but this error did not reliably increase as a function of time interval over which the judgments were made.

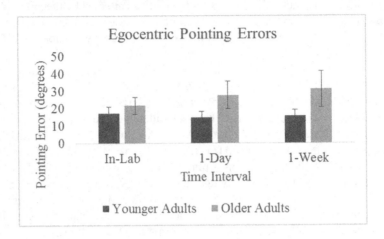

Fig. 6. Average egocentric pointing errors for both age groups across the three time intervals with standard error bars.

Pointing Trials: Allocentric. Participants completed allocentric pointing trials at each testing time interval for all pairs of landmark locations. These trials had participants imagine standing at one location, facing one landmark, and then pointing to another. Allocentric pointing performance reflects the knowledge of object-to-object relations that were stored and maintained in the cognitive map. Allocentric pointing error was calculated between the response and correct angle. Directional bias within the pointing task was analyzed using the same ANOVA Model as above, with no significant effects found for any of the factors (all p's > 0.05). ANOVA results for the absolute allocentric pointing errors showed significant differences between age groups [$F(1,18) = 94.54$, $p < 0.001$, *partial* $\eta^2 = 0.117$]. However, there were no reliable differences observed between the testing time intervals for older adults [$F(2,9) = 2.10$, $p = 0.124$, *partial* $\eta^2 = 0.012$] or for younger adults [$F(2,9) = 1.46$, $p = 0.234$, *partial* $\eta^2 = 0.008$]. Similarly, no significant interaction between age group and time interval was found, $p > 0.100$. These results suggest that older adults were consistently worse than younger adults for allocentric pointing accuracy, regardless of the testing time interval that the judgments were made. This finding is not surprising, as previous research has shown that older adults have a more difficult time than their younger peers on allocentric tasks [12, 17]. Means and standard deviations of the allocentric pointing trials can be found in Table 3 below.

Table 3. Average allocentric pointing errors and standard deviations for both age groups across the three time intervals.

Allocentric pointing data (in degrees)			
Age group	Time interval	Mean	Standard deviation
Older	in-lab	59.52	41.19
Older	1-day	63.10	41.57
Older	1-week	52.42	40.47
Younger	In-lab	32.14	20.86
Younger	1-day	35.78	20.24
Younger	1-week	36.36	21.13

4 Discussion

The present research was designed to evaluate differences that manifest in cognitive map decay between older and younger adults, and to characterize the decay function through several measures of spatial behavior. This was accomplished through examining differences in sketch maps (physical representations of cognitive maps) and performance on egocentric and allocentric pointing trials between younger and older adults over multiple time periods. The methodological paradigm was designed in a way that all tasks were done after forming a highly accurate baseline. Given that previous research has found that cognitive map formation is impacted by age, it was postulated here that the maintenance of the same spatial knowledge would also be affected by age. This prediction was partially supported by the outcomes of this study as older adult showed reduced spatial knowledge as compared to younger adults on the same tasks. The data clearly reflect a trend that older adults exhibit a greater decay in spatial knowledge of the learned environment over time as compared to younger adults.

Results also showed that it took older adults about twice as long to learn the environments than their younger counterparts. The complexity of the environment was designed to be challenging for the older adults but in this study, we emphasized landmark configuration complexity over road network configuration complexity. This design choice was made to ensure that we could collect a robust data set for the egocentric and allocentric pointing judgments, which relied more on knowledge of landmark configuration than road network complexity. The decision to allow all participants time to form an accurate baseline cognitive map is a unique component of the current methodological approach that was implemented in order to ensure consistency between individuals during the formation process. If a fixed time limit had been imposed during the learning phase, it would not have been possible to ensure that all participants were operating from an accurate baseline representation. As a result, the cognitive maps of the older adults may have suffered from increased formation error compared to the younger participants, which would have compromised the efficacy of comparing the decay functions between groups. In sum, guaranteeing an accurate initial baseline provides a robust technique that supports strong statistical efficacy for detecting any changes in cognitive map accuracy over the subsequent time-delayed testing intervals for each task (map sketching, egocentric pointing, and allocentric pointing). With this design, any changes in performance during delayed testing can be attributable to the decay process, rather than to problems in cognitive map formation. Evidence for forming this accurate baseline for the older adults can be observed in Figs. 4 and 6, where the in-lab performance (tested spatial knowledge) nearly matched that of the younger adult group.

Conducting the bi-dimensional regression analysis on the sketch maps elucidated differences that exist in the underlying cognitive maps between older and younger adults. The cognitive maps of older adults were shown to be more susceptible to errors and overall distortion of landmark placements and road layouts as compared to younger adults. The magnitude of decline for older adults was specifically attributed to age-related effects on the decay process, given that all participants were required to develop their initial cognitive maps to accurate baselines. Increased distortion for older adult cognitive maps was evident from both landmark placement and road layout accuracy in their physical map recreations. Many of the same underlying mental structures for memory are used for storage and access of cognitive maps. As such, it is reasonable to expect that the methodological paradigm employed in the current work could also be applied to other spatial tasks that may change as a function of the aging process.

The loss of cognitive map accuracy may reduce the ability for older adults to successfully navigate using this internal spatial information. As previous research has shown, cognitive maps are key to accurate navigation and older adults clearly display losses in this long-term store of spatial knowledge after accurate learning of the environment, as evidenced by the current results. Other types of memory formation have demonstrated decay of information over time as following a logarithmic trend. In the current study, there were no reliable mathematical trends in the data. However, in-line with previous findings, the closest predictive trend from our data was a logarithmic function. Due to the high standard deviations and small sample size, the effect of time interval for older adults may have only been numeric, but the large absolute difference between the distortion values from the immediate time interval testing (11.2) and the combined average of the two time delayed testing intervals (32.2) is notable. The performance differences on map recreation between immediate and delayed sketch maps provides an indication that decay is occurring in the older adults' cognitive maps as time passes.

The decay of cognitive maps had a slightly different effect on other measures of interest related to physical map recreation. For instance, reliable differences in scale were not observed but significant differences in rotational errors were evident. These results suggest that older adults accurately maintain the distance relations between landmarks within their cognitive maps in a similar manner as younger adults. Likewise, neither younger nor older adults exhibited reliable compression or expansion effects for the spatial relations of the stored landmark knowledge over time. Rotational errors for landmark placements and road layouts were found to be significantly greater as a function of age during recreation, indicating that the cognitive maps of older adults are more susceptible to distortions in these factors as compared to their younger counterparts. The amount of rotational error also increased significantly over the time intervals tested for older adults. This outcome indicates that the cognitive maps of older adults are more susceptible to rotational error, but that the overall inter-landmark relations are maintained. From a practical standpoint, imagine placing a physical map onto a table lined up with true north. If you then rotate the map, the angles of the individual landmarks as they relate to the global environment are now incorrect, but within the map the landmark-to-landmark distances and angles are stable. The current data suggests that the same overall rotation of a cognitive map would lead to navigational difficulties for older adults.

Egocentric pointing data also revealed strong age group differences as well as numeric differences in error as a function of time delayed testing. Significantly worse pointing responses for older adults represents inaccuracies of landmark placement within the stored cognitive maps as compared to younger adults. These results further explain the significance of rotational errors within the cognitive maps demonstrated from the bi-dimensional theta values. As mentioned above, older adult cognitive maps seem to reflect greater rotational error of the stored landmark locations. These egocentric pointing errors reflect the same increase in rotation of landmark relations for older adults as were observed in the bi-dimensional regression analysis. Previous research has found that egocentric spatial abilities tend to be preserved for older adults as compared to allocentric pointing [4, 5]. However, some recent work by Giudice and colleagues has found exceptions, demonstrating declines in egocentric performance for older adults after learning multi-target haptic arrays [12]. The current results support the Giudice et al. findings in the haptic domain and extend the finding of age-related egocentric deficits between older and younger participant groups after visual learning of multi-target layouts. High variability within the egocentric pointing errors certainly contributed to the lack of significance observed for time interval; however, the in-lab errors averaged about 21° and the two time-delayed errors averaged about 30°. This gap between immediate and time delayed errors reflects a strong numeric pattern suggesting a temporal effect on remembered landmark locations. As with the distortion values, no mathematical trend was significant for egocentric pointing errors from older adults over time. However, the logarithmic function was the closest to significant as a predictor for pointing errors.

There were however, greater errors for allocentric pointing for older adults as compared to their egocentric performance. In this sense, older adults performed better with the egocentric task than the allocentric trials, but their egocentric errors were still significantly greater than those exhibited by the younger adults. Allocentric pointing also showed age group differences with older adults averaging about 58° of error and younger adults about 35°. Recent work by Giudice et al. (2017) also found significant differences between age groups for allocentric pointing [12]. The means for the older adult group (34°) and younger adult group (18°) for that work were however on a lower scale than the errors found here. Overall, the errors for this allocentric pointing task showed that both age groups exhibited relatively poor performance, with even the younger adults averaging about 35° of error and the older adults showing highly variable performance between time intervals (see Table 3 for exact means). This could be due to the method of execution for the allocentric trials. In order to accommodate the time delayed testing, the pointing trials were done on paper and this technique may have introduced increased allocentric errors for both age groups.

In conclusion, the current study elucidated differences in remembered cognitive map accuracy between younger and older adults. The results demonstrated that older adults were disadvantaged compared to younger adults, including a pattern of performance decline for older adults across the temporally delayed testing intervals of one-day and one-week. The methodological paradigm used in this research to evaluate cognitive map decay lays the groundwork for additional research on spatial decay functions. The characterization of the decay function will be further examined with methodological changes made to strengthen the mathematical trend analysis (including larger sample sizes and additional time interval testing).

Acknowledgements. We thank everyone at the VEMI lab for their assistance creating the driving simulator. We specifically thank Sam Gates and Scott Richards for development of the VR environment used during this research. We acknowledge funding support for this project provided by NSF grant CHS-#1425337 and a University of Maine Aging Research and Technology Seed Grant awarded to Dr. Nicholas Giudice.

References

1. Bennett, A.T.: Do animals have cognitive maps? J. Exp. Biol. **199**(1), 219–224 (1996)
2. Golledge, R.G.: Wayfinding Behavior: Cognitive Mapping and Other Spatial Processes. JHU Press, Baltimore (1999)
3. Tolman, E.C.: Cognitive maps in rats and men. Psychol. Rev. **55**(4), 189–208 (1948)
4. Klencklen, G., Després, O., Dufour, A.: What do we know about aging and spatial cognition? Reviews and perspectives. Ageing Res. Rev. **11**(1), 123–135 (2012)
5. Moffat, S.D.: Aging and spatial navigation: what do we know and where do we go? Neuropsychol. Rev. **19**(4), 478–489 (2009)
6. Harris, M.A., Wolbers, T.: Ageing effects on path integration and landmark navigation. Hippocampus **22**(8), 1770–1780 (2012)
7. Head, D., Isom, M.: Age effects on wayfinding and route learning skills. Behav. Brain Res. **209**(1), 49–58 (2010)
8. Iaria, G., et al.: Age differences in the formation and use of cognitive maps. Behav. Brain Res. **196**(2), 187–191 (2009)
9. Park, D.C.: The basic mechanisms accounting for age-related decline in cognitive function. In: Park, D.C., Schwarz, N. (eds.) Cognitive Aging: A Primer, vol. 11, pp. 3–19. Psychology Press, Philadelphia (2000)
10. Park, D.C.: Cognitive Aging: A Primer. Psychology Press, Philadelphia (2000)
11. Park, D.C., et al.: Models of visuospatial and verbal memory across the adult life span. Psychol. Aging **17**(2), 299–320 (2002)
12. Giudice, N.A., et al.: Spatial updating of haptic arrays across the lifespan. Exp. Aging Res. **43**, 274–290 (2017)
13. Rubin, D.C., Wenzel, A.E.: One hundred years of forgetting: a quantitative description of retention. Psychol. Rev. **103**(4), 734 (1996)
14. Bennett, C.R., Corey, R.R., Giudice, U., Giudice, N.A.: Immersive virtual reality simulation as a tool for aging and driving research. In: Zhou, J., Salvendy, G. (eds.) ITAP 2016. LNCS, vol. 9755, pp. 377–385. Springer, Cham (2016). https://doi.org/10.1007/978-3-319-39949-2_36
15. Nasreddine, Z.S., et al.: The montreal cognitive assessment, MoCA: a brief screening tool for mild cognitive impairment. J. Am. Geriatr. Soc. **53**(4), 695–699 (2005)
16. Brooks, J.O., et al.: Simulator sickness during driving simulation studies. Accid. Anal. Prev. **42**(3), 788–796 (2010)

17. Antonova, E., et al.: Age-related neural activity during allocentric spatial memory. Memory **17**(2), 125–143 (2009)
18. Gardony, A.L., Taylor, H.A., Brunye, T.T.: Gardony map drawing analyzer: software for quantitative analysis of sketch maps. Behav. Res. Methods **48**(1), 151–177 (2016)
19. Tobler, W.R.: Bidimensional regression. Geogr. Anal. **26**(3), 187–212 (1994)
20. Friedman, A., Kohler, B.: Bidimensional regression: assessing the configural similarity and accuracy of cognitive maps and other two-dimensional data sets. Psychol. Methods **8**(4), 468 (2003)

Is Order Memory of Routes Temporal or Spatial? An Individual Differences Study

Ineke J.M. van der Ham[1(✉)], Suze de Zeeuw[2], and Merel Braspenning[2]

[1] Department of Health, Medical, and Neuropsychology, Leiden University,
Leiden, The Netherlands
c.j.m.van.der.ham@fsw.leidenuniv.nl
[2] Department of Experimental Psychology, Utrecht University, Utrecht, The Netherlands

Abstract. Memory for order has been shown to be a separate component of navigation ability. The current study is aimed at characterizing order memory in navigation and to assess the impact of individual differences. In total, 589 participants performed an experiment in which they studied a video of a route through a realistic virtual environment, after which they were asked about the relative and absolute order of scenes in the route. Results suggest that order memory performance in navigation resembles the spatial layout of a route, rather than its temporal layout. Order memory appears to be relatively robust, as it is affected only by age and spatial experience, but not by gender or spatial anxiety. Participants showed an increase in performance into mid adulthood, directly followed by a decrease in performance. Spatial experience only affected performance for children; the more they navigated by themselves in daily life, the better their order memory.

Keywords: Order memory · Navigation · Spatial memory · Temporal memory · Individual differences

1 Introduction

Our ability to find the way is highly complex. In order to travel to a given destination many different processes are executed simultaneously. We perform tasks like creating mental maps, recognizing our environment, and adopting different perspectives on our environment (e.g. Stankiewicz and Kalia 2007; Iaria et al. 2007; Igloi et al. 2009). Many of these functions have received a lot of attention in literature. In order to understand navigation as a cognitive construct it is crucial to understand the cognitive properties of each of these different processes. The current study therefore concerns one of these processes; order memory. Order memory is an aspect of human navigation that has been dealt with only scarcely, but has been shown to be essential for successful navigation (Ekstrom et al. 2011; Van der Ham et al. 2010).

Order memory concerns the memory specifically for the order in which items are encountered. In multiple studies a dissociation has been found between order memory and other aspects of memory, such as recognition and memory load (Fabiani and Friedman 1997; Hannesson et al. 2004a; Hannesson et al. 2004b; Hampstead et al. 2010). These findings highlight the distinct nature of order memory. These dissociations

© Springer International Publishing AG 2017
T. Barkowsky et al. (Eds.): KogWis/Spatial Cognition 2016, LNAI 10523, pp. 86–101, 2017.
https://doi.org/10.1007/978-3-319-68189-4_6

have not only been found in behavioral measures, but in neuroanatomical correlates as well. The prefrontal cortex has been linked to temporal order memory, but not to recognition. Moreover, the parietal cortex and the hippocampus are related to temporal distinctiveness, which in turn, is linked to how order memory is applied during navigation (Marshuetz and Smith 2006).

For navigation in particular, the few reports on order memory support the dissociation between temporal order memory and other memory aspects like memory for spatial layout, (Ekstrom et al. 2011). In a limited number of studies on route learning, tasks focusing on performance resembling order memory are used. Denis and colleagues (2014) have highlighted the importance of environment richness for order memory performance. Schinazi and Epstein (2010) studied path memory to a limited extent by showing specific involvement of the retrosplenial cortex in processing building pairs congruent and incongruent with a newly learned route. Wiener et al. (2012) apply a similar approach in showing aging effects specifically in route retracing as compared to route repetition. Moreover, in a neuropsychological case study (Van der Ham et al. 2010) we have shown that impairment restricted to order memory for scenes along routes is sufficient to cause severe problems of getting lost in daily life. Despite this apparent significant role in human navigation, the properties of order memory of routes are largely unknown.

It is important to note that order memory in navigation can be considered distinctive from order memory in other memorization tasks. In straightforward working memory paradigms, usually memorizing letters or simple objects, order memory is typically assessed with tasks in which the temporal order of items should be remembered (e.g. Barker et al. 2007; Hampstead et al. 2010; Postma et al. 2006). Yet in navigation, order memory could also concern spatial order. The major difference between standard working memory paradigms and navigation tasks is that they concern static versus dynamic contexts in which information is to be remembered. When moving along a route, remembering the order of landmarks could logically rely on the temporal order in which they were encountered, as landmarks are by definition encountered at different points in time. However, the spatial order of landmarks typically coincides with this temporal order, with the requirement that the route is travelled at constant speed. Although the few studies that included measures of order in human navigation experiments usually define it as 'temporal order' (e.g. Barker et al. 2007; Ekstrom et al. 2011; Van der Ham et al. 2010), there is no empirical support for the use of this term. With the current study we aim to examine the nature of order memory and whether it is appropriate to label it 'temporal'.

Our main approach to dissociate temporal from spatial order lies with the fact that a route is typically travelled at constant speed. Temporal order can be selectively affected by manipulating the navigation speed when travelling along the route. Therefore, if speed manipulations influence the quality of memory for landmark order, a considerable temporal memory process is present. However, if speed manipulation does not affect order memory, it does not seem appropriate to consider order memory in navigation 'temporal order memory'. Although the term 'temporal order' is commonly used for remembering the order of items along a route, it could well be that order memory is based on spatial information instead. Spatial input is more stable and available through the mental map that is built during learning the environment of a particular route (see e.g. Tversky 2003). It could therefore well be a more reliable source of information.

Order memory of routes can be assessed in different ways. An important distinction is that of relative versus absolute order. When asking for relative order, a participant is typically presented with multiple items and asked to arrange them in the correct order, relative to each other. In contrast, absolute order concerns the order of an individual item with respect to the route as a whole. In this case a participant can indicate where a particular scene was encountered on an abstract representation of the route, e.g. by marking a position on a horizontal line. The speed manipulation is therefore ideally used in a test of absolute order, as distortions of order position can be easily assessed in such a task. If order memory is distorted by an increased speed for a given item, a participant may position this item along the line in a distorted manner. Such an effect cannot be detected with the relative order measure, but with the absolute order measure such effects can be effectively measured. Moreover, the use of different measures allowed us to compare scores on the absolute and relative measures, overall and for each scene individually, to gain more insight into the characteristics of order memory.

The secondary goal of the current experiment was to study individual differences in order memory of routes. Within the field of spatial cognition and of navigation ability in particular, large variation in individual performance is often found. Factors like age, gender, spatial experience, and spatial anxiety commonly affect navigation performance. Therefore, those factors are taken into account in the current study.

For age, both development and aging should be considered. As children grow older, their general memory for routes is commonly thought to improve. For instance, there is a significant improvement in encoding landmarks between the ages of 8 and 12 (Heth et al. 1997). Moreover, order memory for non-spatial information has been shown to increase considerably in this same age range (Brown et al. 1999). Therefore, we hypothesized a substantial increase in performance in order memory during navigation in the 8 to 12 years age range, with potential further improvement into adulthood. With regard to aging, older adults have been shown to be worse in a landmark-ordering task after memorizing a route (Wilkniss et al. 1997). This finding was further substantiated by an elaborate assessment of aging effects on survey and route knowledge by Head and Isom (2010). They found that order memory, in addition to location memory and memory for directional information connected to landmarks declined with old age (20 vs 70 years of age). Furthermore, this age related decline was associated with caudate nucleus volume. We therefore expect a clear decline in order memory with older age. Based on existing literature, it is hard to predict what would happen at specific ages, as those studies typically include participants either limited in age range or categorized in loosely defined age groups. Therefore, the current experiment will allow for a much more detailed approach, as we will not only use multiple measures to assess order memory performance, but we have a sample of participants that is diverse and large enough to allow for a detailed analysis of age effects in the range of 7 to 81 years old.

With regard to gender differences in general navigation ability, typically, males make more use of geometric cues, whereas females pay more attention to landmarks (e.g. Sandstrom et al. 1998), yet this is a strategic difference, resulting in different performance levels, depending on the task at hand. Some have found that gender effects are restricted to survey knowledge showing similar route knowledge in males and females (Castelli et al. 2008). Choi et al. (2006), also report no gender difference in route learning, when a specific route needs to be retraced. Yet, others have found a male advantage in route learning (Schmitz 1997; Saucier et al. 2002). As order memory can be considered an aspect of route learning, literature either predicts no difference between males and females, or a male advantage. With the wide age range in this study we can furthermore assess gender effects across lifespan.

Spatial experience could well have a positive effect on order memory performance. The more we encounter different spatial situations, the better we may be at memorizing various route properties, analogous to what has been found for experienced taxi drivers (e.g. Maguire et al. 2000). Spatial anxiety might have an opposite effect; when anxiety is high, participants may pay less attention to details in the environment and remember them less (e.g. Lawton 1994; Eysenck et al. 2007; Van der Ham et al. 2013). However, very little is known about anxiety specifically for spatial situations. Therefore, the inclusion of this characteristic is of an exploratory nature. The size of the current sample of participants allows for a substantial range in and therefore meaningful examination of spatial experience and spatial anxiety.

In short, we will attempt to find out whether order memory during navigation is based on temporal or spatial information by manipulation of speed during encoding of a route through an environment. Also, a comparison of absolute and relative measures of order memory is performed to further clarify the concept of order memory. A large sample of participants of a wide age range is included to study developmental as well as aging effects. Order memory performance is thought to clearly increase between the ages of 8 and 12, and to decrease with older age. For gender, there are two plausible outcomes; either there is no difference between males and females as they do not differ in route memory, or males perform better. The factors of spatial experience and spatial anxiety are approached in a more explorative manner. Spatial experience increases with age, with a clear increase when children learn to explore their environment autonomously, which could well benefit their navigational skills, including order memory. Spatial anxiety could in turn reduce spatial performance.

2   Methods

2.1   Participants

In total 589 participants took part in the experiment. Details concerning age, gender, and education level (for adults) are provided in Table 1. The experiment was part of 'Science Live', an initiative of Nemo Science Center in Amsterdam. Therefore, all participants were visitors of this science museum, who were asked to participate during their visit. All participants, or their parents when underage, were required to sign an informed consent form prior to participation.

Table 1. Descriptives of all participants. Standard deviations in parentheses. Education level (range 1–7) based on Verhage (1964).

		Children	Younger adults	Middle-aged/older adults
N		281	102	206
% male		51.0	44.0	51.0
Age (in years)	Mean	10.2 (2.0)	32.7 (7.0)	49.1 (8.7)
	Range	7–17	18–40	41–81
Education level		–	5.8 (0.8)	5.9 (1.0)

2.2 Materials

For all adults, a brief questionnaire was used containing questions concerning city of residence, spatial anxiety, and frequency of travel. 'What is your city of residence?' could be answered with four options: small village (1), large village (2), small city (3), and large city (4). This division was made in order for children to be able to answer this question as well. Spatial anxiety was measured with the spatial anxiety questions taken from the Wayfinding Questionnaire reported by Van der Ham et al. (2013): 'I am afraid to lose my way somewhere', 'I am afraid to get lost in an unknown city', 'In an unknown city, I prefer to walk in a group rather than by myself', 'When I get lost, I get nervous', 'How uncomfortable are you in the following situations: a. Deciding where to go when you are just exiting a train, bus, or subway station. b. Finding your way in an unknown building (for example a hospital). c. Finding your way to a meeting in an unknown city or part of a city. Frequency of travel was chosen to reflect spatial experience and partic- ipants indicated how many times a week they traveled over 10 km.

All children indicated their city of residence with the same four categories as the adults. Furthermore children reported their level of spatial anxiety by indicating their anxiety when travelling to an unknown place 'How afraid are you to go to places you have not been before' and when travelling by themselves 'How afraid are you to travel by yourself by bike or on foot'. Children were also asked how often they travelled to school alone. This item is thought to reflect spatial experience as travelling alone forces a child to make their own spatial decisions, whereas adult supervision or the company of other children eliminates the need for spatial decision making. In the Netherlands, the vast majority of children live within walking or biking distance from their schools, therefore it is physically possible for them to travel to school by themselves from an early age.

Some of the participants were foreign tourists and did not speak Dutch. To ensure consistency in questionnaire answers, they did not fill out the questionnaire. For the experiment itself, a version with English instructions was used and sufficient command of English was required for inclusion.

For the experiment, the virtual Tübingen environment was used (see e.g. Van Veen et al. 1998 and Van der Ham et al. 2010). A route through this realistic environment was selected, with a length of 350 m, including 8 decision points. Participants watched the route in a video clip with a duration of 4 min and 49 s and were asked to memorize this as well as they could, without reference to specific questions that could be asked afterwards. The route was shown through the perspective of an adult of average height, at normal walking speed. Participants were randomly assigned to one of two versions of the video: baseline and altered speed. The altered speed video showed the exact same route, but the speed of the first half of the route was presented at 88% of the speed of the baseline video and the second half at 120% of the speed of the baseline video, resulting in a video with exactly the same duration and exactly the same spatial layout. 11 screenshots from the video were used as scenes in the experimental tasks. These screenshots were taken at points on the route that were exactly 10% of the total route distance apart (0%–10%–20%–30%–40%–50%–60%–70%–80%–90%–100%). Visual complexity was highly comparable across the different screenshots, as they all included a path of similar width with several buildings on both sides.

2.3 Design

Order memory of the route was tested in two different ways. Participants were asked to indicate relative order by clicking each of nine scenes (scenes at 0% and 100% were not used) in their order of appearance. All nine images were presented simultaneously and when an image was clicked it would disappear, correction was not possible. 9 instead of 11 images were chosen as they were presented simultaneously on the screen and 9 allowed for better visibility of all images. For each scene, the indicated position was registered. As this task concerned relative order memory, each scene was scored based on its relation to the scene selected directly after it; if the next selected scene was taken from a point later along the route, a point was awarded. This leads to a score range of 0–8. For instance, the sequence 8-3-4-5-6-7-9-1-2 would be awarded 6 points (8-3 and 9-1 receive no points).

Absolute order memory was assessed with a slider as a response tool. Participants were shown each of the eleven scenes, one at a time, along with a horizontal slider. They were instructed to indicate where along the route they had encountered the scene. Note that it was ensured that the instruction did not refer to distance or time explicitly. With the mouse participants could provide their response; a red bar appeared in the slider starting from the left, which could be extended to where the participant thought the scene was. The score for this task was the mean deviation in percentage points. Two scores were calculated: one based on the spatial layout of the route (0%–10%–20%–30%–40%–50%–60%–70%–80%–90%–100%) and one on the temporal layout of the route (0%–12%–24%–36%–48%–60%–68%–76%–84%–92%–100%). For example, if the second scene was positioned at 23%, this would result in 13% spatial deviation and 11% temporal deviation. If this score is lower for the temporal reference score than for the spatial reference score, this is in favor of a more temporal coding of position. For each participant, regardless of the version of the video they had seen, both scores were calculated, termed measures (distance, time) in the analyses.

Lastly, as an additional measure of spatial and temporal memory of the route, participants were asked to provide an estimation of the total distance of the route in meters and the total duration of the video in minutes.

2.4   Procedure

Prior to participation, participants or their parents filled out the informed consent form and were informed about the content of the experiment. The questionnaire was filled out before or after the experiment. Participants were assigned to either the baseline or adjusted speed version of the video, based on their gender and age. Comparable distribution of gender and age between both versions was ensured. The experiment took place in a museum, in which there was a dedicated research area, comparable to a standard laboratory setting. Visual and auditory distractions were kept to a minimum. Each participant performed the experiment individually, at least two experimenters were present at all times to instruct and observe the participants. After viewing the video, half the participants, also controlled for age and gender, started with the relative order task, the other half started with the absolute order task. After the order tasks, they were asked to estimate distance and duration. After completion of the experiment, participants were debriefed and informed about the goal of the experiment.

3   Results

3.1   Spatial Versus Temporal Order

In order to compare the deviation based on distance and speed, a repeated measures general linear model (GLM) was performed with measure (distance, time) as dependent variable and version (baseline, adjusted speed) as independent variable, for all adults aged 18–40. This age group was selected as it reflects the age range of adults typically used in this type of experiment. The younger and older participants are considered in later analyses to gain specific insight into developmental and aging processes. The analysis showed a significant main effect of measure, $F(1,100) = 11.10$, $p < .01$, partial $\eta2 = 0.10$. The deviation in the measure based on distance was smaller than the deviation in the measure based on time. The main effect of version, $F < 1$, partial $\eta2 = 0.001$, and the interaction of measure and version, $F < 1$, partial $\eta2 = 0.005$, were not significant. So, version, or speed of presentation, clearly did not significantly affect order memory as tested here. This pattern of results is illustrated in Fig. 1.

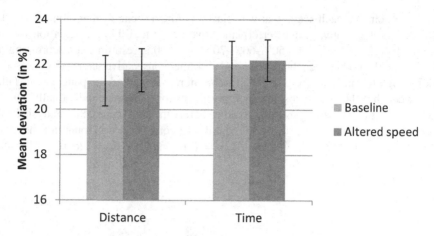

Fig. 1. Mean deviation in percentage points for the absolute order memory task. Performance is split up by video speed (baseline or altered speed) and reference score (based on either distance or time). Error bars represent standard error of the mean (SEM).

It could be possible that the temporal manipulation used was not strong enough to induce effects. Therefore the two groups of participants (baseline or adjusted speed version) were also compared on duration and distance estimation. Outliers were removed (more than 3 standard deviations above the mean). A significant difference between these two groups was found: estimated duration was much longer for the altered speed group (12.86 min) than for the baseline group (7.07 min), $F(1,96) = 9.93$, $p < .01$ (actual duration of the video: 4.82 min). Estimation of distance was highly comparable between both groups ($F < 1$). This highlights that the speed manipulation was clearly strong enough to induce differences within the temporal domain.

One potential objection to our temporal manipulation could be that the difference in exposure time to the individual scenes between the first and second half of the route allows for differences in performance, which do not appear in the baseline condition. Therefore we directly compared performance on the first and second half of the route for both the manipulated speed (19.1% vs 25.0%) and baseline condition (17.4% vs 27.7%). This resulted in a significant main effect of half, $F(1,100) = 34.8$, $p < .001$, partial $\eta2 = 0.258$, in which deviation was larger in the second half of the route, and no significant main effect of version ($F < 1$) or interaction of half and version ($p > .10$).

3.2 Comparison Relative and Absolute Order Memory

With our task design we were able to compare two types of order memory: absolute and relative. As version did not affect performance, the scores of all participants, regardless of version were included in the analyses described below. First of all, the correlation between the two measures was weak, but significant, $R = -0.306$, $p < .001$. The negative correlation indicates that with higher scores on the relative order memory task, participants show less deviation on the absolute order memory task. In addition, we recalculated the score on the absolute task in the same manner as for the relative task; by awarding a point for each scene that was placed before a scene further along the route. Analogous to the relative order performance, we performed this recalculation for the scenes at 10%–20%–30%–40%–50%–60%–70%–80%–90%, resulting in a score ranging 0–8. The correlation between the relative and absolute 'consecutive scene' score was also weak but significant, R = .15, p < .001. Furthermore, we studied the pattern of correlation between the relative and absolute memory scores for each scene individually. Due to the nature of the calculation (position should be before the next scene), this analysis could be performed for all scenes at 10%–80%. Significant correlation was found for the scene at 10%, R = .163, p < .001, 20%, R = .136, p = .001, and 70%, R = .126, p < .01. Mean scores per scene are depicted in Fig. 2.

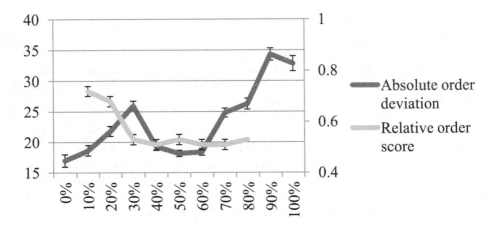

Fig. 2. Performance for each scene for both measures of order memory. The 0% and 100% scenes were not used in the relative order memory task. Error bars represent standard error of the mean.

3.3 Age and Gender

Our sample allowed for a detailed analysis of the influence of age and gender on performance. For both main performance measures, relative and absolute order memory, the effects of age and gender were assessed. For age, participants were grouped by age in single years for the ages 7–15 years, and grouped by 5 years for older participants. An ANOVA showed a significant, quadratic main effect for relative order, $F(1, 566) = 11.01$, $p < .01$, as well as absolute order memory, $F(1, 566) = 36.87$, $p < .001$. Performance increased with increasing age for the younger participants, peaked around the age of 35 and decreased with increasing age for participants over 35. The age effects are illustrated in Fig. 3A and B. The same pattern was found for both measures of order memory. No significant effects of gender were found.

3.4 Spatial Experience and Spatial Anxiety

To assess the effects of spatial experience and spatial anxiety, participants were split up into children, younger adults, and middle-aged/older adults. Average scores are provided

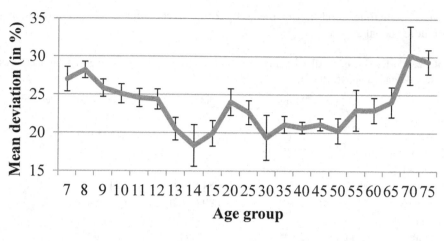

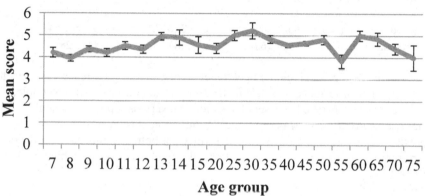

Fig. 3. Mean performance for all age groups for (A) the relative and (B) the absolute order memory measures. Age groups represent 1-year-groups for the ages 7–15 and 5 year groups for the ages 20–75. Error bars represent standard error of the mean (SEM).

in Table 2. For children, spatial experience was expressed by how frequently they travelled to school together. Also, residence was taken into account. Spatial anxiety reflected how anxious they felt when travelling to an unknown place and when travelling alone. A univariate ANOVA with spatial experience, residence and spatial anxiety as between subject factors showed only a significant main effect of spatial experience, $F(3, 197) = 3.00$, $p < .05$, partial $\eta2 = .044$, for performance on the relative order memory task. This effect showed that the difference in performance between the responses 'sometimes' and 'often' (in response to the question 'How often do you go to school by yourself?') was at trend level, $p = .054$, with better performance for 'often'. No other effects were significant. A very similar pattern was found when the same analysis was performed for absolute order memory performance: a significant main effect of spatial experience, $F(3, 197) = 3.08$, $p < .05$, partial $\eta2 = .045$, with a significant difference between the responses 'never' and 'often', $p < .05$, and a difference at trend level between 'sometimes' and 'never' p = .087. Both effects indicate a better performance with more spatial experience.

Table 2. Performance of all participants on the questionnaire and experimental measures. Standard deviation in parentheses.

	Children	Adults	Middle-aged/older adults
Questionnaire			
Residence (1–4)	2.33 (1.14)	2.39 (1.17)	2.46 (1.07)
Alone to school (0–3)	1.37 (1.11)	–	–
Anxiety (1–4)	2.47 (1.86)	–	–
Frequency of travel (1-4)	–	2.84 (1.17)	2.84 (1.10)
Anxiety (0–6)	–	3.89 (1.50)	4.20 (1.44)
Experiment			
Absolute order test (in %)	25.05 (8.12)	21.5 (7.3)	21.64 (6.90)
Relative order test (0–27)	11.23 (4.28)	12.4 (4.57)	12.2 (3.87)
Estimated distance (in m.)	566.74 (682.8)	1049.2 (677.17)	962.04 (669.54)
Estimated time (in min.)	8.58 (6.68)	10.38 (9.40)	11.44 (9.28)

For both the younger and middle-aged/older adults, spatial experience was reflected by travel frequency, residence was also taken into account as a separate variable, and spatial anxiety was measured by a set of questions on various aspects of spatial anxiety. For the relative order memory performance, a univariate ANOVA with spatial experience, residence, and spatial anxiety was performed for both absolute and relative order memory scores, showing no significant effects of any of the between subject variables (all p's > .05).

3.5   Quality of Route Memory

Lastly, participants were asked for their estimations of the duration and length of the route. The mean estimations per age group are depicted in Fig. 4A and B. The horizontal lighter grey lines indicate the actual duration and length. The figures indicate very clearly that participants substantially overestimate both properties of the route. With a multivariate ANOVA, the effects of age group and gender were assessed for both estimations. It showed a significant main effect of age group for the length estimation, $F(20, 472) = 4.50$, $p < .001$, partial $\eta2 = .160$, and a trend level effect of gender for the duration estimation, $F(1, 472) = 3.69$, $p = .055$, partial $\eta2 = .008$. Length estimation is larger and therefore less accurate for older participants and duration estimation is lower and therefore more accurate for males.

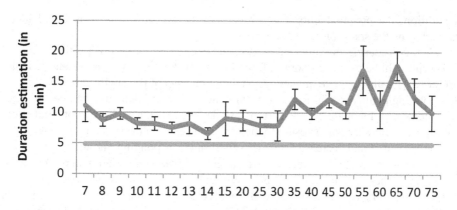

Fig. 4. Mean estimations for all age groups of (A) distance and (B) duration of the route. Age groups represent 1 year groups for the ages 7–15 and 5 year groups for the ages 20–75. Error bars represent standard error of the mean (SEM).

4 Discussion

The current experiment was aimed at creating a better understanding of order memory in navigation, as multiple sources of evidence agree that order memory is a separate memory component and should be considered a separate component of navigation ability as well (e.g. Ekstrom et al. 2011; Van der Ham et al. 2010). The main question concerned the nature of order memory: is it temporal, as most publications imply, or might it be more spatial? The secondary question concerned the role of individual differences in order memory performance: what is the contribution of age, gender, spatial experience, and spatial anxiety to order memory performance in a navigation task?

By manipulating the speed in one of the two route videos participants memorized, the impact of temporal changes could be assessed. The temporal manipulation had no effect on participants' performance, which indicates that the use of 'temporal order memory' may be out of place. Responses overlapped more with the spatial layout of the route, suggesting that order memory could be a more spatial process. The null effects of the temporal manipulation show very small effect sizes (.001 and .005), found in a relatively very large sample of participants, substantiating the lack of effect of the temporal manipulation. Furthermore, the effectiveness of the speed manipulation was demonstrated by a substantial effect on duration estimation; the altered speed version led to estimations almost twice as long than the baseline version. Nonetheless, the distance estimation was highly similar between both conditions. It is striking that there is an apparent tendency to overestimate the duration of the route, regardless of condition. We cannot exclude the possibility that a proportion of participants might have responded this question with their estimation of how long they thought it would take to walk the route themselves. The baseline speed of the route was somewhat above average walking speed, which could result in longer temporal estimations overall. However, on average such a distortion would be identical for all participants, regardless of experimental group.

In addition, the potential impact of differences in exposure time was found to be unaffected by the speed of the video shown.

When considering the order tasks at hand, it may not be surprising that a spatial approach might be used. Temporal information is by definition less stable and reliable, and moreover, during route memorization a mental map of the environment is created, incorporating mainly spatial features, from which order of landmarks can be deduced. It should be noted though, that the current task design does not exclude a potential effect of temporal differences in exposure to the specific scenes on the route. It is a possibility that the increased and decreased speed resulted in corresponding variation in memorization of those parts of the route. However, at group level such variation in performance is not found when individual scenes are considered.

Order memory can be assessed with relative and absolute measures, which were weakly related in the current experiment. This was analyzed into more detail by splitting up performance for each scene. For separate scenes, only the scores for the scenes at the beginning (10% and 20%) and end of the route (70%) were significantly correlated. This can be explained by the type of response participants provided, by responding with the slider, this reference tool could easily induce responses with a deviation towards the middle of the slider. This effect has greater impact for the scenes taken from the beginning and the end of the route. Furthermore, it is important to realize that the relative measure specifically concerned the relation between the individual scenes, whereas the absolute measure focused on the relation between a particular scene and the route as a whole, disregarding the other scenes.

In a general sense, these findings can be placed in the context of understanding how humans interact with landmarks, or scenes, during route learning. Although some have studied route learning characteristics such as path memory and route retracing (e.g. Schinazi and Epstein 2010; Wiener et al. 2012), with the current study we have specifically focused on memory for order of particular scenes along a route. This particular focus on the landmark property of order is relatively novel, but could contribute to ongoing research on landmark processing in general (see e.g. Waller and Lippa 2007).

Apart from overall group effects, individual differences were also taken into account. Age has shown to be an important factor; participants showed a clear increase in performance into adulthood, until the age of around 35, after which performance decreased again, as expected. It is important to note that the pattern of increasing performance does extend beyond the 8–12 year old age range, up until 35 years of age. Also, the commonly found decrease of performance in the elderly appears to already start at the age of 35, much earlier than is commonly found for spatial tasks in general (for a review see Klencklen et al. 2012). However, the results also indicate that the decline in performance is larger for ages 60 and up. The general pattern of lower performance in route learning with age has been found when performance relies more heavily on route memory (e.g. Head and Isom 2010; Cushman et al. 2008).

Some have argued that this aging pattern is mainly linked to route planning (e.g. Salthouse and Siedlecki 2007; Allain et al. 2005; Lipman and Caplan 1992). Planning of a route could well have a functional connection to order memory of that particular route. It should be noted that due to the current task design, no measures of general route knowledge were available. Therefore it is not possible to determine whether this aging pattern is specific for order memory, or for route learning in general. To explore this option further, we consulted performance from healthy middle-aged/older adults through another dataset from our lab (N = 59, age 43–87 years, mean age 59.31) (manuscript in preparation). They performed several general neuropsychological tests concerning spatial and verbal working memory, processing speed, and estimated verbal intelligence level. Furthermore, an elaborate navigation test battery was administered. Order memory performance in this group did not correlate significantly with any of the neuropsychological tests and with all but one navigation test. It showed to only correlate significantly with route continuation memory. Although this concerns a different sample of participants, it shows that order memory performance is at least partially independent from general cognition measures and other measures of navigation.

In contrast, gender did not affect performance in any of the analyses. Therefore, the previous findings of no differences in route performance appear to apply for order memory as well (Castelli et al. 2008; Choi et al. 2006).

The addition of spatial experience and spatial anxiety to the analyses were more exploratory. For children, experience as expressed by navigation autonomy plays a significant role. Children who often navigate autonomously have better order memory. The current data do not allow analysis of causality, but it appears plausible that autonomous navigation improves the quality of order memory. It would be worthwhile to study whether this effect is also present for other aspects of navigation. For adults, however, experience does not play a role anymore. Neither does spatial anxiety. It should be noted however that the anxiety measure was restricted to self-report.

The performance on the duration and length estimation tasks was also affected by individual variation. First of all, there was a striking overall overestimation on both measures. Furthermore, age was related to distance estimation: the older the participant was, the larger their estimation was. Yet, the youngest participants were very accurate, so with age, overestimation emerged. In contrast, duration estimation was affected by gender. Overall, males reported lower and therefore more accurate estimations of duration.

5   Conclusion

Taken together, the present findings show that order memory in navigation is mainly based on spatial features. This implies that a spatial mental map is consulted to answer questions pertaining to order of route elements. The commonly used term temporal order should therefore be reconsidered. Order memory seems to be quite a robust cognitive ability as the impact of individual variation is limited. There are clear effects of age, with a peak in performance around 35 years of age. Improvement therefore continues after childhood, and decline sets in earlier than most reports on aging imply. Furthermore, order memory performance is not affected by gender or spatial anxiety. Spatial experience does have an impact: children with higher spatial autonomy outperform children with less spatial autonomy.

Acknowledgments. The authors wish to thank the Science Live initiative at Nemo Science, Amsterdam for the opportunity to use their facilities, Rimalda van Beurden and Christel Peeters for their assistance in testing the participants, and Edwin Dalmeijer for his help in programming the experiment. This work was supported by NWO (Netherlands Organisation of Scientific Research) under Veni grant (451.12.004).

References

Allain, P., Nicoleau, S., Pinon, K., Etcharry-Bouyx, F., Barré, J., Berrut, G., Dubas, F., Le Gall, D.: Executive functioning in normal aging: a study of action planning using the Zoo Map Test. Brain Cogn. **57**, 4–7 (2005)

Barker, G.R.I., Bird, F., Alexander, V., Warburton, E.C.: Recognition memory for objects, place, and temporal order: a disconnection analysis of the role of the medial prefrontal cortex and perirhinal cortex. J. Neurosci. **27**, 2948–2957 (2007)

Brown, G.D.A., Vousden, J.I., McCormack, T., Hulme, C.: The development of memory for serial order: a temporal-contextual distinctiveness model. Int. J. Psychol. **34**, 389–402 (1999)

Castelli, L., Corazzini, L.L., Geminiani, G.C.: Spatial navigation in large-scale virtual environments: gender differences in survey tasks. Comput. Hum. Behav. **24**, 1643–1667 (2008)

Choi, J., McKillop, E., Ward, M., L'Hirondelle, N.: Sex-specific relationships between route-learning strategies and abilities in a large-scale environment. Environ. Behav. **38**(6), 791–801 (2006)

Cushman, L.A., Stein, K., Duffy, C.J.: Detecting navigational deficits in cognitive aging and Alzheimer disease using virtual reality. Neurology **71**, 888–895 (2008)

Denis, M., Mores, C., Gras, D., Gyselinck, V., Daniel, M.-P.: Is memory for routes enchanced by an environment's richness in visual landmarks? Spat. Cogn. Comput. **14**, 284–305 (2014)

Ekstrom, A.D., Copara, M.S., Isham, E.A., Wang, W., Yonelinas, A.P.: Dissociable networks involved in spatial and temporal order source retrieval. NeuroImage **56**, 1803–1813 (2011)

Eysenck, M.W., Derakshan, N., Santos, R., Calvo, M.G.: Anxiety and cognitive performance: attentional control theory. Emotion **7**, 336–353 (2007)

Fabiani, M., Friedman, D.: Dissociations between memory for temporal order and recognition memory in aging. Neuropsychologia **35**(2), 129–141 (1997)

Hampstead, B.M., Libon, D.J., Moelter, S.T., Swirsky-Sacchetti, T., Scheffer, L., Platek, S.M., Chute, D.: Temporal order memory differences in Alzheimer's disease and vascular dementia. J. Clin. Exp. Neuropsychol. **32**(6), 645–654 (2010)

Hannesson, D.K., Howland, J.G., Phillips, A.G.: Interaction between perirhinal and medial prefrontal cortex is required for temporal order but not recognition memory for objects in rats. J. Neurosci. **24**(19), 4596–4604 (2004a)

Hannesson, D.K., Vacca, G., Howland, J.G., Phillips, A.G.: Medial prefrontal cortex is involved in spatial temporal order memory but not spatial recognition memory in tests relying on spontaneous exploration in rats. Behav. Brain Res. **153**, 273–285 (2004b)

Head, D., Isom, M.: Age effect on wayfinding and route learning skills. Behav. Brain Res. **209**, 49–58 (2010)

Heth, C.D., Cornell, E.H., Alberts, D.M.: Differential use of landmarks by 8- and 12-year-old children during route reversal navigation. J. Environ. Psychol. **17**, 199–213 (1997)

Iaria, G., Chen, J.-K., Guariglia, C., Ptito, A., Petrides, M.: Retrosplenial and hippocampal brain regions in human navigation: complementary functional contributions to the formation and use of cognitive maps. Eur. J. Neurosci. **25**(3), 890–899 (2007)

Igloi, K., Zaoui, M., Berthoz, A., Rondi-Reig, L.: Sequential egocentric strategy is acquired as early as allocentric strategy: parallel acquisition of these two navigation strategies. Hippocampus **19**(12), 1199–1211 (2009)

Klencklen, G., Després, O., Dufour, A.: What do we know about aging and spatial cognition? Reviews and perspectives. Aging Res. Rev. **11**, 123–125 (2012)

Lawton, C.A.: Gender differences in wayfinding strategies: relationship to spatial ability and spatial anxiety. Sex Roles **30**(11–12), 765–779 (1994)

Lipman, P.D., Caplan, L.J.: Adult age differences in memory for routes: effects of instruction and spatial diagram. Psychol. Aging **7**, 435–442 (1992)

Maguire, E.A., Gadian, D.G., Johnsrude, I.S., Good, C.D., Ashburner, J., Frackowiak, R.S.J., Frith, C.D.: Navigation-related structural change in the hippocampi of taxi drivers. Proc. Natl. Acad. Sci. U.S.A. **79**, 4398–4403 (2000)

Marshuetz, C., Smith, E.E.: Working memory for order information: multiple cognitive and neural mechanisms. Neuroscience **139**, 195–200 (2006)

Postma, A., Van Asselen, M., Keuper, O., Wester, A.J., Kessels, R.P.C.: Spatial and temporal order memory in Korsakoff patients. J. Int. Neuropsychol. Soc. **12**, 327–336 (2006)

Salthouse, T.A., Siedlecki, K.L.: Efficiency of route selection as a function of adult age. Brain Cogn. **63**, 279–286 (2007)

Sandstrom, N.J., Kaufman, J., Huettel, S.A.: Males and females use different distal cues in a virtual environment navigation task. Cogn. Brain. Res. **6**, 351–360 (1998)

Saucier, D.M., Green, S.M., Leason, J., MacFadden, A., Bell, S., Elias, L.J.: Are sex differences in navigation caused by sexually dimorphic strategies or by differences in the ability to use the stratgies? Behav. Neurosci. **116**(3), 403–410 (2002)

Schinazi, V.R., Epstein, R.A.: Neural correlates of real-world route learning. NeuroImage **53**, 725–735 (2010)

Schmitz, S.: Gender related strategies in environmental development: effect of anxiety on wayfinding in and representation of a three-dimensional maze. J. Environ. Psychol. **17**, 215–228 (1997)

Stankiewicz, B.J., Kalia, A.A.: Acquistion of structural versus object landmark knowledge. J. Exp. Psychol. Hum. Percept. Perform. **33**(2), 378–390 (2007)

Tversky, B.: Structures of mental spaces. Environ. Behav. **35**, 66–80 (2003)

Van der Ham, I.J.M., van Zandvoort, M.J.E., Meilinger, T., Bosch, S.E., Kant, N., Postma, A.: Spatial and temporal dimensions of navigation impairments: a case study. NeuroReport **21**, 685–689 (2010)

Van der Ham, I.J.M., Kant, N., Postma, A., Visser-Meily, J.M.A.: Is navigation ability a problem in mild stroke patients? Insights from self-reported navigation measures. J. Rehabil. Med. **45**, 429–433 (2013)

Van Veen, H.J., Distler, H.K., Braun, S., Bülthoff, H.H.: Navigating through a virtual city: using virtual reality technology to study human action and perception. Future Gener. Comput. Syst. **14**, 231–242 (1998)

Verhage, R.: Intelligentie en leeftijd. Dissertation. Assen, The Netherlands (1964)

Waller, D., Lippa, Y.: Landmarks as beacons as associative cues: their role in route learning. Mem. Cogn. **35**, 910–924 (2007)

Wiener, J.M., Kmecova, H., de Condappa, O.: Route repetition and route retracing: effects of cognitive aging. Front. Aging Neurosci. **4**(7), 1–7 (2012)

Wilkniss, S.M., Jones, M.G., Korol, D.L., Gold, P.E., Manning, C.A.: Age-related differences in an ecologically based study of route learning. Psychol. Aging **12**, 372–375 (1997)

Spatial Memory

The Difference in Cognitive Processing Between Route and Survey Descriptions Used by Visuo-Spatial Working Memory

Hironori Oto[✉]

Department of Communication and Psychology, Faculty of Psychological Sciences,
Hiroshima International University, 555-36 Kurose-Gakuendai, Higashi-Hiroshima,
Hiroshima 739-2613, Japan
h-ootou@he.hirokoku-u.ac.jp

Abstract. This study was carried out using a correlational method to determine whether visual (visual cache) and spatial (inner scribe) components in visuo-spatial working memory constrain the construction of spatial representations through spatial description. In the experiment, participants listened to a description explaining the layout of the city from either a ground-level viewpoint walking through the city (route descriptions) or a bird's eye-view looking down on the interrelationships of the landmarks within it (survey descriptions). They were asked to imagine the described scenes and to memorize directions and landmarks for later recall. Visual and spatial span tests were executed to evaluate visual and spatial capacities of participants, respectively. The results indicate that spatial span correlates mainly with the recall score of route descriptions and that visual span is related mainly to survey descriptions. Moreover, the findings also suggest that components that are not mainly used are also related to the composition process of spatial representations; however, the effect becomes positive or negative depending on the imposed memory load.

Keywords: Spatial descriptions · Perspectives · Visuo-spatial working memory · Cognitive resources

1 Introduction

Imaging a place or area that is visible from where we are now is important for understanding the large-scale environment surrounding oneself and for traveling through it. This spatial representation or image governs our behavior (Boulding 1956). It also helps us to comprehend the environment and the behavior of others through textual means in such a way that the reader imagines the described scene or the movement of a character as being in a world set in a story. What, however, determines the ability to construct this spatial representation? This study focuses on specifically this issue.

Spatial representation can be distinguished into route and survey, depending on the perspective from which a person mentally represents a place or area (Thorndyke and Hayes-Roth 1982). Route representation refers to an inferred environment by simulating traveling within it from the person's viewpoint. Survey representation, on the other hand,

© Springer International Publishing AG 2017
T. Barkowsky et al. (Eds.): KogWis/Spatial Cognition 2016, LNAI 10523, pp. 105–117, 2017.
https://doi.org/10.1007/978-3-319-68189-4_7

refers to an environment represented in the mind from above, such as in looking at maps. Which perspective is used depends both on the way of learning, i.e., by map or by navigation, and the perspective-related goal of taking either a route or survey perspective (Taylor et al. 1999). Spatial representations are also constructed through verbal descriptions (Taylor and Tversky 1992, 1996). Tayler and Tversky (1992) found that readers formed isomorphic mental models of environments with representations described from either route or survey perspectives. It costs extra reading time to switch perspective from reading to a described one. After reading and retrieving from the memory of the environment, however, the time it takes to switch perspectives diminishes or disappears altogether (Lee and Tversky 2001, 2005).

It is presumed that people form spatial representations from verbal descriptions using their working memory resources. It is well known that such construction is constrained by visuo-spatial capacity as well as by verbal capacity in working memory. Several studies have also suggested that there can be differential involvement of the working memory in the construction of route and survey representations from texts. However, when it comes to the subdivided components of visuo-spatial working memory, i.e., visual and spatial components, little is clear about the role of each type of capacity in spatial representation. The aim of this study is to investigate whether the capacity of visual and spatial components underpins the ability to construct route and survey representations through spatial description.

The multiple working memory systems proposed by Baddeley and Hitch (1974) work for temporal retention and for the processing of information with verbal and visuo-spatial components. Later, Logie (1995) revised their working memory model from one based on a singular visuo-spatial component to one that subdivided visuo-spatial working memory into visual and spatial components. In this model, the visual component called the visual cache retains visual information such as color and figure. The spatial component called the inner scribe, on the other hand, stores spatial information, such as the sequential positions of objects and their movements.

Several studies have revealed the engagement of working memory in text comprehension using a dual task method. In this method, participants listen to spatial descriptions that describe a person traveling somewhere engaging visuo-spatial or verbal tasks concurrently. Typical results show that both concurrent tasks interfere with comprehension. Instead, when participants listen to non-spatial abstract descriptions, only concurrent verbal tasks will interfere with this (De Beni et al. 2005; Meneghetti et al. 2011; Pazzaglia et al. 2007). This interference is generally explained by the competition for the common resource of a working memory component that occurs between main and concurrent tasks (e.g., Baddeley 1986; Logie 1995). This result implies that the contents of spatial descriptions are retained in the visuo-spatial component as well as in the verbal component, whereas non-spatial descriptions are maintained only in the verbal component.

The studies using a dual task method have also demonstrated the existence of differential processing in the process of route and survey description. Pazzaglia et al. (2010) found that both concurrent spatial (spatial tapping) and verbal (articulatory suppression) tasks interfered with text comprehension in route descriptions, whereas only the verbal task interfered with it in survey descriptions. Brunyé and Taylor (2008) also reported similar results, suggesting that spatial components play an important role when compre-hending route descriptions. Altogether, these studies have showed that the capacity of the spatial component in visuo-spatial working memory constrains the processing of route descriptions, but not survey descriptions. However, what about the capacity of the visual component?

In this context, the role of the visual component is less clear compared to that of the spatial component. Although Pazzaglia and Cornoldi (1999) have investigated the role of visuo-spatial working memory on route and survey descriptions, they failed to find the difference between these two descriptions in respect to the function of the visual component. Deyzac et al. (2006) conducted further research in relation to the comparison of methods used in the processing of information between landmarks and moves/loca-tions in spatial descriptions. In their experiments, participants listened to verbal descrip-tions of the urban-like environments gained from walking through it (route perspective) or looking down it from above (survey perspective) and were asked to draw maps after that. The results for the spatial component (experiment 1) showed the interference effect of tapping on the route-description test and the weaker negative effect on the survey-description test, indicating that the degree of its involvement on processing of the spatial descriptions was different between route and survey. However, they failed to show the interference effect of concurrent visual tasks on both route and survey descriptions. The results for the visual component (experiment 3), contrary to what was predicted, showed a promoting effect on the survey description test. Altogether, since suggestions about the role of the visual component are not clear, further investigation is required.

Though the dual task is a well-used and sophisticated method in the working memory literature, it has one potential risk, which is that imposing a concurrent task may itself cause changes in cognitive processes. This is because the participants may try to avoid any lowering of their performance. Meneghetti et al. (2011) showed that imposing the concurrent spatial task while listening to spatial descriptions tends to lead participants to use less visuo-spatial strategies compared to participants with no concurrent task. Besides this, people can take a different perspective from the one in which they learn the environment (e.g., navigation vs. map) (Thorndyke and Hayes-Roth 1982) or the described environment (Taylor et al. 1999). Furthermore, the cost of shifting perspective from memory is not necessarily large when spatial representation is constructed through spatial descriptions (Lee and Tversky 2001). These all raise the potential risk for partic-ipants in change processing strategies, including taking a perspective that is against the experimenter's intention. It is especially likely to force adaptation when participants face a situation in which they find it hard to engage in a spatial task in the way they usually do or do as the experimenter instructs them. It seems difficult to get rid of this problem completely when using the dual task method.

Thus, it is plausible to research the impact of visuo-spatial working memory on spatial descriptions using other approaches. Using the alternative approach of the dual task method, the role of working memory in complex tasks has been investigated using a correlational method focusing on individual differences between subjects (e.g., Daneman and Carpenter 1980, 1983; Just and Carpenter 1992). Daneman and Carpenter (1980) found that a participant's working memory span as measured by the reading span test is highly correlated with reading comprehension scores. Oto (2015) reported on data suggesting that the capacity of the visual component has an effect on map learning. He measured participants' visual and spatial working memory spans and investigated the correlation between each span and the performance of distance judgments based on memorized maps. The results showed that distance error was correlated only with visual span. This implies that the capacity of the visual component in visuo-spatial working memory is more critical than that of the spatial component.

Due to the correlation method never imposing additional work on participants, by using it we can escape the risk of intervention in the strategy that participants use in constructing spatial representations for comprehending spatial descriptions. Therefore, this study used the correlational method to determine the subtle visuo-spatial working memory components for route and survey representations constructed from spatial description. A visual pattern test and a Corsi block test were used for the assessment of visual and spatial working memory capacity (Logie 1995; Logie and Pearson 1997). Two hypotheses were developed for this study: the first is that, in route description, the capacity of the spatial component mainly predicts the comprehension performance of a participant, because route perspectives induce sequential simulations of body movements and the change in relative positions between landmarks and the body; and second, in survey descriptions, the capacity of the visual component mainly predicts the participant's performance, because the survey perspective offers overall visual views containing the interrelationships among landmarks.

2   Experiment

2.1   Participants

53 undergraduates (29 males, 24 females) from Hiroshima International University participated in the experiments. They were all between 18 and 22 years old.

2.2   Materials

The Spatial Description Test
Six descriptions were prepared by referring to the material used by Deyzac et al. (2006). Half of them were for route, and half were for survey descriptions. All of them were constructed in Japanese (see Appendix for the translated version in English). For the route descriptions, each navigational route within the city was described from the perspectives seen on the ground, and directions were expressed as appropriate actions to be taken at each corner, such as going straight or turning right or left. For the survey descriptions, routes were described from a bird's eye perspective, and directions were expressed using the terms south, north, east, and west. Each description was constructed with six sentences. Commonly, the first sentence contained one landmark at the start location, and each of the following sentences contained one landmark at a corner and one direction to go to the next landmark or goal location. Therefore, each description contained six landmarks and five directions. All descriptions were read aloud and recorded, then used as an acoustic stimulus in the experiment. Finally, six answer sheets were constructed. On each sheet was printed a description identical to one of the six

descriptions developed for the test, except that the directions and landmarks within it were blanked out and underscored.

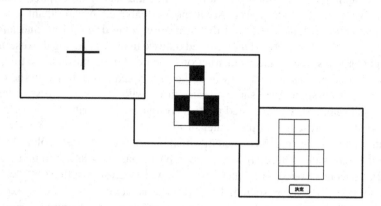

Fig. 1. An example of the presentation stimulus for the visual pattern test

Visual and Spatial Span Test

Two-span tests were used as a measure of the visual and spatial components in visuo-spatial working memory. A visual pattern test was used to assess each participant's visual span, and a Corsi Block Test was used to evaluate their spatial span. Both tests were conducted on a computer (Figs. 1 and 2). The detail of each test is explained in the next section.

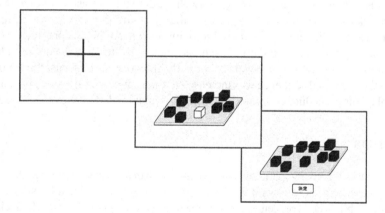

Fig. 2. An example of the presentation stimulus for the Corsi Block Test

Procedure

In the spatial description test, each participant listened to a spatial description consisting of six sentences at first. After that, each was given an answer sheet and required to answer questions in which the directions and landmarks in the description were blanks to be filled in. To confirm that the participants represented the layout of the city in the described perspective, each was required to use the imagery obtained during the process of listening to each description. For the route descriptions test, each participant was asked to "imagine you are walking on a road." For the survey descriptions test, each participant was told, "Imagine you can see a map from above." A participant given route imagery instruction listened to one of three different route descriptions and answered questions as a practice trial at first then carried out two main trials using the rest of them. A participant given survey imagery instruction executed three trials in the same manner using survey descriptions. Twenty-seven of the participants were tested in the order of route descriptions first and then survey descriptions, with 26 in the reverse order.

The visual span test was executed using a computer as described below. At first, a fixation point was presented at the center of the computer screen for two seconds. A 2×2 matrix pattern was then presented in which half of the cells were colored in black, and the other half were colored in white. Each participant was asked to memorize the pattern. Two seconds later, another matrix pattern with a decision button ("決定" button in Japanese) below it was presented. This matrix was identical to the first, except that all the black cells were changed to white. Each participant was required to point to all the cells that had been previously been shown as black. Each identified cell was marked by a cross mark, and subsequent manipulation could not cancel this. After pointing, each participant had to push the decision button. If a participant succeeded in answering correctly in two of the three trials, a black cell and a white cell were added to the former matrix pattern, and the participant was given another three trials. This procedure continued until the participant failed in two out of three trials.

In the Corsi Block Test, the fixation point was presented at first as in the visual span test. Nine blocks on a board were then presented. Some of these blocks were flashed sequentially at the rate of one per second. Each participant was asked to memorize the flashed blocks and the sequence. After that, the identical nine blocks were presented again, and each participant was required to point at all those blocks previously flashed in the same sequence. After pointing, each participant had to push the decision button. If a participant succeeded in answering correctly in two of three trials, the number of blocks in the presented sequence was increased to three, and he or she was given another three trials. This procedure continued until the participant failed in two out of three trials.

3   Results

Scoring for the two visuo-spatial working memory span tests and the spatial description test was carried out as follows: the visual span score was calculated by summing the number of the black cells presented in the three most complex patterns for which changed squares were successfully recalled, and the spatial span score was calculated by summing the length of the three longest sequences that the participants successfully recalled. The recall scores for each spatial description test of the directions and landmarks were computed by summing the number of items correctly recalled.

Table 1. The mean ratio and standard deviations of the recall scores of directions and landmarks for both route and survey descriptions

	Route		Survey	
	Directions	Landmarks	Directions	Landmarks
Mean	63.8	58.9	55.7	53.0
SD	27.3	25.5	16.1	15.6

At first, to compare the recall scores in relation to directions and landmarks, a 2 (Perspective: Route, Survey) $\times$ 2 (Items: Directions, Landmarks) analysis of variance (ANOVA) for repeated measures was carried out using the mean ratio of the recall scores as a dependent variable. The results showed that there were significant main effects of items, indicating a higher recall ratio of directions than of landmarks ($F(1, 52) = 6.57$, $p = .01$). No other main effects or their interaction were significant (Table 1).

Next, a correlation analysis was conducted to confirm to what degree each span score is related to the route and survey mean recall scores. To measure the strength of the pure connection, partial correlation coefficients were calculated between each correct recall score and each span score, while controlling for the other span scores and the order of presenting descriptions. Contrasting results were obtained for the described perspectives. In route descriptions, the recall scores of both landmarks and directions were significantly correlated with spatial span score, but no positive correlations were found with visual span score. However, in the survey descriptions, the recall scores of both landmarks and directions were significantly correlated with the visual span score, but none were presented with the spatial span score even though it was found that the recall score of landmarks was negatively correlated with spatial score at a marginally significant level (Table 2).

Table 2. Partial correlation coefficients between each correct recall score (route and survey) and each span score (visual span test (VPT) and Corsi block test (Corsi)) while controlling for other span scores and the order of presenting descriptions

	Route		Survey	
	Directions	Landmarks	Directions	Landmarks
Visual (VPT)	.22	.13	.45[*]	.48[*]
Spatial (Corsi)	.28[*]	.35[*]	−.06	−.27[+]

[*]$p < .05$, [+]$p < .10$

Finally, the identical correlation analysis computed above was conducted by adding the serial position factor so that each item was presented when the participant was listening to a description. This additional analysis was designed to confirm whether increasing the cognitive load caused the participants to change their processing strategies. Generally speaking, memorizing items in the middle section of the serial position resulted in an increased burden because of reduced benefits of elaborative rehearsal compared to the first part and reduced benefits of immediate recall compared to the last part of the serial position. Therefore, memorizing the middle part of the serial position might have resulted in participants relying on other components in addition to the effective components that are used for memorizing items with a lower cognitive load. Forcibly changing the strategies used by participants was not expected to result in better performance.

Before conducting the additional analysis, it was confirmed that the serial position effect occurred in this experiment. For this purpose, a 2 (Perspective: Route, Survey) × 2 (Items: Directions, Landmarks) × 5 (Serial Position: 2, 3, 4, 5, 6) ANOVA for repeated measures was computed using the mean ratio of recall scores as a dependent variable. Data of items presented in the first sentence were excluded from the analysis to equalize the number of serial positions that were presented between directions and landmarks. The result indicated significant effects of the serial position, which confirmed the existence of the serial position effect ($F(1, 52) = 26.9, p < .0001$) (Fig. 3).

Then, partial correlation coefficients were calculated between each correctly recalled score and each span score for each serial position, while controlling for other span scores and the order of presenting descriptions. The results indicated that the positive correlation between spatial span scores and recall scores were the strongest for route descriptions of items in the middle part of the serial position. Moreover, the correlation between visual span scores and recall scores of landmarks were marginally significant in the same part of the serial position, although its effect was negative. Similarly, positive correlation between visual span scores and recall scores were the strongest for survey descriptions of items in the middle part of the serial position. Moreover, there was a significant negative correlation between visual span scores of landmarks in the same part of the serial position. Interestingly, in both types of descriptions, items at the top or bottom positions also indicated significant correlations with span scores that had negative correlations with items in the middle part of the serial position. In the case of items at the top or bottom positions, however, these effects were not always negative and were sometimes positive (Table 3).

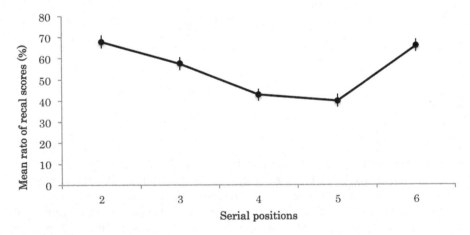

Fig. 3. The mean ratio and standard error bars of recall scores for serial positions

4 Discussion

The present study used correlation methods to determine the subtle visuo-spatial working memory components for route and survey representations constructed from spatial descriptions. The result of overall correlation analysis showed that clearly different components constrained recall performance corresponding to description type. Recall scores of both landmarks and directions in route descriptions were correlated only with spatial span scores. Conversely, recall scores of both of those in survey descriptions were associated only with visual span scores. The results suggest that different visuo-spatial components mainly support the construction of route and survey representations through spatial descriptions as expected in the present study. Information about landmarks was recalled more often than that about directions. Deyzac et al. (2006) also report the same pattern of results. This might mean that directional information is more essential for the construction of spatial representation through description.

Table 3. Partial correlation coefficients between each correct recall score (route and survey) and each span score including the visual span test (VPT) and the Corsi block test (Corsi) for serial positions, while controlling for other span scores and the order of presenting descriptions.

Route

	Direction					Landmark					
	2	3	4	5	6	1	2	3	4	5	6
Visual (VPT)	.32*	0.7	0.9	.13	.17	.02	.35*	−.10	−.27+	−.02	.29*
Spatial (Corsi)	.06	.43*	.42*	.18	−.06	.20	−.11	.28*	.44*	.05	.16

Survey

	Direction					Landmark					
	2	3	4	5	6	1	2	3	4	5	6
Visual (VPT)	.32*	.28*	.40*	.29*	.19	.20	.17	.26+	.44*	.16	.13
Spatial (Corsi)	.02	.09	−.03	−.09	−.14	.18	−.03	−.06	−.28*	−.15	−.32*

$^*p < .05,\ ^+p < .10$

Moreover, supplemental analysis calculated the coefficients for each serial position and produced two more findings. First, participants tended to rely on both visual and spatial components when the memorization load was high due to items presented in the middle part of descriptions. Furthermore, the newly relied component did not contribute to recall performance at all but rather had an adverse effect on recall performance. These negative effects seem to reflect the fact that participants could not afford to store the items using components that were more effective for performing the task. Second, situations with low a memorization load, such as when items are presented first or last, would also lead the participants to rely on both components of visuo-spatial working memory. However, in such situations, the newly relied component would at times contribute to recall performance. The working memory model presented by (Baddeley 1986; Baddeley and Hitch 1974) suggests that processing and storing information compete for working memory resources. Therefore, when the memorization load is low, a person might be able to afford trying additional cognitive processing that is expected to help performance, such as using better elaboration methods.

Taken together, the results suggest a certain degree of variability in the processing of spatial descriptions. This viewpoint is consistent with the findings of the research using the dual task method (Meneghetti et al. 2011). The study indicated that a high memory load during the main task causes people to change their usual strategy for completing the main task to what permits them to avoid the competence of cognitive resource between main and concurrent tasks. Besides this, the results of the present study suggest that even if the memory load is small, participants may change their usual strategies for seeking the one best fit for the task.

Using the dual task method, Deyzac et al. (2006) found that the visual component was involved in the processing of route descriptions as well as survey descriptions, while an overall correlation of visual span and the recall score of route test did not appear in the present study. This may because the dual task method could detect even slight involvements of the visuo-spatial component on the task. When little visual capacity is needed to take the route perspective, individual differences in capacity are unlikely to reflect memory performance. Nevertheless, even such a small engagement can presumably be detected by imposing dual tasks carrying a heavy load. Thus, only the previous study could find an influence from the visual component on the processing of route descriptions.

Although the results of correlation analysis conducted in this study showed the involvements of visual and spatial component in visuo-spatial memory with the processing of spatial representation, the calculated correlation coefficients were not high and all were below .50. Therefore, there could be other important factors for the processing of spatial description. From the viewpoint of the working memory model, there are two possible factors. One possible factor is the function of verbal working memory (the phonological loop). In the spatial description test used in the present study, participants were required to recall the blanked-out parts of spoken spatial descriptions, so they were thus able to answer the test by rote memorization rather than by using imagery. This may have encouraged participants to retain spatial descriptions phonologically in verbal working memory and weakened the involvement of visuo-spatial working memory on the processing of the descriptions. Even if this was the case, however, this does not explain the difference of the results between route and survey descriptions regarding visuo-spatial working memory, because participants can memorize by rote the spatial description in the same phonological manner regardless of how the environment is described. Rather, obtained results seem to reflect the difference in the type of spatial representation, i.e., route and survey representation, constructed through spatial descriptions as assumed in the present study. Hence, verbal working memory seems to have had limited influence, if any, on the results of the present study.

A second possible factor is the function of the central executive. Pearson (Pearson 2001; Pearson et al. 1999) has proposed a working memory model that supposes a buffer within visuo-spatial working memory as a workspace for imagery. He also insists that conscious image is retained in it primarily based on resources of the central executive system. In his model, visual component (visual cache) was presumed to hold non-conscious visual information and to be transferred into the buffer when conscious manipulation and inspection was needed. In addition, a spatial component (inner scribe) is assumed to be involved in the manipulation of the image within the buffer. Taking this model into account, individual differences in the capacity of the central executive may possibly influence the processing of route and survey descriptions as well as visual and spatial capacity. For the processing of route representation, while the spatial component supports the transformation of the image according to imaginal traveling, the central executive may also play a critical role in retaining the image in buffer. For the processing of survey representation, the central executive seems to have the same role, while the visual component worked as back-up storage for imagery and transferred visual information into the buffer when the construction of conscious map-like images fades. Further research is necessary to clarify the degree of contribution of the central executive to the processing of route and survey descriptions.

Altogether, the present study has demonstrated that the route and survey representations constructed through spatial descriptions mainly rely on different visuo-spatial components more clearly than has been previously considered. Moreover, components that are not mainly used are also related to the composition process of spatial representations; however, the effect becomes positive or negative depending on the imposed memory load. The viewpoint of the present study seems logical when considering the flexibility of human thought and our memorizing strategies. This study thus offers useful fundamental data for the consideration of individual differences in the processing of route and survey descriptions.

Appendix

Spatial descriptions for the translated version in English.

Route description

1. There is a karaoke club at your back.
2. Go straight, and there is an appliance store.
3. Turn left, and there is a bar.
4. Turn left, and there is a luggage store.
5. Turn right, and there is a station.
6. Turn right, and you arrive at a bowling alley.

1. There is a community center at your back.
2. Turn right, and there is a family restaurant.
3. Turn left, and there is an amusement park.
4. Go straight, and there is a cafeteria.
5. Turn left, and there is a police office.
6. Turn right, and you arrive at a coffeehouse.

1. There is a meat market at your back.
2. Go straight, and there is a fire department.

3. Turn left, and there is a game center.
4. Turn left, and there is a flower shop.
5. Turn right, and there is a university.
6. Turn right, and you arrive at a kindergarten.

Survey description

1. There is a library.
2. Go south, and there is a drugstore.
3. Go south, and there is a parking area.
4. Go east, and there is a city hall.
5. Go north, and there is a pet shop.
6. Go west, and you arrive at a fish store.

1. There is an elementary school.
2. Go east, and there is a supermarket.
3. Go north, and there is a bookstore.
4. Go east, and there is a bank.
5. Go south, and there is a nursery school.
6. Go south, and you arrive at a camera shop.

1. There is a hotel.
2. Go north, and there is a museum.
3. Go west, and there is a park.
4. Go south, and there is a department store.
5. Go west, and there is a convenience store.
6. Go east, and you arrive at a cycling shop.

References

Baddeley, A.D.: Working Memory. Oxford University Press, Oxford (1986)

Baddeley, A.D., Hitch, G.J.: Working memory. In: Bower, G.H. (ed.) The Psychology of Learning and Motivation: Advances in Research and Theory. Academic Press, New York (1974)

Boulding, K.E.: The Image: Knowledge in Life and Society. University of Michigan Press, Ann Arbor (1956)

Brunyé, T.T., Taylor, H.A.: Working memory in developing and applying mental models from spatial descriptions. J. Mem. Lang. **58**, 701–729 (2008)

Daneman, M., Carpenter, P.A.: Individual differences in working memory and reading. J. Verbal Learn. Verbal Behav. **19**, 450–466 (1980)

Daneman, M., Carpenter, P.A.: Individual differences in integrating information between and within sentences. J. Exp. Psychol. Learn. Mem. Cogn. **9**, 561–584 (1983)

De Beni, R., Pazzaglia, F., Gyselinck, V., Meneghetti, C.: Visuospatial working memory and mental representation of spatial descriptions. Eur. J. Cogn. Psychol. **17**, 77–95 (2005)

Deyzac, E., Logie, R.H., Denis, M.: Visuospatial working memory and the processing of spatial descriptions. Br. J. Psychol. **97**, 217–243 (2006)

Just, M.A., Carpenter, P.A.: A capacity theory of comprehension: individual differences in working memory. Psychol. Rev. **98**, 122–149 (1992)

Lee, P., Tversky, B.: Costs of switching perspectives in route and survey description. In: Proceedings of the 23rd Annual Conference of the Cognitive Science Society, Edinburgh, Scotland (2001)

Lee, P.U., Tversky, B.: Interplay between visual and spatial: the effect of landmark descriptions on comprehension of route/survey spatial descriptions. Spat. Cogn. Comput. **5**, 163–185 (2005)

Logie, R.H.: Visuo-Spatial Working Memory. Lawrence Erlbaum Associates Ltd., Hove (1995)

Logie, R.H., Pearson, D.G.: The inner eye and the inner scribe of visuo-spatial working memory: evidence from developmental fractionation. Eur. J. Cogn. Psychol. **9**, 241–257 (1997)

Meneghetti, C., De Beni, R., Gyselinck, V., Pazzaglia, F.: Working memory involvement in spatial text processing: what advantages are gained from extended learning and visuo-spatial strategies? Br. J. Psychol. **102**, 499–518 (2011)

Oto, H.: Effect of visuo-spatial working memory on distance estimation in map learning. GSTF J. Psychol. **2**, 56–60 (2015)

Pearson, D.G.: Imagery and the visuo-spatial sketchpad. In: Andrade, J. (ed.) Working Memory in Perspective, pp. 33–59. Psychology Press, Hove (2001)

Pearson, D.G., Logie, R.H., Gilhooly, K.J.: Verbal representation and spatial manipulation during mental synthesis. Eur. J. Cogn. Psychol. **11**, 295–314 (1999)

Pazzaglia, F., Cornoldi, C.: The role of distinct components of visuo-spatial working memory in the processing of texts. Memory **7**, 1–17 (1999)

Pazzaglia, F., De Beni, R., Meneghetti, C.: The effects of verbal and spatial interference in the encoding and retrieval of spatial and nonspatial texts. Psychol. Res. **71**, 484–494 (2007)

Pazzaglia, F., Meneghetti, C., De Beni, R., Gyselinck, V.: Working memory components in survey and route spatial texts processing. Cogn. Process. **11**, 359–369 (2010)

Taylor, H.A., Naylor, S.J., Chechile, N.A.: Goal-specific influences on the representation of spatial perspective. Mem. Cogn. **27**, 309–319 (1999)

Taylor, H.A., Tversky, B.: Spatial mental models derived from survey and route descriptions. J. Mem. Lang. **31**, 261–292 (1992)

Taylor, H.A., Tversky, B.: Perspective in spatial discourse. J. Mem. Lang. **35**, 371–391 (1996)

Thorndyke, P.W., Hayes-Roth, B.: Differences in spatial knowledge acquired from maps and navigation. Cogn. Psychol. **14**, 560–589 (1982)

Psychophysics of Place Recognition

Hanspeter A. Mallot[1](✉), Stephan Lancier[1], and Marc Halfmann[2]

[1] Department of Biology, University of Tübingen, Tübingen, Germany
hanspeter.mallot@uni-tuebingen.de
[2] Leibniz-Institut für Wissensmedien, Tübingen, Germany

Abstract. Places are locations of special significance represented in spatial memory. Place recognition is a central task in spatial cognition that combines perception of local position information and ego-motion with working memories of adjacent places and long-term memory codes of the target place. In this paper, we examine the role of visual position information and place recognition and thus attempt to link spatial cognition to visual psychophysics. We present two experimental paradigms for assessing the visual processing involved in the formation of memory codes of place and the content of such memory codes. We also present a maximum likelihood model of place recognition from distant landmarks allowing detailed quantitative testing of the general assumptions. We conclude that place recognition is based on a visual working memory containing raw "snapshot" information as well as local depth maps of surrounding landmark objects.

1 Introduction

1.1 Place Recognition

Place vs. Location. The concept of place, i.e. of locations of special significance, is central to the understanding of spatial cognition. Origins of spatial memory in the animal kingdom are associated with a life-style known as central-place foraging (Papi 1992) in which animals keep and remember a "home" location from which they make excursions for feeding. Indeed, the representation of this central place may be the simplest case of a spatial long-term memory in the animal kingdom. Finding back to the central place can be based on various mechanisms including search, laid-out trails (chiton), path integration (ants, spiders, honeybees), or landmark-based matching (digger wasp, honey-bee). In any case, the animal will have to know when the home is reached, in which case some change in behavior will occur, e.g. the animal will decide to stop moving or to start a final search routine.

In rodents and other mammals, multiple places or location in general are thought to be represented in the activity of hippocampal place cells. For example, Wilson and McNaughton (1993) demonstrate that the current location of

Supported by the German Federal Ministry of Education and Research within the Tübingen Bernstein Center for Computational Neuroscience (Grant 01GQ1002A).

T. Barkowsky et al. (Eds.): KogWis/Spatial Cognition 2016, LNAI 10523, pp. 118–136, 2017.
https://doi.org/10.1007/978-3-319-68189-4_8

a rat in a maze can be reconstructed from a population of ongoing place-cell recordings, given that the firing fields of these neurons had been determined in a previous measurement. Still, firing fields do not simply pave environmental space in a homogeneous way. Rather, density and overlap of place cell firing fields is increased at places which have an increased significance for the animal. For example, Hollup et al. (2001) showed that in rats trained to find a hidden platform in an annular watermaze, more firing fields are found in the vicinity of the platform than in mid-water. Firing field density changes as the platform is relocated.

In primates, place recognition also involves other brain regions, including among others the parahippocampal place area (Epstein and Kanwisher 1998, Epstein 2008). Places represented in the parahippocampal place area are discrete entities characterized not just by their location (expressed e.g. by geometric coordinates) but by invariant features such as landmark objects or the overall geometrical layout of a scene.

Cognitive Graphs. Cognitive models of spatial behavior on the navigational or way-finding scale are often based on places as a central data format or "spatial primitive". For example, the base level of Kuipers' (2000) "spatial semantic hierarchy" is formed by places which are recognized and approached by the minimization of some measure of perceptual distance between the place and the agent's current location. The place representations are connected by action links allowing the agent to travel from one place to the next. Tolman's "means-ends-field" (Tolman 1932) is also a graph-like structure in which the nodes are states of the animal which may include the recognition of being at a particular place as well as goals which the animal is currently pursuing. Again, the states are linked by "means-ends-relations" allowing to plan state transitions. A developmental argument for the relevance of places as a building block in spatial memory has been presented by Siegel and White (1975). Graph approaches underly a large part of the wayfinding literature in which routes are generally considered chains of recognized places and actions, see for example O'Keefe and Nadel (1978), Gillner and Mallot (1998), and Hartley et al. (2003).

Despite the central role of "places" in many representational formats of space, other structures with similar roles may exist in spatial memory. One possibility is the oriented "view" visible from a location. View-specific neurons have been found in the primate hippocampus by Rolls et al. (1998) and have been used as nodes for cognitive graphs e.g. by Schölkopf and Mallot (1995) and Gaussier et al. (2002). Spatial graphs may also be composed of regional nodes representing groups of places in a hierarchical scheme (Wiener and Mallot 2003) or patch maps including a local reference frame (Meilinger 2008). Views, places, and regions differ in the granularity of spatial representations. In the experiments reported here, the extension of a place is mostly treated as an uncertainty, quantified by a confusion area, i.e. the statistical error ellipse of the place judgments. A more comprehensive theory of place recognition should probably treat the extension as a property of a mentally represented place.

Views, as well as places, as elements of a spatial ontology are associated with a geometrical location in the sense that they are perceived when the agent is located at or looking from this location. The situation is different for landmarks and boundaries, which may also be elements of the spatial graph and associated with specific locations, but which need not be reachable for the navigating agent. In this paper, we consider reachable places which are encoded in memory during an actual visit at this place and are recognized during subsequent encounters. Landmarks and boundaries will show up only as descriptors of places, not as nodes of the cognitive graph.

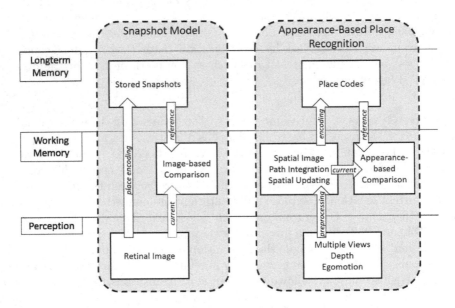

Fig. 1. Two approaches to place recognition

1.2 Models and Mechanisms

Figure 1 summarizes two basic approaches to place recognition. In the snapshot approach suggested by Cartwright and Collett (1982), left part of Fig. 1, the memory code for a particular place is closely related to the retinal image visible at the encoded place. Since this image may change substantially with the illumination, the time of day or year etc. (Zeil et al. 2003), some preprocessing is essential to yield a sufficient level of invariance. Such preprocessing of the retinal image has indeed been suggested by Cartwright and Collett (1982), who assume that the retinal image passes an edge detector before being stored as a snapshot. Other preprocessing operations include detection of "landmark" pixels (Lambrinos and Möller 1997), sky-line detection (Graham and Cheng 2009; Basten and Mallot 2010), average egocentric position of landmark objects ("center-of-gravity", O'Keefe 1991), local distance map derived from motion parallax (Dittmar et al. 2010), etc. In any case, the actual recognition step is carried out as a comparison or matching operation between the stored and a current snapshot, both preprocessed in the same way. Algorithms for this comparison operation include feature correspondence search (Cartwright and Collett 1982), pixel-based root-mean-square minimization with and without image warping (Franz et al. 1998) etc. For review see Möller and Vardy (2006).

In human spatial cognition place recognition can be based on snapshot-like mechanisms (Gillner et al. 2008). However, it is quite clear that under normal circumstances, extra-retinal information provided by one or several working memory stages will also play a role. These working memories contain information from outside the current field of view and are updated upon observer motion (Loomis et al. 2013; Burgess and Hitch 2005; Schindler and Bartels 2013; Röhrich et al. 2014). They provide a description of the local spatial layout which may be conceptualized as a local map or environment model surrounding the subject. Behavioral experiments with configurations of isolated landmark objects show that local charts of such landmark objects play a role in place recognition (Waller et al. 2000; Pickup et al. 2013). Here, we will use the term "spatial appearance" to characterize the spatial working memory of a place. Place codes for long-term memory (LTM) will then be derived from the spatial appearance and recognition will be based on comparisons of such LTM codes with the current spatial appearance (right part of Fig. 1).

While the idea of appearance-based place recognition does not seem to be particularly controversial, it allows for a number of systematic questions that may be used to structure the psychophysics of place recognition. These questions are:

1. Depth of processing: which image processing steps are needed to extract the place code from the raw retinal image? Possibilities include various early vision operations (edge detection, parallax) as well as the recognition of more abstract landmark structures such as the sky-line or recognizable objects.
2. Structure of the spatial working memory: which information is maintained and used for place recognition? Possibilities include panoramic views, collections of local views, objects localized in a local, egocentric but two-dimensional map, three-dimensional spatial layouts, etc.
3. Mechanisms of comparison and decision making. These will depend on the structure of the working memory and may include pointwise snapshot matching, comparisons of local maps, identification of landmark objects, etc.
4. Structure of long-term memories of places. This includes the role of local metric charts, geometric layout of he surrounding scene, and context from larger representations of space.

1.3   Experimental Procedures

The classical place recognition experiment in animals has been developed by Kruyt and Tinbergen (1938) in a study on digger wasps returning repeatedly to each of a number of borrows in which a larva awaits feeding. In this case, the place is selected by the animal and no learning or specific training is required during the experiment. Tinbergen and Kruyt (1938) marked a borrow by a circle of pine cones and displaced this circle after the digger wasp had left from the borrow. When returning, the wasp would search in the center of the displaced circle, indicating that the cones were used as landmarks.

In the Morris water maze task for rodents (Morris 1981) a goal location is rewarded by the fact that a rat can rest from swimming when it reaches the submersed platform in a water basin. Place learning in the water maze assesses both the recognition performance and the learning speed. The experiments can last for extended time, suggesting that a long-term memory of the place of the submersed platform is built and tested. For human subjects, various versions of the Morris water maze have been realized in virtual reality. For example, Hamilton and Sutherland (1999) used a virtual pool surrounded by two sets of landmarks (A, B) to study blocking in landmark learning. When trained with both sets together (A + B), subjects performed well even after one set was removed. However, when trained with one set only (A) and given the additional set B later, removal of set A lead to performance loss, indicating that the landmarks B had not been learned in this situation. Hort et al. (2007) adapted the water-maze paradigm to humans using a circular arena of 2.9 m diameter with landmarks projected variably by a beamer. This setup was used to demonstrate deficits in spatial cognition associated with early stages of dementia.

In this paper, we will study place recognition by two different experimental tasks. In the first one, "return-to-cued-location" (Gillner et al. 2008), a subject in a virtual environment is presented with the visual surround visible from a goal location. The virtual viewpoint tracker is then switched to a starting point from which the goal has to be approached by interactive navigation in the virtual environment. The task is similar to the tasks used in the geometric module literature (Cheng et al. 2013), but goal places can occur anywhere in the maze. Since the memory of the goal location is built during a brief inspection period prior to the performance, the "return-to-cued-location" task addresses a working memory of place. In the second paradigm, "incidental place learning" subjects are required to navigate to a goal from different starting points, using routes which all share a central crossing point. In the learning phase, this crossing point is always passed, but never mentioned as a special point to remember. In the test phase, however, subjects are explicitly instructed to navigate to the central crossing point. This paradigm has the advantage that subjects have to discover the central point themselves. It emphasizes spatial long-term memories.

The problem of place recognition is closely related to place learning, and experimental paradigms will generally involve both performances. It is important to note, however, that different learning schemes may lead to different place representations. One respect in which these representations may differ is their characterization as long-term or working memories. A second respect is place selection which is arbitrary in supervised schemes such as the Morris water maze or the walk-to-cues-location paradigm but may be influenced by the availability of landmarks etc. in free place choice.

2   Depth of Processing

Place recognition from visual cues involves the standard processes of early vision, including among others the detection of image features and depth, the understanding of scenes, and the recognition of objects. Here we use stereoscopic dynamic random dots to study the role of pure depth information in place recognition. Results indicate that place recognition can be based on pure depth information and (at least in our experimental environment) is not substantially improved by cues from other visual sub-modalities such as texture or localized objects (room corners).

2.1   Local Position Information

The recognition of places is generally thought to rely on a combination of landmark cues visible from the target place and spatial context such as traveled distances from neighboring places (e.g., O'Keefe and Nadel 1978). For the landmark component, various types of "local position information" can be extracted from the visual input and have been shown to play a role in place recognition. These types include barely processed "snapshots" (for review, see Gillner et al. 2008) as well as visual information requiring higher amounts of image processing such as landmark configurations (see next section), room geometry and three-dimensional spatial layout (Cheng et al. 2013; Epstein 2008), or identified landmark objects (Janzen and van Turennout 2004). Visual depth, i.e. the perceived distance to objects of the surrounding scene, is relevant for a number of these cues, especially if indoor-environments are considered. Here we use psychophysical approaches from the study of early visual processes (stereopsis, motion parallax) to investigate the role of perceived depth in place recognition (Halfmann 2016).

2.2   Methods

Subjects and Procedure. 40 students from the University of Tübingen passed a simple test for stereo vision and participated in this study. The experiments were carried out in a virtual environment simulating a kite-shaped room with edged or rounded corners. In the "return-to-cued-location task" (Gillner et al. 2008), participants were placed at one of three goal locations in the kite-shaped room. In the following inspection phase subjects studied the local appearance of the room by looking around and performing small translational movements. They were then set back to a start position and used a joy-stick to return to the goal. After indicating goal recognition by the button hit, subjects were moved to the correct goal position, and the next trial started from there. In all, twelve decisions were recorded per subject and condition, i.e. two cycles of all six possible transitions between the three goal locations. In the results reported here, the virtual environment was presented with an Oculus-Rift stereoscopic head-mounted display (HMD), but controls with a mirror stereoscope and monocular viewing were also performed. In addition to the stereo disparities presented on

right eye   *left eye*   *right eye*

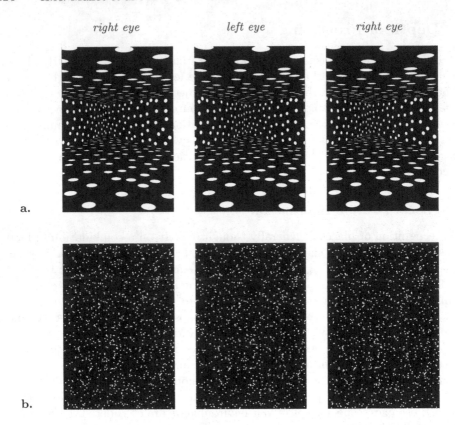

a.

b.

Fig. 2. Sample view of the kite-shaped room arranged for free stereoscopic viewing. For crossed fusion use leftmost columns, for uncrossed fusion use rightmost columns. **a.** Texture condition. **b.** Dot condition (sample frame of the dynamic random dot display). Both stereograms show the room with edged corners. Note that the texture condition gives a much better stereoscopic impression that the dot condition. However, in the actual experiment, motion parallax was present as an additional cue, leading to a clear perception of the room layout.

the stereoscope, the HMD setup provided a higher level of immersion including closed-loop movements of the head and body that might lead to better perception of structure-from-motion.

Stimuli and Conditions. Two factors, "visual cues" and "room shape", were varied in a full factorial design. In the *cue-condition "texture"*, rooms were defined by a texture of large spots (about 10 cm diameter in the virtual environment) pasted to the room walls, floor, and ceiling as a wallpaper. This texture provided stereo disparity, motion parallax upon observer motion, texture gradients and information about room corners (Fig. 2a). In the *cue-condition "dots"*,

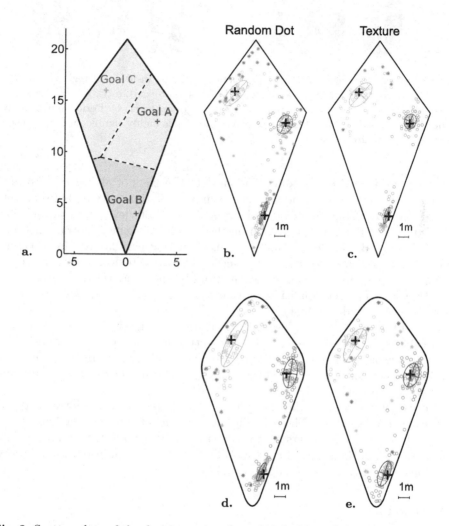

Fig. 3. Scatter plots of the decision points from 240 decisions (20 subjects × 12 decisions per subject). **a.** Layout of the kite-shaped room with goal locations A, B, C, and nearest-neighbor cells. Dimensions in meters. **b., c.** Edged corner room, **d., e.** rounded corner room. Dot colors indicate goal positions A, B, C. Tokens indicate: + true goal location, ○ decision points within goal region ("correct decision"). ∗ decision point outside goal region ("qualitative error"). Error ellipses are calculated over the within-region decisions only and reflect one standard deviation. (Color figure online)

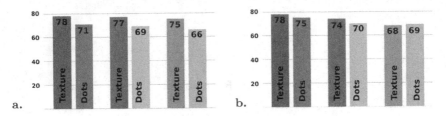

Fig. 4. Absolute numbers of correct decisions (decisions inside goal region) out of a total of 80 decisions per target (accumulated over all subjects). **a.** Edged corner room, **b.** rounded corner room. Colors indicate goal locations A, B, C. Performance above chance level defined by the relative area of Voronoi cell is highly significant for all cases. (Color figure online)

surfaces were defined by dynamic random dots (Sperling et al. 1989) uniformly distributed in the image plane and with a limited lifetime varying between 100 and 200 ms. Outdated dots or dots leaving the field of view were continuously replaced so that the dot distribution on the screen was kept uniform. The dots provided stereo disparities, a small amount of motion parallax (during dot lifetime), but no texture gradients (see Sperling et al. 1989). Room corners might have been inferred from the depth information, but not from the dot distribution itself (Fig. 2b). The cue conditions were performed in a blocked, within-subject design (texture condition first).

Even if the example stimulus of Fig. 2b is properly fused, the structure of the room is barely visible. In the experimental setup, however, the dots would start to move as soon as the observer changes his or her viewpoint. In this situation, the three-dimensional structure of the room becomes much clearer, since motion parallax can be used.

We used two *shape-conditions* "edged", and "rounded", as shown in Fig. 3 (between subjects factor). These conditions were included to test the hypothesis that the better defined corners in the "edged" condition provide better landmark information than the rounded corners in the "rounded" condition, predicting a superior performance in the "edged" condition.

2.3   Results

Figure 3 shows the decision points in the four conditions, accumulated over all subjects. Decision points scatter about the goal positions with a moderate variance, and variance is not substantially different in the four conditions. We also find a fair number of "qualitative errors" in which the subjects choose a place closer to one of the non-goals than to the current goal. The respective nearest-neighbor cells (Voronoi tessellation around goal points) are also indicated in Fig. 3a. These errors are equivalent to the "rotation errors" discussed in the geometric-module literature (see Cheng et al. 2013 for review). Figure 4 shows the number of correct decisions for the various conditions, again accumulated over all subjects. Note that the numbers given there are absolute counts out of

80 trials and do therefore not carry error bars. If subjects would ignore the visual information, the chance level for choosing a decision point in the correct Voronoi cell would be about 33% compared to an average recorded performance rate of about 91% shown in Fig. 4. A binomial test with chance level as null hypothesis reveals high significance ($p < 0.001$) in all cases. No significant differences between conditions were found.

A comparison with the stereoscopic and monocular viewing conditions (data not presented in this paper) shows similar results. Performance is well above chance even for the monocular condition, albeit slightly poorer than in the HMD-data reported here.

2.4   Discussion

The results indicate that subjects can use pure depth information as is provided by dynamic random dots to recognize places in a room. Additional texture cues providing more reliable depth information seem to lead to some improvement, which, however, is not statistically significant. This is even more surprising since texture cues provide still another cue for place recognition, i.e. snapshot matching. Indeed, since the texture was "painted to the wall", the subjects might have tried to remember the pattern of black and white wall patches appearing at each goal location and try to match it to their memory when they return. If they did use this strategy, it did not lead to a substantial improvement in performance. The sharpness of the corners of the room ("edged" vs. "rounded" conditions) do not seem to play an important role in self-localization, indicating that subjects rely more on the distances to walls than to the corners. Overall, the results fit nicely to the idea that places are represented by a local map of the environment which is updated as the subject moves around (Byrne et al. 2007; Loomis et al. 2013; Röhrich et al. 2014).

3   Place Recognition from Distant Landmarks

In this section, we present experimental data and a probabilistic model of place recognition from a configuration of distant landmarks surrounding a goal. The model assumes that landmark positions are perceived with hyperbolic distance compression and added noise, depending on current observer position. Position-dependent recognition rate is modeled as the likelihood of perceiving the expected (stored) landmark configuration from each position. The model reproduces key features of experimental results including a systematic localization bias towards the most distant landmark, the shape and orientation of the error ellipses, and effects of approach direction. We conclude that place recognition is based on a comparison between a place code (landmark distance and angles) and a working memory of surrounding space suffering from systematic depth distortions and distance-dependent drop in resolution.

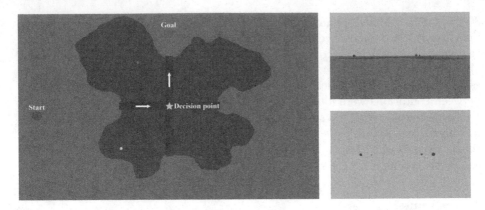

Fig. 5. Experimental setup for Experiment 2. *Left:* Aerial view of pond and plus-shaped bridge with a start and a goal location. In the experiments, four start and goal locations close to the ends of the bridge arms were used in all possible combinations involving a left or right turn at the decision point (bridge center). Four landmark objects can be seen in the four quadrants defined by the bridge. *Top right:* Subjects' view during learning phase. Note the landmark objects hovering above the pond. *Bottom right:* Subject's view during test phase. Only the landmark objects remain visible while the pond and bridge are covered by fog.

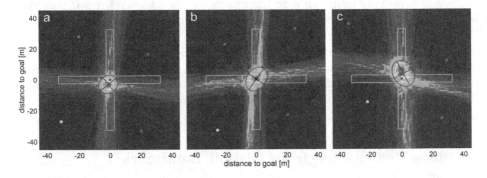

Fig. 6. Position choices for three landmark configurations. The landmarks are shown with their actual position and color. **a.** Standard configuration (20 subjects, 954 decisions), **b.** Parallelogram configuration (16 subjects, 761 decision), **c.** Peaked configuration (16 subjects, 754 decisions). The error ellipses are displaced from the goal (control and peaked condition) and elongated in the direction of the most distant landmark. See Lancier (2016).

3.1   Summary of Experimental Data

The accuracy of the place recognition in an open environment comprising four distant, distinguishable landmarks was studied in a behavioral experiment with human subjects navigating a virtual environment (Fig. 5). The environment included a plus-shaped bridge crossing a pond and four colored spheres hovering in mid-air above the pond, one in each quadrant defined by the bridge

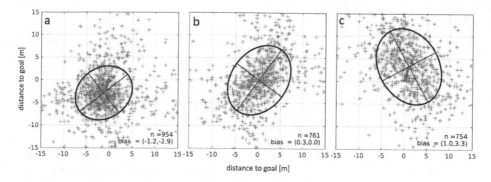

Fig. 7. Detailed decision points for the data appearing in Fig. 6. **a.** Standard configuration (20 subjects, 954 decisions), **b.** Parallelogram configuration (16 subjects, 761 decision), **c.** Peaked configuration (16 subjects, 754 decisions). The read bar marks the mean deviation from the bridge center ("bias"); it was significantly different from zero for the standard and peaked conditions (Hotelling's T-Square test).

arms. Subjects started at one bridge entry and had to find a goal that involved either a left or a right turn at the bridge center ("decision point"). All possible starting points and turn directions were used. In the test phase, bridge, pond, and goals were rendered invisible by simulated ground fog and the subjects were asked to navigate to the now invisible center of the bridge and indicate place recognition by button hit. This performance was based essentially on the four landmarks which remained visible at all times. In order to prevent subjects from using path integration, the starting points at each of the four bridge entries were varied using a random positional scatter. Experimental results are summarized in Fig. 6 (Lancier 2016). For the model, the following constraints can be derived:

1. Decision points show both a systematic bias and a statistical error. The systematic bias as well as the major axis of the error ellipses point roughly in the direction of the most distant landmark (Figs. 6 and 7).
2. If a point-symmetric configuration of landmarks is used, the systematic bias goes away (Figs. 6b and 7b).
3. If the landmark sizes, and therefore the perceived landmark distances, are manipulated between training and test session, decision points are shifted towards down-scaled landmarks and away from the up-scaled ones (data not shown). I.e. subjects try to adjust remembered and perceived distances.

3.2   Model

In a world coordinate system centered around the target point (the center of the bridge), the landmark positions are denoted by l_i, $i = 1, \ldots, 4$. Let x denote the current observer position. The true landmark vectors from the current observer position are $m_i = l_i - x$. We assume that these positions are represented in

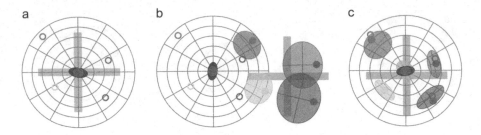

Fig. 8. Place recognition model. **a.** Layout with bridge (shown in light brown) and four landmarks arranged as in the "peaked" condition (Fig. 6c), shown as open circles. The polar grid symbolizes the egocentric landmark memory of an observer inspecting the bridge center. In this grid, the landmark positions are stored as a place code. **b.** Approaching observer with place code (open colored circles). Solid colored disks: true landmark positions; transparent ellipses: distribution of landmark measurement according to Eq. 2. Note the displacements of the distributions relative to the true landmark positions, which reflects the assumed hyperbolic distance compression. **c.** Probabilistic match of place code and observed landmark positions. The green distribution in the center is the joint likelihood $p(l_1, \ldots, p(l_4|x)$ from Eq. 4. (Color figure online)

an egocentric coordinate system with allocentric orientation. This allocentric orientation can be provided by the overall orientation of the bridge and landmark configuration (Fig. 8).

In order to model the systematic bias, we will need to assume that the actual perceived landmark distance is not veridical but hyperbolically compressed according the equation

$$\boldsymbol{\mu}_i = \frac{A}{A + \|\boldsymbol{m}_i\|} \boldsymbol{m}_i \tag{1}$$

(Gilinsky 1951). A is a constant set to 60 m in our simulations. This compression does not affect the stored landmark position which is assumed to be derived from triangulation and spatial updating processes and may therefore be assumed veridical. Indeed, Philbeck and Loomis (1997) demonstrate that the distance walked to a visually presented target in the "walking-without-vision" task is not affected by the hyperbolic compression reported by Gilinsky (1951). The stored place code is therefore given by the true landmark positions l_i.

Consider the probability of perceiving a landmark i at a position $\boldsymbol{m}_i$, given that the current observation position is $\boldsymbol{x}$. This measurement $\boldsymbol{m}_i$ is given in a Cartesian, egocentric coordinate system oriented to some allocentric "North" orientation. It comprises information about the perceived egocentric distance (with hyperbolic compression) and allocentric bearing, i.e. bearing with respect to a reference direction defined, for example, by the overall orientation of the virtual environment. The probability density function is assumed to be

$$p(\boldsymbol{m}_i|\boldsymbol{x}) = \phi(\boldsymbol{m}_i; \boldsymbol{\mu}_i(\boldsymbol{x}), \Sigma_i(\boldsymbol{x})), \tag{2}$$

i.e. the two-dimensional normal distribution with mean $\boldsymbol{\mu}_i$ and covariance matrix Σ_i. Note that both mean and covariance depend on the current observer position $\boldsymbol{x}$. For the mean, we have specified this dependence in Eq. 1 above. The covariance matrix Σ_i will have an eigenvector in the direction $(\boldsymbol{l}_i - \boldsymbol{x})$, i.e. the depth direction from the current view-point to the true landmark position, and an orthogonal one in the width direction. Denoting the local bearing of the i-th landmark by ϕ_i, ($(\cos\phi_i, \sin\phi_i) = (\boldsymbol{l}_i - \boldsymbol{x})/\|\boldsymbol{l}_i - \boldsymbol{x}\|$), we obtain:

$$\Sigma_i(\boldsymbol{x}) = \begin{pmatrix} \cos\phi_i & -\sin\phi_i \\ \sin\phi_i & \cos\phi_i \end{pmatrix} \begin{pmatrix} \sigma_{id}^2 & 0 \\ 0 & \sigma_{iw}^2 \end{pmatrix} \begin{pmatrix} \cos\phi_i & \sin\phi_i \\ -\sin\phi_i & \cos\phi_i \end{pmatrix}. \tag{3}$$

The eigenvalues in the distance and width directions are assumed to scale with distance according to $\sigma_{id}(\boldsymbol{x}) = 0.01\,\|\boldsymbol{l}_i - \boldsymbol{x}\|^2$ and $\sigma_{iw}(\boldsymbol{x}) = 0.3\,\|\boldsymbol{l}_i - \boldsymbol{x}\|$. Thus, the angular error of perceived landmark bearing does not depend on viewing distance. For small distances the angular errors are larger than the depth errors $(\sigma_{iw} > \sigma_{id})$ as is necessary to reproduce the shape of the experimental distributions. This may reflect the fact that inter-landmark angles have to be inferred from multiple views and are therefore more error-prone than the distance estimates.

As the observer moves, the probability densities $p(\boldsymbol{m}_i|\boldsymbol{x})$ will be shifted to their new bearing and (hyperbolically compressed) distance. In addition, they will be rotated to keep the principle axis associated with σ_{id} aligned with the landmark bearing. The place code for the goal position $\boldsymbol{x} = 0$ will be $\{\boldsymbol{l}_i, i = 1, \ldots, 4\}$. The probability of measuring this place-code, given that the observer is actually at $\boldsymbol{x}$, is obtained by substituting $\boldsymbol{m} = \boldsymbol{l}_i$ in Eq. 2 and taking the product over all four landmarks:

$$p(\boldsymbol{l}_1, ..., \boldsymbol{l}_4|\boldsymbol{x}) = \prod_{i=1}^{4} \phi(\boldsymbol{l}_i; \boldsymbol{\mu}_i(\boldsymbol{x}), \Sigma_i(\boldsymbol{x})). \tag{4}$$

The function $LL(\boldsymbol{x}) := \log p(\boldsymbol{l}_1, ..., \boldsymbol{l}_4|\boldsymbol{x})$ is plotted as the model prediction in Fig. 9 for the error distributions for the three landmark configurations appearing in Figs. 6 and 7.

Note that the likelihood function $p(\boldsymbol{l}_1, ..., \boldsymbol{l}_4|\boldsymbol{x})$ will always take its maximum at $\boldsymbol{x} = 0$ if we omit the hyperbolic distance compression (Eq. 1). In this case, we have $\boldsymbol{\mu}_i = \boldsymbol{l}_i - \boldsymbol{x}$ and the product in Eq. 4 is taken over four Gaussians all of which are centered at $\boldsymbol{x} = 0$. The systematic bias found in our experiments cannot be explained in this case.

The simulations of Fig. 9 are in good quantitative agreement with the experimental results appearing in Figs. 6 and 7. In particular, they reproduce the bias towards the most distant landmark in the standard and peaked configurations, and the orientation of the error distributions. A quantitative test of the model was obtained with the directional statistics of the decision points appearing in Fig. 10. Each decision point judgment was transformed into a unit vector and counted in a circular histogram. Figure 10 shows the resulting distributions together with the landmark bearings (colored circles) and the direction of the

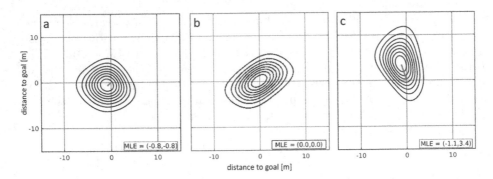

Fig. 9. Likelihood function (Eq. 4). **a.** Control condition, **b.** Parallelogram condition **c.** peaked condition. The red bar indicates the maximum likelihood estimator (MLE) for the bias. The direction and roughly also the length of the predicted biases agree with the experimental results (Fig. 7). Note that the likelihood distributions in **b.** and **c.** also show the elongation towards the most distant landmark. (Color figure online)

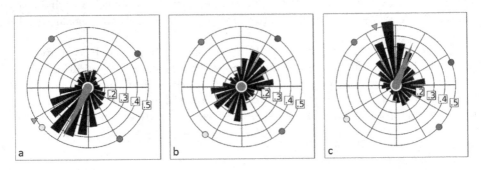

Fig. 10. Circular statistics of the bias direction for the control (**a.**), parallelogram (**b.**) and peak conditions (**c.**). The black columns show the approximate densities in expected cases per radian. The red needle shows the resultant vector, i.e. it points towards the circular mean while its length is a measure of concentration. The colored discs show the direction to the landmarks for each configuration. The green triangle indicates the bias direction predicted by the model. Note that for the parallelogram condition (**b.**) no bias is predicted, in agreement with the experimentally found resultant vector. (Color figure online)

bias predicted by the model (green triangle). Note that no bias is predicted in the parallelogram condition, Fig. 7b. The red needles show the circular mean of the distributions. The orientation of the distributions towards the predicted bias direction (green triangles) was tested against the null hypothesis of non-oriented distribution using the circular V-test (Batschelet 1981) and reveals significant deviations from the null hypothesis for the control ($V(954) = 0.389$, $p < 10^{-4}$) and peaked conditions ($V(754) = 0.291$, $p < 10^{-4}$). Since the model does not predict a bias for the parallelogram condition, we tested this condition with the most distant landmark direction as a predicted bias, but no significant effect was found ($V(761) = 0.021$, n.s.).

We conclude that place recognition from distant landmarks is based on a comparison of two components, (i) a referential place code containing veridical landmark distances and inter-landmark angles, and (ii) a visual working memory of the complete surroundings with distance-dependent resolution and systematic depth compression. A simple model of these components is able to quantitatively predict the statistical distribution of decisions made by human subjects. Effects of approach direction can be modeled by increasing the variances of the less seen landmarks.

The most surprising result of this study is the systematic bias found for the asymmetric landmark configurations. This bias can be modeled if we assume that the landmark distance instantaneously perceived during place recognition is hyperbolically compressed while the landmark distance represented in long-term memory is not. We think that this assumption is justified since the long-term place code (the landmark positions $l_1, ..., l_4$) is a result of many encounters of the goal location arriving from all four directions. It is thus a consolidated memory taking into account multiple views and motion parallax during approach. In contrast, the perception during recognition is mostly instantaneous, with only limited access to the depth cues provided by motion parallax.

4 Conclusion

Place recognition is a simple, well-defined task in which a subject moves to a place (in reality or in virtual reality) and reports arrival by button hit. The main dependent variable is the observer position x at button hit, to which simple bivariate statistics apply. Place recognition is interactive and continuous much like an adjustment task in classical psychophysics with the adjusted parameter being observer position. Button hit is triggered by a comparison operation involving memory content. In this respect, place recognition is more like a match-to-sample task in which the sample has to be remembered. It differs from match-to-sample in the continuity of the position parameter that allows gradual similarity. Also, the memory content may change during the experiment due to spatial updating processes accompanying the approach movement.

In this paper, we discussed two experiments on place recognition addressing the various stages of the appearance-based place recognition model of Fig. 1. The results are consistent with a simple model of spatial working memory (Eq. 4) making the following assumptions:

1. The landmarks are distinguished and identified (index i in model).
2. Both landmark distance and bearing are represented in an egocentric but geo-oriented reference frame.
3. Landmark distance in working memory is systematically biased according to hyperbolic distance compression (Eq. 1).
4. Landmarks outside the field of view are also represented at an updated position, but statistical error is larger than for actually perceived landmarks.

This last assumption, i.e. the increased error of representations of landmarks out of sight is not relevant for the results presented here, but has been used to model the effects of different approach directions by Lancier (2016).

Similar assumptions are made in most models of spatial working memory. For example, Loomis et al. (2013) assume that object knowledge is maintained and updated in a spatial working memory. While this is well in line with our results, it does not lend itself easily for quantitative predictions, as are sought in this study. The Byrne et al. (2007) model assumes a map-like representation in which walls or other objects are represented as activity in pixels of the map. The model nicely explains spatial updating but it is not obvious how to represent object identities. In contrast, object identities are easily accounted for in the Röhrich et al. (2014) model which is based on views of the environment and therefore automatically represents visual landmark properties. However, it lacks a mechanism for spatial updating which would have to based on some sort of ego-motion dependent view transformations.

In summary, our results call for an improved model of spatial working memory, accommodating both object identities and spatial updating in a way allowing quantitative predictions.

References

Basten, K., Mallot, H.A.: Simulated visual homing in desert ants natural environments: efficiency of skyline cues. Biol. Cybern. **102**, 413–425 (2010)

Batschelet, E.: Circular Statistics in Biology. Academic Press, London (1981)

Burgess, N., Hitch, G.: Computational models of working memory: putting long-term memory into context. Trends Cogn. Sci. **9**, 535–541 (2005)

Byrne, P., Becker, S., Burgess, N.: Remembering the past and imagining the future: A neural model of spatial memory and imagery. Psychol. Rev. **114**, 340–375 (2007)

Cartwright, B.A., Collett, T.S.: How honey bees use landmarks to guide their return to a food source. Nature **295**, 560–564 (1982)

Cheng, K., Huttenlocher, J., Newcombe, N.S.: 25 years of research on the use of geometry in spatial reorientation: a current theoretical perspective. Psychon. Bullet. Rev. **20**, 1033–1054 (2013)

Dittmar, L., Stürzl, W., Baird, E., Boeddeker, N., Egelhaaf, M.: Goal seeking in honeybees: matching of optic flow snapshots? J. Exper. Biol. **213**, 2913–2923 (2010)

Epstein, R., Kanwisher, N.: A cortical representation of the local visual environment. Nature **392**, 598–601 (1998)

Epstein, R.A.: Parahippocampal and retrosplenial contributions to human spatial navigation. Trends Cogn. Sci. **12**, 388–396 (2008)

Franz, M.O., Schölkopf, B., Mallot, H.A., Bülthoff, H.H.: Where did I take this snapshot? Scene-based homing by image matching. Biol. Cybern. **79**, 191–202 (1998)

Gaussier, P., Revel, A., Banquet, J.P., Babeau, V.: From view cells and place cells to cognitive map learning: processing stages of the hippocampal system. Biol. Cybern. **86**, 15–28 (2002)

Gilinsky, A.S.: Perceived size and distance in visual space. Psychol. Rev. **58**, 460–482 (1951)

Gillner, S., Mallot, H.A.: Navigation and acquisition of spatial knowledge in a virtual maze. J. Cogn. Neurosci. **10**, 445–463 (1998)

Gillner, S., Weiß, A.M., Mallot, H.: Visual place recognition and homing in the absence of feature-based landmark information. Cognition **109**, 105–122 (2008)

Graham, P., Cheng, K.: Ants use panoramic shyline as a visual cue during navigation. Current Biol. **19**, R935–R937 (2009)

Halfmann, M.: Place Recognition and Navigation in Virtual Environments. PhD thesis, Faculty of Science, University of Tübingen, Germany (2016)

Hamilton, D.A., Sutherland, R.J.: Blocking in human place learning: Evidence from virtual navigation. Psychobiology **27**, 453–461 (1999)

Hartley, T., Maguire, E.A., Spiers, H.J., Burgess, N.: The well-worn route and the path less traveled: distinct neural bases of route following and wayfinding in humans. Neuron **37**, 877–888 (2003)

Hollup, S.A., Molden, S., Donnett, J.G., Moser, M.-B., Moser, E.I.: Accumulation of hippocampal place fields at the goal location in an annular watermaze task. J. Neurosci. **21**, 1635–1644 (2001)

Hort, J., Laczo, J., Vyhnalek, M., Bojar, M., Bures, J., Vlcek, K.: Spatial navigation deficit in amnestic mild cognitive impairment. Proc. Nat. Acad. USA **104**, 4042–4047 (2007)

Janzen, G., van Turennout, M.: Selective neural representation of objects relevant for navigation. Nat. Neurosci. **7**, 673–677 (2004)

Kuipers, B.: The spatial semantic hierarchy. Artif. Intell. **119**, 191–233 (2000)

Lambrinos, D., Maris, M., Kobayashi, H., Labhart, T., Pfeifer, R., Wehner, R.: An autonomous agent navigating with a polarized light compass. Adapt. Behav. **6**, 131–161 (1997)

Lancier, S.: Spatial Memories in Place Recognition. PhD thesis, Faculty of Science, University of Tübingen, Germany (2016)

Loomis, J.M., Klatzky, R.L., Giudice, N.A.: Representing 3D space in working memory: Spatial images from vision, hearing, touch, and language. In: Lacey, S., Lawson, R. (eds.) Multisensory Imagery: Theory and Applications, pp. 131–156. Springer, New York (2013). https://doi.org/10.1007/978-1-4614-5879-1_8

Meilinger, T.: The network of reference frames theory: a synthesis of graphs and cognitive maps. In: Freksa, C., Newcombe, N.S., Gärdenfors, P., Wölfl, S. (eds.) Spatial Cognition 2008. LNCS (LNAI), vol. 5248, pp. 344–360. Springer, Heidelberg (2008). https://doi.org/10.1007/978-3-540-87601-4_25

Möller, R., Vardy, A.: Local visual homing by matched-filter descent in image distances. Biol. Cybern. **95**, 413–430 (2006)

Morris, R.G.M.: Spatial localization does not require the presence of local cues. Learn. Motiv. **12**, 239–260 (1981)

O'Keefe, J.: The hippocampal cognitive map and navigational strategies. In: Paillard, J. (ed.) Brain and Space, pp. 273–295. Oxford University Press, Oxford (1991)

O'Keefe, J., Nadel, L.: The Hippocampus as a Cognitive Map. Clarendon, Oxford, England (1978)

Papi, F. (ed.): Animal Homing. Chapman and Hall, London (1992)

Philbeck, J.W., Loomis, J.M.: Comparison of two indicators of perceived egocentric distance under full-cue and reduced-cue conditions. J. Exp. Psychol. Hum. Percept. Perform. **23**, 72–75 (1997)

Pickup, L.C., Fitzgibbon, A.W., Glennerster, A.: Modelling human visual navigation using multiview scene reconstruction. Biol. Cybern. **107**, 449–464 (2013)

Röhrich, W., Hardiess, G., Mallot, H.A.: View-based organization and interplay of spatial working and longterm memories. PlosONE **9**(11), e112793 (2014)

Rolls, E.T., Treves, A., Robertson, R.G., Georges-François, P., Panzeri, S.: Information about spatial view in an ensemble of primate hippocampal cells. J. Neurophysiol. **79**, 1797–1813 (1998)

Schindler, A., Bartels, A.: Parietal cortex codes for egocentric space beyond the field of view. Current Biol. **23**, 177–182 (2013)

Schölkopf, B., Mallot, H.A.: View-based cognitive mapping and path planning. Adapt. Behav. **3**, 311–348 (1995)

Siegel, A.W., White, S.H.: The development of spatial representations of large-scale environments. In: Reese, H.W. (ed.) Advances in Child Development, vol. 10, pp. 9–55. Academic Press, New York (1975)

Sperling, G., Landy, M.S., Dosher, B.A., Perkins, M.E.: Kinetic depth effect and the identification of shape. J. Exp. Psychol. Hum. Percept. Perform. **15**(4), 826–840 (1989)

Tinbergen, N., Kruyt, W.: Über die Orientierung des Bienenwolfes (Philanthus triangulum Fabr.) III. Die Bevorzugung bestimmter Wegmarken. Zeitschrift für vergleichende Physiologie, vol. 25, pp. 292–334 (1938)

Tolman, E.C.: Purposive behavior in animals and men. The Century Company, New York (1932)

Waller, D., Loomis, J.M., Golledge, R.G., Beall, A.C.: Place learning in humans: The role of distance and direction information. Spatial Cogn. Comput. **2**, 333–354 (2000)

Wiener, J.M., Mallot, H.A.: 'Fine-to-coarse' route planning and navigation in regionalized environments. Spatial Cogn. Comput. **3**, 331–358 (2003)

Wilson, M.A., McNaughton, B.L.: Dynamics of the hippocampal ensemble code for space. Science **261**, 1055–1058 (1993)

Zeil, J., Hoffmann, M.I., Chahl, J.S.: Catchment areas of panoramic snapshots in outdoor scenes. J. Opt. Soc. Am. A: **20**, 450–469 (2003)

Environmental and Idiothetic Cues to Reference Frame Selection in Path Integration

Qiliang He[1], Timothy P. McNamara[1(✉)], and Jonathan W. Kelly[2]

[1] Vanderbilt University, Nashville, TN, USA
t.mcnamara@vanderbilt.edu
[2] Iowa State University, Ames, IA, USA

Abstract. The current study investigated the ways in which environmental and idiothetic cues affect the nature of the reference frame (i.e., egocentric or allocentric) in path integration in a virtual environment. Participants navigated to multiple waypoints and then attempted to walk or point to the first waypoint. We manipulated the environmental geometry, complexity of the outbound path, availability of idiothetic cues (vestibular, proprioceptive, & efferent motor information) and initial heading in the virtual environment to examine the reference frame in path integration. Experiments 1 and 2 showed that when idiothetic cues were present, participants adopted an egocentric reference frame regardless of the environmental geometry and outbound path complexity. Experiments 3 and 4 showed that when idiothetic cues were absent, participants adopted the initial heading as the reference direction. We concluded that unlike their marked influence on reference directions in spatial memory, environmental cues had little impact on the reference frame in path integration regardless of the availability of idiothetic cues.

Keywords: Path integration · Reference frame · Environmental cues · Idiothetic cues · Virtual environment

1 Introduction

Path integration refers to the process by which navigators integrate sensory cues continuously to estimate their current location and orientation relative to a destination in the absence of position-informative information [1,2]. Path integration has long been studied in many species [3–6]. Recent research indicates that path integration in mammals may be supported by interactions among grid, place, and head-direction cells [7–10]. Investigations of path integration typically require the organism to navigate from a home location to a destination (outbound path) and then to return to home using the shortest available path (return path). The present study investigated the reference frame involved in the computation of the return path in a virtual environment. Specifically, we tried to identify the nature of this reference frame (egocentric or allocentric) and how environmental and idiothetic cues (internal sensory cues provided by body

© Springer International Publishing AG 2017
T. Barkowsky et al. (Eds.): KogWis/Spatial Cognition 2016, LNAI 10523, pp. 137–156, 2017.
https://doi.org/10.1007/978-3-319-68189-4_9

movement, including vestibular, proprioceptive and efferent motor information [11–13]) influenced reference frame selection in path integration.

The use of an egocentric reference frame in path integration refers to the process whereby the navigator represents and updates its position in the environment using a reference system centered on the body [14,15]. By contrast, the use of an allocentric reference frame refers to the process whereby the navigator represents and updates its position in the environment using a reference system external to the body and anchored in the environment [2,13]. Figure 1A illustrates the use of an egocentric reference frame in which the principal reference axes are defined by facets of the body. The correct turning angle to home is the egocentric bearing of home, or the angle between egocentric front and the vector from the body to home (γ). Figure 1B illustrates the use of an allocentric reference system in which the principal reference axes are fixed in the environment. The correct turning angle to home is not explicitly represented, and must be computed from the allocentric bearing of home and the allocentric heading of the navigator ($\gamma = \beta - \alpha$).

In an egocentric reference frame, the navigator's heading is always parallel to the principal reference direction, and hence the return angle computation (or retrieval) is equivalent across different headings. In an allocentric reference system, however, if the navigator's heading or home location's bearing is parallel to the principal reference direction (i.e., α or β is $0°$), the computation (or retrieval) of the correct return angle is assumed to be facilitated [16]. In the present study, we manipulated the alignment between the navigator's heading when the return angle needed to be computed and the assumed principal reference direction to identify which reference frame people use in path integration: If performance was comparable across all headings, we assumed that people adopted an egocentric reference frame; if performance was better for headings or return directions parallel to the assumed principal reference direction than for other headings or directions, we assumed that people adopted an allocentric reference frame.

Results from Kelly et al. [17] and Mou et al. [18] suggest that people use an allocentric reference direction to represent the self-to-object spatial relations even when idiothetic cues are available. Kelly et al. [17] had participants learn a layout of objects from a fixed perspective in a room, and then point to the learned objects in the same or a different room. They found that participants generally performed better when the imagined perspective was aligned with the learning perspective, regardless of the room conditions. Moreover, Mou et al. [18] found that participants used an allocentric reference direction to represent the self-to-object spatial relation regardless of the alignment between the imagined perspective and the body orientation. Results from both studies suggest that when idiothetic cues are available people update spatial relations between their bodies and objects in the environment using an allocentric reference frame, and this conclusion was echoed by other studies [13,19]. On the other hand, results from Klatzky et al.'s [20] study suggested that participants used an egocentric reference frame during path integration when idiothetic cues were available, but failed to update their heading when idiothetic cues were absent. However, the

A.   B.

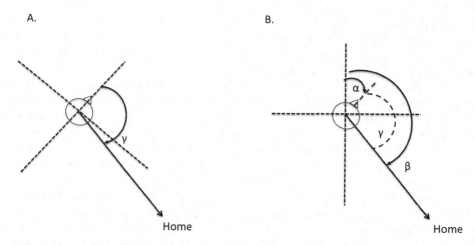

Home   Home

Fig. 1. The circle and the triangle represent a navigator and the facing orientation. (A) Egocentric reference system. γ is the correct turning angle to face home. (B) Allocentric reference system. α is the navigator's allocentric heading. β is the allocentric bearing of home. γ is the correct turning angle to face home.

virtual environment in Klatzky et al.'s [20] study was almost featureless, and it remains to be seen whether the environmental cues, as well as the interaction between environmental and idiothetic cues, would affect the selection of reference frame during path integration. In the current study, we manipulated the availability of idiothetic cues by having participants physically walk or use a joystick to navigate in the virtual environment.

Evidence shows that environmental cues such as the symmetry of the environment can determine the reference direction in spatial memory [19,21]. People favor the axis which divides the environment into symmetrical halves (principal axis) and tend to use the principal axis as the reference direction to organize the object-to-object spatial relations. In Experiment 1 of the present study, we rendered the environment as square (four principal axes) and trapezoidal (single principal axis) to examine whether the regular geometric shape and the small number of principal axes might cause participants to use an allocentric reference frame even when idiothetic cues were present.

Another factor that could influence the selection of the reference frame is spatial updating strategy. Researchers have proposed that there are two spatial updating strategies that humans can employ during path integration: continuous and configural [22]. Continuous updating refers to a strategy of computing and updating the homing vector while navigating the outbound path. Properties of the outbound path, such as the length of the path and the number of turns, are not committed to memory. Configural updating refers to a strategy of representing the configuration of the outbound path during navigation. The homing vector is computed at the end of the outbound path prior to executing the return path. If navigators use this strategy, they should have memories of path properties at the end of the outbound path, even after executing the return path. There is evidence showing that humans can use either configural updating [19,22] or continuous updating [22,23] under proper instructions or depending on the complexity of the outbound path [24].

We conjecture that the spatial updating strategy could influence the reference frame used in path integration. If the homing vector is updated continuously (i.e., continuous updating strategy), with the constantly changing body orientation during navigation, it is more efficient to compute the homing vector using an egocentric reference frame than an allocentric reference frame, due to the additional retrieval of headings and computations required by the use of an allocentric reference frame. However, if the configuration of the outbound path is constructed and represented during navigation (i.e., configural updating strategy), it is more efficient to use a single reference direction than multiple reference directions, as the latter would require mental rotation or other transformations to bring the forms into alignment. Therefore, we hypothesize that if people use a continuous updating strategy in path integration, they are more likely to compute the homing vector using an egocentric reference frame; and if they use a configural updating strategy, they are more likely to adopt an allocentric reference frame. Results of previous studies [23,24] implied that when the outbound path became sufficiently complex, people switched from a configural to a continuous updating strategy. In Experiment 2, we decreased the number of legs in the outbound path to encourage participants to use a configural updating strategy and examined whether this change would make them switch to an allocentric reference frame even when idiothetic cues were available.

Klatzky et al.'s [20] results indicated that people cannot update their heading when idiothetic cues are absent. In Experiments 3 and 4, we employed a procedure similar to Klatzky et al.'s [20] condition in which idiothetic cues were absent, and (a) examined whether participants could update their headings when idiothetic cues were not available but environmental cues were available, and (b) assessed whether the reference direction was determined by the initial heading or environmental cues by placing the two in conflict.

To anticipate our findings, Experiments 1 and 2 showed that when idiothetic cues were present, participants relied on an egocentric reference frame regardless of the number of principal axes in the environment or the number of legs in the outbound path. Experiments 3 and 4 showed that when idiothetic cues were absent, participants used the initial heading instead of the environmental cues as the reference direction (Table 1).

Table 1. The idiothetic and environmental cues, number of path legs, response method and the adopted reference frame in each experiment.

	Exp. 1A	Exp. 1B	Exp. 2A	Exp. 2B	Exp. 3	Exp. 4
Idiothetic cues	Yes	Yes	Yes	Yes	No	No
Enclosure geometry	Square	Trapezoid	Trapezoid	Trapezoid	Trapezoid	Trapezoid
Red lines	No	Yes	Yes	Yes	Yes	Yes
Number of legs	5	5	3	3	3	3
Response method	Walking	Walking	Walking	Pointing	Pointing	Pointing
Reference frame	Egocentric	Egocentric	Egocentric	Egocentric	Allocentric	Allocentric

2 Experiments

2.1 Experiment 1A

Experiment 1A was designed to examine the reference frame used in path integration when salient environmental cues and idiothetic cues were available.

Method

Participants. Twelve students (6 women, 6 men) from Vanderbilt University participated in this experiment in return for extra credit in psychology courses.

Materials and Design. The experiment was conducted in the Learning in Immersive Virtual Environments Laboratory (LIVE Lab) at Vanderbilt University. The virtual environment was presented through an nVisor SX60 (from NVIS, Reston, VA) head-mounted display (HMD), which presented stereoscopic images at 1280×1024 pixel resolution, refreshed at 60 Hz. The HMD field of view was $47°$ horizontal by $38°$ vertical. Graphics were rendered by a 3.0 GHz Pentium 4 processor with a GeForce 6800 GS graphics card using Vizard software (WorldViz, Santa Barbara, CA). A three-axis orientation sensor (InertiaCube2; Intersense, Bedford, MA) tracked head orientation, and an optical tracking system (PPTX4; WorldViz, Santa Barbara, CA) tracked head position. Graphics displayed in the HMD were updated based on sensed head position and orientation. As such, participants' physical movements resulted in smooth visual movements through the virtual environment.

The virtual environment was a $7\,m \times 7\,m$ square room with 2.5 m high walls. There were 15 possible locations of waypoints (Fig. 2). Room walls were textured with a repeating tile pattern and the floor was textured with a repeating carpet pattern. The ceiling was textured with light blue. Participants started at the back of the room facing the same orientation in every trial.

Four experimental conditions were created by manipulating the facing direction at the end of the outbound path and the correct return path direction (Fig. 3): Random, in which the participant's final heading and the correct return

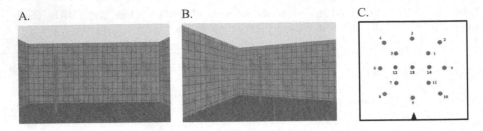

Fig. 2. The virtual environment and the layout of posts in Experiment 1A. (A) Participants' initial view in Experiment 1A showing the first waypoint. (B) Participants' view after rotating to face the first waypoint. (C) Layout of post positions. Participants only saw one post at a time. The triangle corresponds to the starting position in every trial. An example path in the RDA condition (see main text) is: starting point → 2 → 8 → 4 → 7 → 12. Participants pointed to 2 from 12. An example path in the random condition is: starting point → 14 → 13 → 10 → 0 → 7. Participants pointed to 14 from 7. (Color figure online)

path direction were not parallel to the assumed principal reference direction; reference direction aligned (RDA), in which the participant's final heading was parallel to the assumed principal reference direction, but the return direction was not; target direction aligned (TDA), in which the participant's final heading was not parallel to the assumed principal reference direction, but the return direction was so parallel; and straight, in which the participant's final heading and the return direction were parallel to the assumed principal reference direction. If participants used an egocentric reference frame to compute the return angle, performance across these four experimental conditions would be equivalent; on the other hand, if participants used an allocentric reference frame to compute the return angle, performance in the RDA and the straight conditions should be better than in the random condition. Performance in the TDA condition could also be better than the random condition (but see [25]).

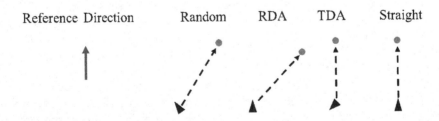

Fig. 3. Illustrations of the four experimental conditions. The dark green arrow represents the assumed principal reference direction anchored to the environment and the red circle represents the first waypoint (not the starting point). The triangle represents the position of the navigator at the end of the outbound path, and the dotted black arrow represents the correct return path. (Color figure online)

Each participant completed 8 blocks of 4 trials each, and each block had one trial in each of the four experimental conditions (8 trials for each condition in total). These trials were presented in a random order. We matched the outbound and return path properties (i.e., outbound path length, overall turning angles; correct return path length and turning angle) across the random, RDA, and TDA conditions to ensure that any significant performance differences were not due to these confounding variables. The average outbound path length was 6.92 m across conditions, and the average return path length was 2.10 m for the random, RDA and TDA conditions. In the straight condition, the return path was approximately half the length of those in the other conditions and the turning angle was by necessity 0°.

The dependent variables were position error, heading error and response time. Position error was defined as the Euclidean distance between the correct home location and participants' actual return location. Heading error was the angular difference between the correct return direction and participants' actual return direction. The actual return direction was determined by participants' position at the end of the outbound path, and the last position in the return path. Response time was the elapsed time between the end of outbound path and the completion of the return path.

Procedure. Participants started every trial at the same location and orientation, as illustrated by the triangle in Fig. 2. A red post appeared and participant walked to it, which disappeared upon arrival. After the disappearance of the red post, four blue posts would appear one by one and participants walked to each one in turn. Posts disappeared upon the participants' arrival. When participants reached the fourth blue post, everything disappeared and participants were asked to walk back to the red post (not the starting point) as they remembered it. Participants were asked to remember the location of the red post, but not the outbound trajectory. When participants believed that they had reached the red post, they pulled the trigger of the joystick to register their response. Then they walked back to the starting location and faced the orientation indicated by a red arrow on the ground. This arrow disappeared and the environment reappeared at the beginning of the next trial. Participants completed four practice trials before starting the experiment. The practice trials were identical to experimental trials except that the destination and waypoints were randomly selected.

Results and Discussion. Position error, heading error and response time were analyzed in 2 (gender) × 4 (experimental conditions) mixed-ANOVAs (Fig. 4). Neither the main effect of gender nor its interaction with condition was significant in any dependent variables, so the data were collapsed across genders in the following analysis.

For position error, the effect of condition was not significant, $F(3, 33) = .648$, MSE $= .026$, $p = .59$, $\eta^2 = .06$.

For heading error, the effect of condition was significant, $F(3, 33) = 10.78$, MSE $= 37.78$, $p < .001$, $\eta^2 = .49$. Pairwise comparisons showed that heading error was higher in the straight condition than in the other conditions, $ts(10) > 3.79$, $ps < .002$. No other comparisons were significant.

For response time, the effect of condition was significant, $F(3, 33) = 31.80$, $MSE = .41$, $p < .001$, $\eta^2 = .74$. Pairwise comparisons showed that response time was shorter in the straight condition than in the other conditions, $ts(10) > 5.84$, $ps < .001$, and that response time in the TDA condition was shorter than in the random condition, $t(10) = 2.26$, $p = .045$. No other comparisons were significant.

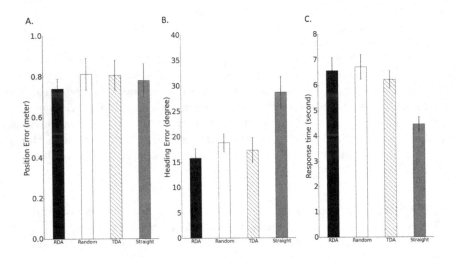

Fig. 4. Position error (A), heading error (B) and response time (C) for Reference direction aligned (RDA), Random, Target direction aligned (TDA) and Straight conditions in Experiment 1A. Error bars are ±1 SEM estimated from data within conditions.

The shorter response time in the straight condition was expected, because the correct return path length in this condition was about as half long as in other conditions. The much higher heading error but comparable position error in the straight condition was probably also due to the shorter return path length in the straight condition. If the dispersion of responses is constant, as indicated by position error, then geometry dictates that heading error will increase as the length of the return path decreases. The response time in the TDA condition was faster than in the random condition, but only by a very small margin. Other than that, none of the dependent variables showed any significant differences among conditions, suggesting that participants used an egocentric reference frame to compute the homing vector.

2.2 Experiment 1B

Participants in Experiment 1A did not appear to use an allocentric reference direction to compute the homing vector despite the presence of regular geometric shape. One possible explanation of this finding is that because the enclosure was square, participants could have used any of the three axes of symmetry (x, y, and diagonal) as the reference direction. The experimental design, however, assumed that only one axis (y) would be used. In Experiment 1B, we changed the room shape and added red lines to the floor to emphasize a single reference direction.

Method

Participants. Twelve students (6 women, 6 men) from Vanderbilt University participated in this experiment in return for extra credit in psychology courses.

Materials, Design and Procedure. Everything was identical to Experiment 1A except that the room was rendered as a trapezoid, with height (i.e., room length front to back) of 5 m and bases of 3 m and 7 m. The room therefore had a single axis of symmetry. We also added red lines on the floor to induce participants to use the principal axis as the reference direction (Fig. 5). The red lines appeared at the beginning of the outbound path, and disappeared at the end of the outbound path.

A.

B.

Fig. 5. (A) Participants' initial view in the virtual environment in Experiment 1B showing the red post. (B) Participants' view after rotating to face the red post. (Color figure online)

Result and Discussion. Position error, heading error and response time were analyzed in 2 (gender) × 4 (experimental conditions) mixed-ANOVAs (Fig. 6).

For position error, only the main effect of gender was significant, $F(1, 10) = 7.05$, MSE $= .116$, $p = . 024$, $\eta^2 = .41$, with men being more accurate than women (men: Mean $= .61$, SE $= .04$; women: Mean $= .87$, SE $= .08$). The main effect of condition was not significant, $F(3, 30) = 1.56$, MSE $= .04$, $p = .22$, $\eta^2 = .14$, and the interaction of gender and condition was not significant, $F(3, 30) = 1.23$, MSE $= .04$, $p = .31$, $\eta^2 = .11$.

For heading error, the main effect of condition was significant, $F(3, 30) = 3.44$, MSE $= 71.93$, $p = .03$, $\eta^2 = .26$, as was the main effect of gender,

$F(1, 10) = 8.81$, MSE $= 112.17$ $p = .014$, $\eta^2 = .47$, with men making smaller heading errors than women (men: mean $= 14.21$, SE $= 1.20$; women: mean $= 23.28$, SE $= 2.52$). Pairwise comparisons revealed that heading errors were smaller in the TDA condition than in the RDA and straight conditions, $ts(10) > 2.79$, $ps < .022$. No other pairwise comparisons were significant. The interaction between gender and condition was not significant, $F(3, 30) = 1.19$, MSE $= 71.93$, $p = .33$, $\eta^2 = .11$.

For response time, only the main effect of condition was significant, $F(3, 30) = 19.21$, MSE $= .68$, $p = .001$, $\eta^2 = .66$. Pairwise comparisons revealed that response time was shorter in the straight condition than in other conditions, $ts(10) > 4.78$, $ps < .001$. No other pairwise comparisons were significant.

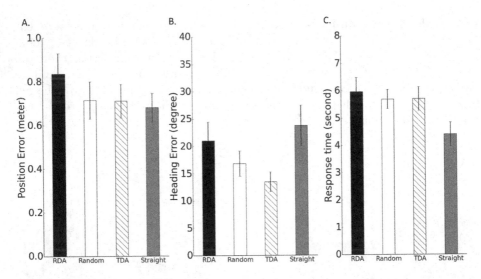

Fig. 6. Position error (A), heading error (B) and response time (C) for RDA, Random, TDA and Straight conditions in Experiment 1B. Error bars are ± 1 SEM estimated from data within conditions.

The significant difference in heading error between the RDA and TDA was unexpected. This effect might have been caused by participants using the red lines to calibrate the return direction, producing a benefit when the return direction was parallel to the red lines (TDA condition). Other than this effect (and the shorter response time in the straight condition), the findings indicated that when the environment had only one principal axis and this axis was highlighted by lines on the floor, performance was comparable across conditions.

2.3   Experiment 2A

The number of legs in the outbound path in Experiment 1 was four, which was larger than the traditional triangle completion task. Longer outbound paths may prompt participants to use a continuous updating strategy and therefore lead to the adoption of an egocentric reference frame. In Experiment 2A, we reduced the number of legs to encourage participants to use a configural updating strategy, which in turn may lead to the adoption of a allocentric reference frame.

Method

Participants. Twelve students (6 women, 6 men) from Vanderbilt University participated in this experiment in return for extra credit in psychology courses.

Materials and Design. The environmental setup and configuration of posts were identical to those in Experiment 1B. The straight condition was removed because of the intrinsic confound in path length, and additional trials were added to the remaining three conditions. As a result, participants in this experiment finished five blocks of 6 trials each, and each block had two trials from each of the three experimental conditions (a total 10 trials per condition). The outbound and return path properties were also matched across experimental conditions. The average outbound path length was 3.08 m and the average return path length was 1.73 m across conditions.

Procedure. The procedure was the same as in Experiment 1 except that participants walked to two blue posts (not four) before they walked back to the red post.

Result and Discussion. Position error, heading error and response time were analyzed in a 2 (gender) × 3 (experimental conditions) mixed-ANOVA (Fig. 7). Neither the main effect of gender nor its interaction with condition was significant in any dependent variable, so the data were collapsed across genders in the following analyses.

The main effect of condition was not significant in position error, $F(2, 22) = .688$, $MSE = .025$, $p = .51$, $\eta^2 = .059$, heading error, $F(2, 22) = .342$, $MSE = 66.26$, $p = .71$, $\eta^2 = .030$, or response time, $F(2, 22) = .184$, $MSE = .173$, $p = .833$, $\eta^2 = .16$.

The pattern of results of Experiment 2A was very similar to that in Experiment 1, which suggests that even with the simpler outbound path, participants still used an egocentric reference frame.

2.4   Experiment 2B

In Experiments 1AB and 2A, participants walked to home to complete the task, which required computing not only homing direction but also distance. Because we assume that the nature of the reference frame primarily influences directional computations, participants in Experiment 2B still walked the outbound path but used a joystick to point to home.

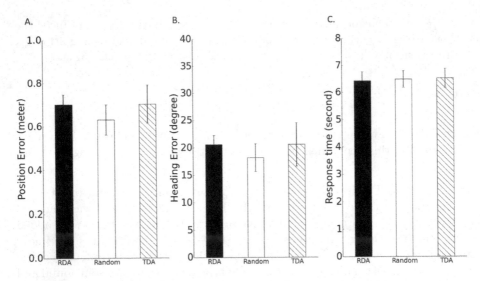

Fig. 7. Position error (A), heading error (B) and response time (C) for RDA, Random, TDA and Straight conditions in Experiment 2A. Error bars are ±1 SEM estimated from data within conditions.

Method

Participants. Twelve students (6 women, 6 men) from Vanderbilt University participated in this experiment in return for extra credit in psychology courses.

Materials and Design. The environmental setup and configuration of posts were identical to those in Experiment 2A. The dependent variables were pointing error, which was the absolute angular difference between the pointing response and the correct direction of the target location, and response time, which was the elapsed time between completion of the outbound path and completion of the pointing response.

Procedure. Participants carried a joystick (Logitech Freedom 2.4 Wireless Joystick) as they walked the outbound path. When they reached the end of the outbound path, they were told to remain in their current position and orientation, and then to deflect the joystick to point to the red post. If the joystick was deflected vertically or horizontally by more than 1 cm, a response would be recorded. Participants then walked to the starting location to start the next trial.

Result and Discussion. Pointing error and response time were analyzed in a 2 (gender) × 3 (experimental conditions) mixed-ANOVA (Fig. 8).

For heading error, the main effect of condition was not significant, $F(2, 20) = .959$, MSE $= 23.128$, $p = .40$, $\eta^2 = .088$; the main effect of gender was not significant, $F(2, 20) = .501$, MSE $= 64.64$, $p = .49$, $\eta^2 = .048$; but the interaction between gender and condition was significant, $F(2, 20) = 7.69$, MSE $= 23.12$, $p = .003$, $\eta^2 = .435$. Simple main effects revealed that men made smaller pointing errors than women in the TDA condition (15.83° vs. 26.31°, $t(10) = 3.02$, $p = .013$).

For response time, the main effect of condition was significant, $F(2, 20) = 6.44$, MSE $= .084$, $p = .007$, $\eta^2 = .392$. Pairwise comparisons revealed that response time was faster in the RDA condition than in other two conditions, $t(10) > 2.34$, $ps < .042$, and no other comparisons were significant.

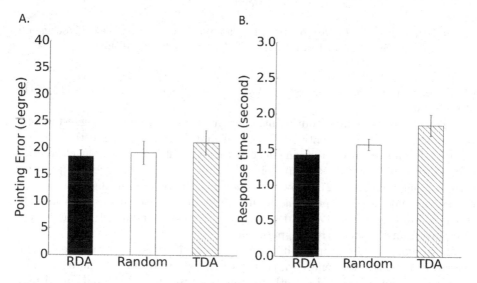

Fig. 8. Position error (A), heading error (B) for RDA, Random, TDA and Straight conditions in Experiment 2B. Error bars are ±1 SEM estimated from data within conditions.

The pointing errors in Experiment 2B showed no significant differences among conditions. When we combined the heading or pointing errors in the RDA, random and TDA conditions across Experiments 1 and 2 (we did not combine response time because walking took much more time than pointing), the results were more evident (Fig. 9): Performance across the three conditions was almost identical (RDA: 18.24°, random: 18.94°, TDA: 18.10°; $F(2, 94) = .211$, MSE $= .46.28$, $p = .81$, $\eta^2 = .004$). We also ran a Bayes factor analysis to confirm the null results [26]. We set the prior odds to 1, a prior which neither favors the null hypothesis nor the alternative. The JZS Bayes factor favoring the null hypothesis was 7.38 (i.e., the null is 7.38 times more likely than the alternative) for the RDA and random conditions, 7.87 for the RDA and TDA conditions, and 8.80 for the TDA and random conditions. All Bayes factors exceeded the

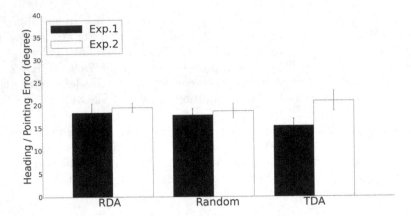

Fig. 9. Heading/pointing error for RDA, Random and TDA conditions in Experiments 1 and 2. Error bars are ±1 SEM estimated from data within conditions.

traditional criterion of 3, suggesting that the null was much more likely than the alternative.

The pattern of results from pointing error in Experiment 2B suggested that participants used an egocentric reference frame, but the response time results implied that a reference direction effect might exist, although reference direction effects are usually manifested in pointing error, or a combination of pointing error and latency [20, 25, 27]. However, due to comparable pointing errors across conditions and the small pointing latency differences between the RDA and the other conditions, we still considered that participants adopted an egocentric reference frame in the current experiment.

In summary, we conclude that when idiothetic cues are available, people favor an egocentric reference frame in path integration. This preference holds when salient environmental directional cues are present and the outbound path is simple.

2.5   Experiment 3

Experiment 3 was designed to examine how the selection of the reference frame in homing vector computation would be affected by the absence of idiothetic cues. Participants in this experiment navigated in the virtual environment using the computer keyboard instead of by walking.

Method

Participants. Twelve students (6 women, 6 men) from Vanderbilt University participated in this experiment in return for extra credit in psychology courses.

Materials and Design. The materials and trials design were identical to Experiment 2.

Procedure. In Experiment 3, instead of navigating in the virtual environment on foot, participants used the computer keyboard to navigate the outbound path, and a joystick for the homing response. Participants pressed a button on the joystick to start a trial, and then used the arrow keys on the keyboard to navigate to posts. They were instructed to first rotate the viewing perspective to face to the post, and then to use the forward key to reach the object. When participants reached the final blue post, everything disappeared and they were told to imagine that they were at the position and facing the direction immediately before everything disappeared. Participants then used the joystick to point to the red post. Participants were not allowed to rotate their body in the experiment. After the response was detected, participants were teleported back to the fixed starting location and started the next trial.

Result and Discussion. Pointing error and response time were analyzed in 2 (gender) × 3 (experimental conditions) mixed-ANOVAs (Fig. 10). Neither the main effect of gender nor its interaction with condition was significant in any of the dependent variables, so data were collapsed across genders in the following analysis.

For pointing error, the main effect of condition was significant, $F(2, 22) = 4.53$, MSE $= 40.99$, $p = .022$, $\eta^2 = .29$. Pairwise comparisons revealed that pointing error in the random condition was significantly larger than in the RDA ($t(10) = 3.79$, $p = .003$) and the TDA conditions ($t(10) = 2.51$, $p = .036$).

For response time, the main effect of condition was not significant, $F(2, 22) = 3.10$, MSE $= .238$, $p = .065$, $\eta^2 = .220$.

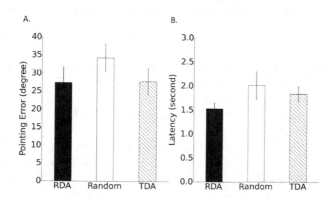

Fig. 10. Pointing error (A) and response time (B) for RDA, Random and TDA conditions in Experiment 3. Error bars are ±1 SEM estimated from data within conditions.

Performance in the TDA condition suggested that participants were able to update their headings in the outbound path. The average final heading in the TDA condition was 115°. If participants were unable to update their heading and pointed to the red post as if they were facing 0°, but pointed accurately, their average error would be 115°, the disparity between their actual and imagined headings. This value is significantly greater than the observed performance in the TDA condition (27.76°, $t(11) = 24.11$, $p < .001$). If this finding is combined with the better performance in the RDA condition than in the random condition, these results show that participants were able to update their heading and relied on an allocentric reference direction to compute the homing direction when idiothetic cues were absent. The good performance in the TDA condition was similar to Experiment 1B, implying that the red lines were used for pointing calibration, and that performance was enhanced when the environmental cues were parallel to the pointing direction.

Experiment 3 cannot differentiate whether the allocentric reference direction was defined by participants' initial heading or the environmental cues, because these two variables always coincided with each other. Experiment 4 was designed to untangle these two factors.

2.6   Experiment 4

Method

Participants. Twelve students (6 women, 6 men) from Vanderbilt University participated in this experiment in return for extra credit in psychology courses.

Materials, Design and Procedure. Everything was identical to Experiment 3, except that participants faced a random orientation (randomly selected from −90° to 90°) to start each trial. The starting location was fixed as in the other experiments.

Result and Discussion. Pointing error and response time were analyzed in 2 (gender) × 3 (experimental conditions) mixed-ANOVAs (Fig. 11). Neither the main effect of gender nor its interaction with condition was significant in any of the dependent variables, so data were collapsed across genders in the following analysis.

For pointing error, the main effect of condition was not significant, $F(2, 22) = 2.93$, MSE $= 74.77$, $p = .074$, $\eta^2 = .210$. For response time, the main effect of condition was not significant, $F(2, 22) = 1.25$, MSE $= .517$, $p = .30$, $\eta^2 = .102$.

The advantage of the RDA over the random condition disappeared when participants faced a random orientation at the beginning of the outbound path, indicating that they used the initial heading, not the environmental cues alone to define the reference direction.

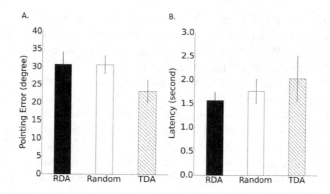

Fig. 11. Pointing error (A) and response time (B) for RDA, Random and TDA conditions in Experiment 4. Error bars are ±1 SEM estimated from data within conditions.

3   General Discussion

The current research aimed to investigate the ways that environmental and idiothetic cues influence the reference frame in path integration. Experiments 1 and 2 showed that when idiothetic cues to locomotion were available, participants relied on an egocentric reference direction for homing vector computation, despite the presence of salient environmental directional cues and use of a simple outbound path. Experiments 3 and 4 showed that when idiothetic cues to locomotion were not available, participants relied on a single reference direction for homing vector computation, and this reference direction was defined by the initial facing orientation instead of environmental cues (Table 1).

In Experiments 1A and 1B, idiothetic cues were available during path integration and the environments were regular and symmetrical. However, the square environment in 1A had multiple axes of symmetry, and hence, multiple possible reference directions, whereas the trapezoidal environment used in 1B had a single axis of symmetry, and hence, one likely reference direction. Despite this difference and the presence of red lines on the floor in 1B, we did not observe any performance differences between the RDA and random conditions, suggesting that this geometrical change has no effect in reference frame selection. In addition, we found that overall performance in the square environment (Exp. 1A) and in the trapezoidal environment (Exp. 1B) was equally good: position errors were .78 m and .74 m ($t(22) = .57$, $p = .57$); heading errors were 20.19° and 18.74° ($t(22) = .53$, $p = .59$); and response time was 5.99 s and 5.43 s ($t(22) = .99$, $p = .33$), for the square and trapezoid, respectively. These findings replicated Kelly et al.'s [28] results, showing that path integration was equally good for room geometries with a small number of rotational symmetries.

Experiment 2 exploited the relations among spatial updating strategy, path complexity, and reference frame selection. As discussed previously, if a continuous updating strategy is used, we conjecture that people are more likely to use an egocentric reference frame. On the other hand, if a configural updating strategy is used, we conjecture that people are more likely to use an allocentric reference frame. We decreased the number of legs in the outbound path in Experiment 2 to encourage participants to use a configural updating strategy [11] and by conjecture an allocentric reference frame. Although we did not have a direct test of the updating strategy used by participants, the reduction in path complexity did not produce any differences among experimental conditions, except for response time in Experiment 2B. The only difference between Experiments 2A and 2B was the response method: Participants in Experiment 2A walked to home, which required distance and direction computation, as well as body rotation; participants in 2B pointed to home, which only required direction computation. It remains to be seen whether response method could change the selection of reference frame and which factors were responsible.

Experiments 3 and 4 were designed to investigate the roles of initial heading and environmental cues in determining the reference direction when idiothetic cues were absent. We observed that participants were able to update their heading in the outbound path and use an allocentric reference frame in Experiment 3. Results from Experiment 4 suggested that the reference direction was defined by the initial heading in the virtual environment instead of by the environmental cues when idiothetic cues were absent. On the other hand, it seems that when idiothetic cues were absent, environmental cues could have been used for pointing or angle calibration, and they were beneficial when these cues were aligned with the correct return direction.

We included gender as a variable in our analyses because gender differences have been observed in some path integration studies [29], although we did not have a priori predictions about gender differences in performance or preferences for reference frames in path integration. We found gender differences in only two of six experiments (1A & 2B) and do not have an explanation of them.

In summary, unlike their substantial influence in determining the reference direction in spatial memory [30,31], environmental cues seem to have little impact on determining the reference frame in path integration, regardless of the presence of idiothetic cues. However, we do not claim that environmental cues have no impact in path integration. We might not have observed an influence of the environmental cues because of the shape and the scale of the environment, as well as the ever-changing home location (the first waypoint) across trials. The regular and small environment in the current research might have made it easy for participants to stay oriented without paying too much attention to the environmental cues, and the ever-changing home location could further discourage participants from memorizing its location with respect to the environmental boundaries. Indeed, studies conducted in complex environments or with multiple stable home locations found that people represented the locations of the objects with respect to the reference frames defined by the environment [32–35]. But at least in a regular and small environment with frequently changing home locations, the reference frame in path integration seemed to be influenced very little by environmental cues.

Acknowledgments. We are grateful to two anonymous reviewers for their helpful comments on the previous version of this article. This research was supported in part by National Science Foundation Grant 1526448.

References

1. Etienne, A.S., Maurer, R., Boulens, V., Levy, A., Rowe, T.: Resetting the path integrator: a basic condition for route-based navigation. J. Exp. Biol. **207**(9), 1491–1508 (2004)
2. Gallistel, C.R.: The Organization of Learning. The MIT Press, Cambridge (1990)
3. Wittlinger, M., Wehner, R., Wolf, H.: The ant odometer: stepping on stilts and stumps. Science **312**(5782), 1965–1967 (2006)
4. Hafting, T., Fyhn, M., Molden, S., Moser, M.-B., Moser, E.I.: Microstructure of a spatial map in the entorhinal cortex. Nature **436**(7052), 801–806 (2005)
5. Fyhn, M., Hafting, T., Treves, A., Moser, M.-B., Moser, E.I.: Hippocampal remapping and grid realignment in entorhinal cortex. Nature **446**(7132), 190–194 (2007)
6. Yartsev, M.M., Witter, M.P., Ulanovsky, N.: Grid cells without theta oscillations in the entorhinal cortex of bats. Nature **479**(7371), 103–107 (2011)
7. Killian, N.J., Jutras, M.J., Buffalo, E.A.: A map of visual space in the primate entorhinal cortex. Nature **491**(7426), 761–764 (2012)
8. Chen, X., He, Q., Kelly, J.W., Fiete, I.R., McNamara, T.P.: Bias in human path integration is predicted by properties of grid cells. Curr. Biol. **25**(13), 1771–1776 (2015)
9. Doeller, C.F., Barry, C., Burgess, N.: Evidence for grid cells in a human memory network. Nature **463**(7281), 657–661 (2010)
10. Jacobs, J., et al.: Direct recordings of grid-like neuronal activity in human spatial navigation. Nat. Neurosci. **16**(9), 1188–1190 (2013)
11. Loomis, J.M., Klatzky, R.L., Golledge, R.G., Cicinelli, J.G., Pellegrino, J.W., Fry, P.A.: Nonvisual navigation by blind and sighted: assessment of path integration ability. J. Exp. Psychol. Gen. **122**(1), 73–91 (1993)
12. Waller, D., Hodgson, E.: Sensory contributions to spatial knowledge of real and virtual environments. In: Steinicke, F., Visell, Y., Campos, J., Lécuyer, A. (eds.) Human Walking in Virtual Environments, pp. 3–26. Springer, New York (2013). https://doi.org/10.1007/978-1-4419-8432-6_1
13. Zhao, M., Zhou, G., Mou, W., Hayward, W.G., Owen, C.B.: Spatial updating during locomotion does not eliminate viewpoint-dependent visual object processing. Vis. Cogn. **15**(4), 402–419 (2007)
14. Fujita, N., Klatzky, R.L., Loomis, J.M., Golledge, R.G.: The encoding-error model of pathway completion without vision. Geogr. Anal. **25**(4), 295–314 (1993)
15. Wang, R.F., Spelke, E.S.: Updating egocentric representations in human navigation. Cognition **77**(3), 215–250 (2000)
16. Klatzky, R.L.: Allocentric and egocentric spatial representations: definitions, distinctions, and interconnections. In: Freksa, C., Habel, C., Wender, K.F. (eds.) Spatial Cognition. LNCS (LNAI), vol. 1404, pp. 1–17. Springer, Heidelberg (1998). https://doi.org/10.1007/3-540-69342-4_1
17. Kelly, J.W., Avraamides, M.N., Loomis, J.M.: Sensorimotor alignment effects in the learning environment and in novel environments. J. Exp. Psychol. Learn. Mem. Cogn. **33**(6), 1092–1107 (2007)

18. Mou, W., McNamara, T.P., Valiquette, C.M., Rump, B.: Allocentric and egocentric updating of spatial memories. J. Exp. Psychol. Learn. Mem. Cogn. **30**(1), 142–157 (2004)
19. Mou, W., Zhang, H., McNamara, T.P.: Novel-view scene recognition relies on identifying spatial reference directions. Cognition **111**(2), 175–186 (2009)
20. Klatzky, R.L., Loomis, J.M., Beall, A.C., Chance, S.S., Golledge, R.G.: Spatial updating of self-position and orientation during real, imagined, and virtual locomotion. Psychol. Sci. **9**(4), 293–298 (1998)
21. Kelly, J.W., McNamara, T.P.: Spatial memories of virtual environments: how egocentric experience, intrinsic structure, and extrinsic structure interact. Psychon. Bull. Rev. **15**(2), 322–327 (2008)
22. Wiener, J.M., Berthoz, A., Wolbers, T.: Dissociable cognitive mechanisms underlying human path integration. Exp. Brain Res. **208**(1), 61–71 (2011)
23. Etienne, A.S., Jeffery, K.J.: Path integration in mammals. Hippocampus **14**(2), 180–192 (2004)
24. Wiener, J.M., Mallot, H.A.: Path complexity does not impair visual path integration. Spat. Cogn. Comput. **6**(4), 333–346 (2006)
25. Rump, B., McNamara, T.P.: Representations of interobject spatial relations in long-term memory. Mem. Cogn. **41**(2), 201–213 (2013)
26. Rouder, J.N., Speckman, P.L., Sun, D., Morey, R.D., Iverson, G.: Bayesian *t* tests for accepting and rejecting the null hypothesis. Psychon. Bull. Rev. **16**(2), 225–237 (2009)
27. Richard, L., Waller, D.: Toward a definition of intrinsic axes: the effect of orthogonality and symmetry on the preferred direction of spatial memory. J. Exp. Psychol. Learn. Mem. Cogn. **39**(6), 1914–1929 (2013)
28. Kelly, J.W., McNamara, T.P., Bodenheimer, B., Carr, T.H., Rieser, J.J.: The shape of human navigation: how environmental geometry is used in maintenance of spatial orientation. Cognition **109**(2), 281–286 (2008)
29. Kelly, J.W., McNamara, T.P., Bodenheimer, B., Carr, T.H., Rieser, J.J.: Individual differences in using geometric and featural cues to maintain spatial orientation: cue quantity and cue ambiguity are more important than cue type. Psychon. Bull. Rev. **16**(1), 176–181 (2009)
30. Shelton, A.L., McNamara, T.P.: Multiple views of spatial memory. Psychon. Bull. Rev. **4**(1), 102–106 (1997)
31. Shelton, A.L., McNamara, T.P.: Systems of spatial reference in human memory. Cogn. Psychol. **43**(4), 274–310 (2001)
32. Manning, J.R., Lew, T.F., Li, N., Sekuler, R., Kahana, M.J.: MAGELLAN: a cognitive map-based model of human wayfinding. J. Exp. Psychol. Gen. **143**(3), 1314–1330 (2014)
33. Meilinger, T., Riecke, B.E., Bülthoff, H.H.: Local and global reference frames for environmental spaces. Q. J. Exp. Psychol. **67**(3), 542–569 (2014)
34. Meilinger, T.: The network of reference frames theory: a synthesis of graphs and cognitive maps. In: Freksa, C., Newcombe, N.S., Gärdenfors, P., Wölfl, S. (eds.) Spatial Cognition 2008. LNCS (LNAI), vol. 5248, pp. 344–360. Springer, Heidelberg (2008). https://doi.org/10.1007/978-3-540-87601-4_25
35. Mou, W., McNamara, T.P., Zhang, L.: Global frames of reference organize configural knowledge of paths. Cognition **129**(1), 180–193 (2013)

Systems and Simulations

EVE: A Framework for Experiments in Virtual Environments

Jascha Grübel[1]([✉]), Raphael Weibel[1], Mike Hao Jiang[1], Christoph Hölscher[1], Daniel A. Hackman[2], and Victor R. Schinazi[1]

[1] Chair of Cognitive Science, ETH Zürich, Zürich, Switzerland
jascha.gruebel@gess.ethz.ch
[2] USC Suzanne Dworak-Peck School of Social Work,
University of Southern California, Los Angeles, CA, USA

Abstract. EVE is a framework for the setup, implementation, and evaluation of experiments in virtual reality. The framework aims to reduce repetitive and error-prone steps that occur during experiment-setup while providing data management and evaluation capabilities. EVE aims to assist researchers who do not have specialized training in computer science. The framework is based on the popular platforms of Unity and MiddleVR. Database support, visualization tools, and scripting for R make EVE a comprehensive solution for research using VR. In this article, we illustrate the functions and flexibility of EVE in the context of an ongoing VR experiment called *Neighbourhood Walk*.

1 Introduction

EVE (Experiments in Virtual Environments) is a user-friendly, novel framework that facilitates the setup, execution, and evaluation of experiments in virtual reality (VR). In contrast to previous frameworks, EVE is not necessarily a Middleware solution (i.e., allowing interaction with hardware from within the software through an abstract interface). Instead, it provides a comprehensive work environment that enables researchers to design different stages of an experiment. EVE is specifically designed for researchers without specialized training in computer science. A friendly graphical user interface (GUI) interface, user manual, and video tutorials are provided to help users with different levels of expertise. One strength of the framework lies in its ability to define, collect, and analyse different types of behavioural (e.g., eye-tracking, avatar control) and physiological (e.g., electrodermal, electrocardiography) data. The framework was originally designed to support spatial cognition and navigation studies but can be easily adapted to any research that uses VR. EVE operates under the platform of the free versions of the game engine and editor Unity [58] and the Middleware framework MiddleVR [35]. The framework capitalizes on Unity's use of the C#-programming language and adds database support, statistical evaluation with R-scripts [40], and Unity-based objects/assets to support different aspects of an experiment.

T. Barkowsky et al. (Eds.): KogWis/Spatial Cognition 2016, LNAI 10523, pp. 159–176, 2017.
https://doi.org/10.1007/978-3-319-68189-4_10

There are several reasons why running experiments in VR can benefit research in experimental psychology and other disciplines. Gaggioli [13] outlines at least four motivations. First, VR can provide for better ecological validity allowing for naturalistic behaviour within a simulated environment. Second, VR systems are flexible and provide programmers the ability to customize the environment and stimuli to the needs of researchers. Third, new VR technology can provide accurate sensorial feedback that can be difficult to capture and manipulate using traditional methods (i.e., videos). Fourth, VR systems can facilitate the accuracy and reliability of data collection, considerably speeding up the entire experimental process. If researchers are capable of accounting for vection (i.e., the perception of self-motion in the absence of physical motion) and presence, VR systems may be capable of achieving a high level of experimental control and ecological validity [26,45].

Despite these advantages, some researchers have argued that VR may not be capable of sufficiently emulating real-world behaviour. For example, Taube and colleagues [56] emphasize that actual locomotion is necessary to realistically capture different aspects of spatial orientation during navigation. While this may be the case for some experiments that require subjects to remain immobile and in a supine position (i.e., fMRI), there is now growing evidence that a correspondence may indeed exist in the navigation behaviour and aesthetic experiences of participants in the real world and VR with limited locomotion [20,23,64]. For example, Weisberg and colleagues [64] tested participants in a virtual replica of a university campus and found a similar pattern of spatial responses (i.e., pointing judgments and model building) as observed in the same real-world environment [48]. Indeed, researchers from various fields have successfully employed VR in their experiments [21,28,61,64].

Previous studies that have used VR often required the programming of custom-made tools specifically designed for the experiment in question [42–44,46,52,63]. Unfortunately, many of these tools were not sufficiently modular (e.g., custom scripts, specific hardware) to be adapted for other experiments and the research community in general. As a direct consequence, many researchers have not been able to produce similar experiments when only minor changes are needed. This can lead to delays and higher costs when preparing an experiment (e.g., the psychologist relies on the computer scientist for addressing every minor adaptation).

Another challenge with previous research occurs when participant data is collected outside the virtual environment (VE) via video or experimenter notes. Manual coding of data can lead to errors in accuracy and also limit the type and richness of data that can be collected, precluding certain research questions and analyses [25,34]. For example, physiological data (e.g., electrodermal activity), often sampled at high frequencies, generates numerous data points that must be properly synchronized to the stimulus presented in the VE. Similarly, navigation studies often rely on the exact position and movement of the avatar for statistical analysis. Here, automatic coding of the data is relatively precise and potentially more reliable than manual coding. Even with automatic coding, some frameworks only allow researchers to store data in text files [2]. This can lead to additional delays and challenges with data organization and analyses.

Some studies have used Middleware frameworks [4,53] to collect data from different types of peripherals. Middleware allows for data retrieval without relying on specific hardware protocols. This is a critical step for collecting information about the participants' interaction with the VE. Middleware frameworks are capable of extracting inputs from sensors (e.g., eye tracker) into a simpler data stream for analyses. Despite the importance of Middleware for managing hardware, it is only one component in the design of a comprehensive experimental framework.

In this paper, we propose a general-purpose framework that allows for the simplification of the various steps involved in the creation, execution, and analysis of experiments in VR. EVE is more than just a Middleware solution. In contrast to previous frameworks (e.g., SNaP [2], CalVR [49]), EVE provides comprehensive support from the early design phases of an experiment through the generation, storage, organization, and analysis of the collected data. EVE is capable of acquiring data from a variety of physical (e.g., eye trackers, physiological devices) and virtual sensors (e.g., position trackers placed directly into the virtual environment) and storing this information into a neatly organized and accessible database for evaluation. We illustrate the functionality of EVE in the context of a complex, ongoing experiment called *Neighbourhood Walk*.

2   Related Work

Existing frameworks for VR tend to be limited to demonstration or visualisation purposes rather than the collection and manipulation of collected data (e.g., behavioural, physiological). Commercial VR frameworks such as EON Studio [10] or Vizard [67] offer development suites for VEs that focus on visualization and game play. Similar to Middleware frameworks such as CAVELib [31], VR Juggler[1] [3], FreeVR [51], and MiddleVR [35], these packages do not currently offer specific support to setup and run scientific experiments in VR.

The scientific community has also attempted to create VR frameworks that offer similar capacities as commercial and Middleware frameworks. Vrui [22] and CalVR [49] are C++-based frameworks offering platforms to develop a variety of visualisation applications. Vrui is often used for visualising volumetric data [4,24] while CalVR is an application typically used to visualise archaeological sites without having to physically visit them [53,60]. However, similar to their commercial counterparts, these packages do not offer sufficient options for the setup and execution of scientific experiments.

There have been some attempts at creating frameworks that are specifically oriented towards the setup and execution of experiments. For example, the SNaP framework [2] provides a limited set of features for collecting metrics focused on the position and orientation of the avatar with respect to the world. However,

---

[1] The project appears to be abandoned.

the environments used in this framework have to be designed with external 3D tools and could not be easily be adjusted/altered within the framework. When editing a specific asset (e.g., a building) in the virtual model, SNaP users are required to load an external application and reload the entire model after each adjustment. This two-step procedure prolongs the development process and makes efficient creation and deployment of experiments difficult. In addition, Virtools [9], the underlying software supporting SNaP, limits the ability to run experiments on arbitrary hardware.

CAVEStudy [14], the precursor to EVE, introduced a general structural layout for experiments and tried to standardize the experiment description in order to guide and facilitate experiment design and execution. CAVEStudy included a large set of physical and virtual sensors, database support, and predefined experimental elements used to develop tasks. However, the development of this framework was halted due to limitations with Vizard-based VR environments. In addition to editing challenges (described above for SNap), Vizard relies on dynamic scripting in Python. This type of dynamical scripting is useful for quick tests but becomes more error-prone when creating a large codebase. These issues are more easily addressed in a statically typed language such as C# used by Unity.

Virtual SILCton [8] is an example of a framework that was specifically developed to investigate individual differences in navigation [64]. A typical experiment in Virtual SILCton consists of learning a novel VE (i.e., a University campus) and completing a series of questionnaires (e.g., mental rotation, sense of direction) and spatial tasks (e.g., distance and direction judgements, model building). Virtual SILCton provides researchers with some flexibility when setting up their experiment. Researchers can select and order (from a preprogrammed set) a series of questionnaires and spatial tasks and define how participants learn the VE (i.e., free exploration or guided navigation). In addition, Virtual SILCton offers a suite of evaluation tools to export the data collected during the experiment. While Virtual SILCton provides a major step forward in the design of VR experiments, it is not sufficiently modular (e.g., all experiments take place in the same virtual world, researchers are limited to the preprogrammed questionnaires) to be adapted or enhanced for other experiments and research paradigms.

Some researchers have relied on modified games [25] at the cost of losing control over some features of the experiment (e.g., the ability to export the exact location of the avatar). Most games also do not provide any information regarding the geometry of the environment, making the analysis of navigation data difficult if not impossible. Although *modding* (i.e., the act of modifying a software to perform a function that was not originally intended by the developer) can overcome some of these difficulties, gameplay is still limited by the main game mechanics (e.g., a driving game cannot be used for pedestrian exploration). In addition, *modding* still falls within a grey zone of software development as it often involves hacking proprietary source code to enable obscure features. However, when properly implemented, some researchers have been capable of using *modded* games for experimental research. This is the case for the studies conducted by

Maguire and colleagues [27], [54] who adapted the video game *The Getaway* in order to conduct neuroscientific research with London taxi drivers.

Lloyd and colleagues [25] used the Sony Playstation 2 game *Driv3r* (Reflections Interactive Ltd.) to simulate a virtual tour of the city of Nice, France. Participants were asked to guide an experimenter who was driving the virtual car by verbally indicating turns along the route. One consequence of such an approach was that performance could only be encoded in the form of turning decisions. Path data (often critical for navigation studies) could not be exported from the gaming console. Other experimenters adapted *Half-Life* in order to investigate spatial integration (i.e., cognitive mapping) in humans [55]. Using the *Valve Hammer Editor*, these researchers were able to design and test participants within the *Half-Life* virtual environment. However, the researchers still relied on video recording to capture participant spatial behaviour during gameplay. Together, these results suggest that using commercial games for research often limits the type of interaction users can have with the VE and the accuracy and type of data that can be exported from the system.

Some researchers [32,33] also try to adapt previous experimental setups to fit the current experimental design [59]. For example, Usoh and colleagues [59] created a two-room environment in order to test immersion in VR. Participants moved from a training room (e.g., a simply furnished room) to a "pit" room. In the pit room, they were instructed to step on a ledge and look through a hole in the floor with a view to the room below. In the original experiment, participants reported their experience with questionnaires, and later variations used physiological sensors as a measure of presence [32]. While adapting previous experiments can have advantages in terms of development costs, these are only expandable to the extent that they fit the research paradigm.

When collecting data in VR, some researchers ask participants to answer questionnaires or complete different tests (in pen and paper format) while the participants are engaged in the VR task [34]. This technique can have important implications for immersion given that participants are forced to switch from the VR to interact with the experimenter. In addition to increasing post processing time, this method is also susceptible to human error during digitalization. Consequently, a framework is needed that allows for self-report questionnaires to be deployed in real-time in a VR context and to be sufficiently accurate so as to minimize any breaks in the sense of immersion.

Altogether, many previous VR studies and frameworks were developed in a task-specific manner and could rarely provide all the necessary elements and be generalized to support new experiments. In contrast, EVE was developed to support multiple experiments by providing features that are common to research in VR and could be adapted to different experimental paradigms from a variety of disciplines. EVE allows for easy handling of common tasks in experiments, promoting greater efficiency and quality of VR experiments. In turn, this enables researchers to focus less on the technical implementation of a study and more on central issues. Among these are experimental design and the creation of immersive VEs that are capable of simulating real-world aspects critical to the research question at hand.

3   Implementation

We will discuss the implementation of EVE in two parts. First, we focus on external software requirements. Second, we analyse how EVE supports scientists during three stages (i.e., setup, runtime, and evaluation) of a typical VR experiment. These stages are outlined in Fig. 1 and discussed in the following subsections.

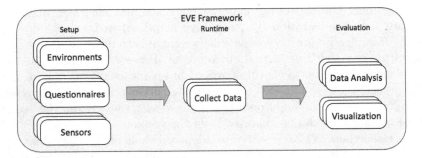

Fig. 1. Overview of the three stages of an experiment that are supported by the EVE framework. In the setup stage, experimenters can upload and manipulate their VE, load XML-based questionnaires, and place their virtual sensors. EVE generates executable files that can be used during runtime to start the experiment and data collection. In the evaluation stage, experimenters can perform different types of analyses and visualizations and export the collected data in different formats.

3.1   Required Software

The EVE framework is based on the Unity game engine and requires a working version of Unity 5 or above. Unity is a widely used game development engine that handles the graphics and physics computations necessary for video game applications. Users should follow the minimum system requirements[2] for developing and running games in Unity. Unity offers a series of step-based tutorials to help users learn the different aspects of the game engine.

EVE integrates with Unity via the C#-programming platform. Data acquisition, management, and evaluation are all provided by a database operating at the backend of the framework. As such, a MySQL database is necessary in order to run the basic version of the framework—although EVE can be easily adapted for other databases (e.g., PostgreSQL). For advanced evaluation purposes, a recent version of the statistical programming language R (e.g. version 3.3.1) along with several R-packages must be installed. The packages DBI [41], RMySQL [39], and dplyr [66] manage the access to the database. Our new package evertools [6] provides additional shorthand functions for accessing specific database entries (e.g., participants' paths) as well as some pre-arranged statistical evaluations. Additionally, evertools uses ggplot2 [65] to visualize the collected

---

[2] https://unity3d.com/unity/system-requirements.

data. EVE also supports Virtual Reality Peripheral Network (VRPN [57]) via *MiddleVR for Unity*. VRPN is a widely used VR standard to define hardware representation in software and access sensor data. MiddleVR must be installed in order to access these non-critical features. MiddleVR allows for data to be collected from any VRPN-enabled sensors via XML configuration files.

3.2   Experiment Setup

This first stage consists of setting up the static VE, creating the interactive parts of the environment, and linking up the sensors necessary to run the experiment. Static environments are the 3D models (e.g., city blocks, building interiors, mazes) that participants interact with (e.g., navigate) during the experiment. Unity provides an editor that allows for the importing and basic manipulation (e.g., moving, rotating, and scaling) of standard 3D model formats (e.g., fbx, dae). While only a limited number of ready-to-use environments are included with EVE (e.g., training scene), the framework provides a variety of tools to setup the interactive parts of a VE. EVE provides a large set of useful experiment-oriented assets (also known as *prefabs* in Unity). In EVE, prefabs can act as virtual sensors that are placed directly into the VE and allow for a variety of data collection options. Generally, virtual sensors allow researchers to define all points of interest in the VE and ensure proper data collection as the participants interact with them.

Interactions can also be attached to virtual sensors further extending their capacity. This includes, but is not limited to, (a) a logging object that records all the movements of the participant's avatar in the VE; (b) hidden markers that record when participants enter or exit a specific zone; (c) invisible walls that keep participants on the designated route and can display guiding messages; (d) visible way-points, goal markers, and collectible items that can guide a subject through the environment; (e) start and end points that can be selected at random and (f) trigger level changes (i.e., completing a part of an experiment and moving on to the next part).

EVE also provides a variety of diegetic and non-diegetic user interface (UI) elements [11] for displaying different types of information to participants. Diegetic UIs allow participants to remain immersed in the VE by embedding the UI in the virtual world. In contrast, non-diegetic UI elements are typically overlaid on top of the participant's view during gameplay. For example, a navigation task can include UI elements such as a mini-map of the environment, a list of goals, a timer, and text pop-ups in the form of floating text (see Fig. 2).

EVE supports the use of questionnaires during all stages of the experiment and can be used in conjunction with the different physical sensors. The basic version of the framework already includes some of the commonly used questionnaires in navigation research (e.g., SBSOD [18]). A novel feature of EVE is the provision of pop-up questionnaires during runtime. These questionnaires can be answered while participants are engaged in the task without diverting their attention. For example, participants can be probed about their current level of arousal via a digital pop-up version of the Self-Assessment Manikin (SAM) [5]

(a) *The mini-map and goal list*   (b) *A highlighted destination*

Fig. 2. EVE's UI elements. (a) Non-diegetic UI: A mini map with a goal list (yellow dots) and the participant's current location (blue dot); (b) Diegetic UI: A text pop-up indicating a destination in a wayfinding task. (Color figure online)

that appears immediately after exposure to a particular stimulus (e.g., a building). Additionally, researchers can use their own questionnaires by providing XML-files tailor fitted to their needs.

The EVE framework gives researchers control over the execution order of the experiment. After the VEs and the questionnaires are prepared, researchers can complement their setup with Unity scenes that are already built into our framework (see Table 1). Here, researchers have to decide the order of events and place each scene into a linear execution order in the Unity editor. The last step consists of selecting and activating the virtual and physical sensors that will be used for data recording. EVE uses the XML-based sensor description in VRPN to describe sensors and enable the framework to properly read and store the associated values.

In addition to VRPN-based sensors, the framework also provides an abstract interface for eye-tracking (currently only deployed with SensoMotoric Instruments [50]), physiological data collection (currently deployed with PowerLab by ADInstruments [1]) and support for HL7 messages [17] used by various medical sensors. Support for additional behavioural and physiological sensors are expected in future versions of the framework.

Table 1. List of available scenes in the basic version of EVE.

Scene	Description
Maze training	A maze environment to train the participants with the navigation controls (e.g., joystick)
Fixation screen	A white screen with a black cross in the middle used to centre gaze and to separate between sections in the experiment
Tutorial	A small room with a video wall explaining basic controls (e.g. how to use a controller)
Video screen	A simple playback screen to show videos during an experiment

3.3   Runtime

After setting up the experiment in the Unity editor, an executable build can be created to run the experiment independent of the editor. The build contains the experiment as an executable file that can be started as a normal application on the respective platform. Unity can generate builds for all platforms allowing for experiments to be conducted on Mac, Windows, Linux, and mobile operating systems such as iOS and Android. Depending on the platform, it may be necessary to adapt the database capabilities of EVE to enable proper data collection. Currently, only the Windows database adapter is implemented. In addition, when VRPN or more complex VR systems like a CAVE [7] are used, MiddleVR must be configured and used to run the executable file. Head-mounted devices such as VIVE [19] and Oculus [37] can also be configured for use within either Unity or MiddleVR.

During runtime, EVE's logging manager records all of the data created during the experiment into a MySQL database (Fig. 3). This data is collected until the end of the experiment and can be retrieved with the R-package *evertools*. The evaluation features are part of the runtime build and will be discussed in the next section.

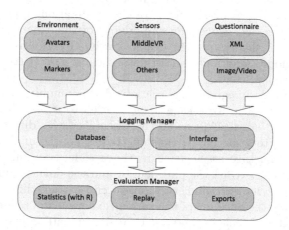

Fig. 3. Overview of the dataflow within the EVE framework. Physical and virtual sensors and questionnaires provide data input. The logging manager stores them in the database and offers an interface to retrieve the data. During evaluation, the data is preprocessed for easier use.

As expected, the framework cannot entirely replace an experimenter during data collection. While EVE will greatly speed up experimental runtime, experimenters still have a central role in overseeing study execution and answering any questions that participants may have.

3.4 Evaluation

The evaluation menu provides access to the underlying database and simplifies the management and visualization of the collected data. EVE's database uses a data layout in the 5th normal form [12]. While this allows for better handling of arbitrary sensor and questionnaire data (from the perspective of a framework), this form makes working with the database a more difficult task for experimenters without knowledge of database management. To overcome this hurdle, the evaluation menu offers a GUI functionality to visually interact with the data collected in the experiment. Instead of going through a series of database queries, experimenters can also use our R-package *evertools* to directly interact with the data (i.e., select, display, analyse, and export).

This functionality can be grouped into three main modules. The first module allows researchers to export data collected during the experiment. Currently, EVE can only export in CSV format. The next versions of the framework will include different export formats (e.g., MatLab, SPSS). The second module covers the visualization of data. A replay mode allows for a detailed inspection of the participants' spatial behaviour (e.g., walked path) from either a first-person or bird's-eye perspective. Researchers may inspect the data for validity or run additional post-processing algorithms including image processing and segmentation (e.g., spatial frequency, contrast). Some of these operations typically have high computational costs that can hinder the fidelity of the experiment if executed during runtime. For this reason, the evaluation build performs these computations in replay mode. Additional sensor data such as gaze patterns can also be overlaid on the replay screen.

The third module integrates the statistical programming language R into the EVE framework. The R-package *dplyr* is used to access the database. An auxiliary R-package *evertools* provides the researcher with direct access to sensor data belonging to a specific participant (bypassing the underlying database structure). The R-package *evertools* currently provides two built-in evaluations. First, researchers can extract the path length and the deviation of a single participant from the cohort. Second, researchers can extract different descriptive statistics regarding the duration of the various experimental phases. These tools can be visualised with *ggplot2* and used to discriminate between participants (e.g., outliers). Researchers may use *evertools* to access the data in their own R-scripts to further customize their analysis.

4 Example Study: Neighbourhood Walk

In this section we present the different features of EVE in the context of the experiment *Neighbourhood Walk* currently being developed as a collaboration among the authors. The experiment investigates whether virtual environments are capable of eliciting different types of behavioural and psychophysiological responses. Previous research has shown that different aspects of neighbourhood environments are related to varying levels of stress reactivity [15,16]. In order to investigate these questions, we designed a virtual city with distinct neighbour-hoods that are differentiated by building types, layout, green space, disorder, and noise among other features that are routinely observed in real world environments [38, 47]. In the experiment, participants were asked to follow a route around the virtual city and collect a series of gems that are placed along the route. Participants also responded to a series of questionnaires about their background and the quality of the environment. Physiological data (i.e., galvanic skin response, heart rate variability and blood pressure) was collected throughout the experiment.

An efficient way to construct an experiment with EVE is to develop a protocol that defines the different stages of the experiment and to use it as a guide when setting up the work in Unity. Figure 4 is a sample protocol from the *Neighbourhood Walk* study. A protocol should contain all the steps of an experiment including those steps that are not directly performed by EVE. This allows researchers to develop a clear timeline and decide their level of interaction. For the *Neighbourhood Walk* study, the protocol contained the steps to be executed by the researcher (SR) and those performed by EVE (SE). The protocol also contained information regarding the placement of alignment windows (W). Alignment windows are Unity scenes provided by EVE that allow for the proper synchronization between the data collected by the physical sensors and the different stages of the virtual experiment (i.e., training, baseline, and main task).

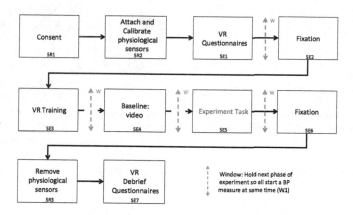

Fig. 4. The protocol describing each execution step of the *Neighbourhood Walk* study. The protocol contains steps to be executed by the experimenter (SR) and by EVE (SE). The protocol also indicates when windows (W) are used to synchronize between the various stages in the experiment.

In a typical experiment session for *Neighbourhood Walk*, the participant arrived at the lab, completed the consent process (SR1) and was connected to the different physiological sensors (SR2). At this stage, the experimenter started the Unity build, and the participant was presented with a digital questionnaire (e.g., background information; SE1; Fig. 5(a)). A fixation screen (SE2) was then used to acquire physiological data before the start of the experiment. Once the fixation screen disappeared, the Unity scene for joystick training was loaded (SE3). Here, participants watched an instruction film on how to manipulate the joystick and later trained their skills on a simple maze environment. This training insured that all participants were sufficiently skilled at navigating the VE before the start of the experimental task. The next stage consisted of acquiring a physiological baseline (SE4). Participants were asked to sit still while watching a nature video. Once the baseline video was complete, the main task was loaded (SE5). For the main tasks, participants were asked to use the joystick to follow a route and collect a variety of gems placed along a virtual city neighbourhood (Fig. 5(b)). After the main task, participants move to a post-task fixation screen (SE6). Note that a Window (W) was used at different stages of the experiment in order to ensure that the physical sensors were synchronized to the stimulus presented on the screen. At the end of the last fixation screen, an information screen was loaded indicating that it was now safe for the experimenter to remove the physiological sensors (SR3). The last scene (SE7) consisted of a series of debriefing questionnaires about the VE.

(a) *An example question used during the* Neighborhood Walk *experiment.*

(b) *First-person perspective of a city block. The gem represents a typical virtual sensor with an interaction.*

Fig. 5. Questionnaire and interactions used in *Neighborhood Walk* study

In the case of the *Neighbourhood Walk*, we created a large virtual city (Fig. 6) in cooperation with external partners from VIS Games [62] and Zatun [68]. VIS Games provided us with the basic city environment (e.g., buildings, streets) while Zatun, in consultation with the authors, added the different assets (e.g., trees, flowers, garbage) that gave each of the city blocks their particular character (e.g., industrial, luxury homes). We also added a variety of virtual sensors and interactions to the different scenes. These virtual sensors allowed us to control different aspects of the experiment (e.g., scene changes, calibration windows) and to collect data about participant behaviour in the environment (e.g., gems collected). Some virtual sensors were also used as checkpoints when participants

Fig. 6. A top-down view of the city used in the *Neighbourhood Walk* study

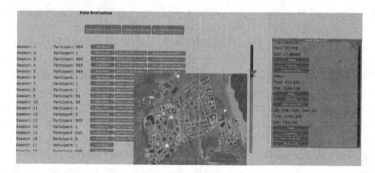

Fig. 7. The evaluation menu including the visualization of a participant's path on a map of the city. The menu also provides basic information about the path and the option to export the data collected by the different sensors.

were navigating the virtual neighbourhood. These sensors encoded the time and location when the participant entered a specific area or street and allowed for a more fine-grained analysis of their spatial behaviour and psychophysiological state.

Data collected in the experiment can be accessed via the evaluation build (Fig. 7). In the case of the *Neighbourhood Walk* study, the experimenter can view and export a variety of data captured by the physical and virtual sensors. The evaluation menu also provides access to a top-down view of the city environment for quick visual inspection of the path walked by the participants. In addition, a first person replay function allows for different post processing analyses (e.g., image analysis) that could not otherwise be performed during runtime. Finally, we use the integrated R functionality of EVE to obtain statistical analysis of the path length and time spent in each section of the city.

5   Summary and Conclusion

In this paper, we describe a new framework to run experiments in VEs. The EVE framework provides a novel way to assist researchers from various disciplines with the setup, execution, and evaluation of experiments in VEs. EVE uses various functionalities offered by the Unity 3D editor to setup the different stages of an experiment. This allows researchers to rely on a powerful 3D-editing environment and game engine to setup and run their experiments. EVE also expands some basic functions in Unity by providing additional research oriented solutions including the collection, storage, visualisation, analysis, and export of experiment data. The framework is specifically designed to process sensor data from peripheral or interactive objects that are placed directly in the VE. EVE is also supported by a database working behind the scenes to organize and store the data collected during the experiment. A key feature of the framework is the evaluation menu that allows researchers to inspect, analyse (via custom made R scripts) and export participant data. The first release of EVE will allow users to export descriptive statistics. Future releases will include data mining functionality and inferential statistics. As such, EVE provides a series of modules that help researchers design and execute an experiment from start to finish.

Our example study, *Neighbourhood Walk*, illustrated some of the features and advantages of designing an experiment with EVE. In the study, the framework was used to support the collection and organization of data from a variety of questionnaires and both physical (e.g., blood pressure) and virtual sensors (e.g., collection of gems, location markers). In addition, EVE provided the necessary functionality to synchronize events occurring in the VE to these sensors. EVE also simplified any type of database management by providing an evaluation menu for the manipulation and exporting of the collected data.

A variety of developments are already planned for future releases of EVE. One such expansion consists of a simulation package for agents (based on avatars) that may be used to improve presence by creating more realistic VEs. These agents will also expand the functionality of EVE to include crowd simulation. An expansion is also under construction that will allow for testing multiple human participants in a single VE via networked computers (both locally and via the Internet). Additional expansions will also enable researchers to import and analyse data from real-world experiments. For example, using a 3D model of a real-world environment, researchers can reconstruct walked paths with the help of computer vision techniques applied to videos recorded from the participants' perspective. This would allow for the systematic analysis and reconstruction of behavioural data acquired in the real-world. Finally, future developments will be aimed at improving the experiment design process by using Finite State Machines (FSM). FSMs are a class of automata that represent sequential processes [29,30,36]. They can describe the experiment protocol in terms of states and transitions and can represent an experiment in graph form that can be visually understood by the experimenter but executed by the machine. FSMs provide a precise description of an experimental design and can reduce ambiguity inherent in text-based descriptions. One clear advantage of such an approach is the ability to implement non-linear protocols during an experiment (e.g., different experiment environments being called in an arbitrary order).

EVE will be provided free of charge to the scientific community. It will be published as an open source project via the code-sharing platform github (https://cog-ethz.github.io/EVE/). The Chair of Cognitive Science at ETH Zürich will maintain and continue to develop the EVE framework. We also encourage researchers to help us improve and extend the framework to meet as many application demands as possible.

Acknowledgements. The authors would like to thank Ioannis Giannopoulos and Tyler Thrash for the valuable comments and suggestions during various drafts of this manuscript. We would also like to thank Katja Wolf and Fabian Schewetofski for the development and design of the evaluation screen, GUI interface, and many other features that have now become an integral part of the EVE framework. We also thank VIS Games for the free provision of the 3D models used in our research. Partial support for Daniel Hackman was provided by the *Robert Wood Johnson Foundation Health and Society Scholars Program* at the *University of Wisconsin-Madison* in the *Department of Population Health Sciences*.

References

1. ADInstruments: Labchart (2016). http://www.adinstruments.com/products/labchart
2. Annett, M., Bischof, W.F.: VR for everybody: the SNaP framework. In: SEARIS Workshop in IEEE Virtual Reality, pp. 131–132 (2016)
3. Bierbaum, A., Just, C., Hartling, P., Meinert, K., Baker, A., Cruz-Neira, C.: VR juggler: a virtual platform for virtual reality application development. In: 2001 Proceedings of Virtual Reality, pp. 89–96. IEEE (2016)
4. Billen, M.I., Kreylos, O., Hamann, B., Jadamec, M.A., Kellogg, L.H., Staadt, O., Sumner, D.Y.: A geoscience perspective on immersive 3D gridded data visualization. Comput. Geosci. **34**(9), 1056–1072 (2016)
5. Bradley, M.M., Lang, P.J.: Measuring emotion: the self-assessment manikin and the semantic differential. J. Behav. Ther. Exp. Psychiatry **25**(I), 49–59 (2016)
6. Chair of Cognitive Science, ETH: EVE: A framework for experiments in virtual environments (2016). https://cog-ethz.github.io/EVE/
7. Cruz-Neira, C., Sandin, D.J., DeFanti, T.A.: Surround-screen projection-based virtual reality. In: Proceedings of the 20th Annual Conference on Computer Graphics and Interactive Techniques, pp. 135–142 (2016)
8. Dara-Abrams, D., Schinazi, V.R.: Virtual SILCton (2016). http://spactial.ci.northwestern.edu/
9. Dassault Systemes: Virtools (2016). http://www.3dvia.com/products/3dvia-virtools/
10. Eon Reality: Eon studio (2016). http://www.eonreality.com/eon-studio/
11. Fagerholt, E., Lorentzon, M.: Beyond the HUD. User interfaces for increased player immersion in FPS games. Ph.D. thesis, Chalmers University of Technology (2016)
12. Fagin, R.: Normal forms and relational database operators. In: Proceedings of the 1979 ACM SIGMOD International Conference on Management of Data, pp. 153–160. ACM (1979)

13. Gaggioli, A.: Using Virtual Reality in Experimental Psychology, vol. 2. IOS Press, Amsterdam (2016)
14. Grübel, J.: Assessing human interface device interaction in virtual environments. Bachelor thesis. ETH Zürich (2016). http://dx.doi.org/10.3929/ethz-a-010544699
15. Hackman, D.A., Betancourt, L.M., Brodsky, N.L., Hurt, H., Farah, M.J.: Neighborhood disadvantage and adolescent stress reactivity. Front. Hum. Neurosci. **6**, 277 (2012)
16. Hartig, T., Mitchell, R., De Vries, S., Frumkin, H.: Nature and health. Ann. Rev. Public Health **35**, 207–228 (2014)
17. Health Level Seven: HL7 Message Standard (2016). http://www.hl7.org/implement/standards/product_brief.cfm?product_id=146
18. Hegarty, M., Richardson, A.E., Montello, D.R., Lovelace, K., Subbiah, I.: Development of a self-report measure of environmental spatial ability. Intelligence **30**(5), 425–447 (2016)
19. HTC: HTC VIVE (2016). https://www.vive.com/
20. Kort, Y.A.W., Ijsselsteijn, W.A., Kooijman, J., Schuurmans, Y.: Virtual laboratories: comparability of real and virtual environments for environmental psychology. Presence Teleoperators Virtual Environ. **12**(4), 360–373 (2016)
21. Kraemer, D.J.M., Schinazi, V.R., Cawkwell, P.B., Tekriwal, A., Epstein, R.A., Thompson-Schill, S.L.: Verbalizing, visualizing, and navigating: the effect of strategies on encoding a large-scale virtual environment. J. Exp. Psychol. Learn. Mem. Cogn. **43**, 611–621 (2016). http://dx.doi.org/10.1037/xlm0000314
22. Kreylos, O.: Environment-independent VR development. In: Bebis, G., et al. (eds.) ISVC 2008. LNCS, vol. 5358, pp. 901–912. Springer, Heidelberg (2008). https://doi.org/10.1007/978-3-540-89639-5_86
23. Kuliga, S.F., Thrash, T., Dalton, R.C., Hölscher, C.: Virtual reality as an empirical research tool - exploring user experience in a real building and a corresponding virtual model. Comput. Environ. Urban Syst. **54**, 363–375 (2016)
24. Laha, B., Sensharma, K., Schiffbauer, J.D., Bowman, D.A.: Effects of immersion on visual analysis of volume data. IEEE Trans. Vis. Comput. Graph. **18**(4), 597–606 (2016)
25. Lloyd, J., Persaud, N.V., Powell, T.E.: Equivalence of real-world and virtual-reality route learning: a pilot study. Cyberpsychol. Behav. **12**(4), 423–427 (2016)
26. Loomis, J.M., Blascovich, J.J.: Immersive virtual environment technology as a basic research tool in psychology. Behav. Res. Methods Instrum. Comput. **31**(4), 557–564 (2016)
27. Maguire, E.A., Nannery, R., Spiers, H.J.: Navigation around London by a taxi driver with bilateral hippocampal lesions. Brain **129**(11), 2894–2907 (2006)
28. Marchette, S.A., Vass, L.K., Ryan, J., Epstein, R.A.: Anchoring the neural compass: coding of local spatial reference frames in human medial parietal lobe. Nature Neurosci. **17**(11), 1598–1606 (2016)
29. McCulloch, W.S., Pitts, W.: A logical calculus of the ideas immanent in nervous activity. Bull. Math. Biophys. **5**(4), 115–133 (2016)
30. Mealy, G.H.: A method for synthesizing sequential circuits. Bell Syst. Tech. J. **34**(5), 1045–1079 (2016)
31. Mechdyne: CAVELib (2016). http://www.mechdyne.com/software.aspx
32. Meehan, M., Brooks, F.P.: Physiological measures of presence in stressful virtual environments. ACM Trans. Graph. (ToG) **21**, 645–652 (2016)
33. Meehan, M., Razzaque, S., Insko, B., Whitton Jr., M., Brooks, F.P.: Review of four studies on the use of physiological reaction as a measure of presence in stressful virtual environments. Appl. Psychophysiol. Biofeedback **30**(3), 239–258 (2016)

34. Meijer, F., Geudeke, B.L.: Navigating through virtual environments: visual realism improves spatial cognition. CyberPsychol. Behav. **12**(5), 517–521 (2016)
35. MiddleVR: MiddleVR for unity (2016). http://www.middlevr.com/
36. Moore, E.F.: Gedanken-experiments on sequential machines. Automata Studies **34**, 129–153 (2016)
37. Oculus VR LLC: Oculus rift (2016). https://www.oculus.com/
38. Odgers, C.L., Caspi, A., Bates, C.J., Sampson, R.J., Moffitt, T.E.: Systematic social observation of children's neighborhoods using Google Street View: a reliable and cost-effective method. J. Child Psychol. Psychiatry **53**(10), 1009–1017 (2012)
39. Ooms, J., James, D., DebRoy, S., Wickham, H., Horner, J.: RMySQL: database interface and 'MySQL' driver for R (2016). https://cran.r-project.org/package=RMySQL
40. R Core Team: R: A language and environment for statistical computing. R Foundation for Statistical Computing, Vienna, Austria (2016). https://www.r-project.org/
41. R Special Interest Group on Databases (R-SIG-DB), Wickham, H., Müller, K.: DBI: R database interface (2016). https://cran.r-project.org/package=DBI
42. Razzaque, S., Kohn, Z., Whitton, M.C.: Redirected walking. In: Proceedings of EUROGRAPHICS. vol. 9, pp. 105–106 (2016)
43. Razzaque, S., Swapp, D., Slater, M., Whitton, M.C., Steed, A.: Redirected walking in place. In: ACM International Conference Proceeding Series, vol. 23, pp. 123–130 (2016)
44. Riecke, B.E., Bodenheimer, B., McNamara, T.P., Williams, B., Peng, P., Feuereissen, D.: Do we need to walk for effective virtual reality navigation? Physical rotations alone may suffice. In: Hölscher, C., Shipley, T.F., Olivetti Belardinelli, M., Bateman, J.A., Newcombe, N.S. (eds.) Spatial Cognition 2010. LNCS (LNAI), vol. 6222, pp. 234–247. Springer, Heidelberg (2010). https://doi.org/10.1007/978-3-642-14749-4_21
45. Riecke, B.E., Schulte-Pelkum, J.: An integrative approach to presence and self-motion perception research. In: Lombard, M., Biocca, F., Freeman, J., ljsselsteijn, W., Schaevitz, R.J. (eds.) Immersed in Media, pp. 187–235. Springer, Cham (2016). https://doi.org/10.1007/978-3-319-10190-3_9
46. Ruddle, R.A., Lessels, S.: For efficient navigational rich visual scene search, humans require full physical movement, but not a rich visual scene. Psychol. Sci. **17**(6), 460–465 (2016)
47. Sampson, R.J., Raudenbush, S.W.: Systematic social observation of public spaces: a new look at disorder in urban Neighborhoods 1. Am. J. Sociol. **105**(3), 603–651 (1999)
48. Schinazi, V.R., Nardi, D., Newcombe, N.S., Shipley, T.F., Epstein, R.A.: Hippocampal size predicts rapid learning of a cognitive map in humans. Hippocampus **23**(6), 515–528 (2016)
49. Schulze, J.P., Prudhomme, A., Weber, P., DeFanti, T.A.: CalVR: an advanced open source virtual reality software framework. In: IS&T/SPIE Electronic Imaging, vol. 8649, pp. 864902–864908 (2016). http://dx.doi.org/10.1117/12.2005241
50. SensoMotoric Instruments: SMI Eye-Tracking (2016). http://www.smivision.com/en/gaze-and-eye-tracking-systems/home.html
51. Sherman, W.R.: FreeVR (2016). http://www.freevr.org/
52. Slater, M., Khanna, P., Mortensen, J., Yu, I.: Visual realism enhances realistic response in an immersive virtual environment. IEEE Comput. Graph. Appl. **29**(3), 76–84 (2016)

53. Smith, N.G., Cutchin, S., Kooima, R., Ainsworth, R.A., Sandin, D.J., Schulze, J., Prudhomme, A., Kuester, F., Levy, T.E., DeFanti, T.A.: Cultural heritage omni-stereo panoramas for immersive cultural analytics - from the Nile to the Hijaz. In: 2013 8th International Symposium on Image and Signal Processing and Analysis (ISPA), pp. 552–557 (2013)
54. Spiers, H.J., Maguire, E.A.: Thoughts, behaviour, and brain dynamics during navigation in the real world. Neuroimage **31**(4), 1826–1840 (2006)
55. Sturz, B.R., Bodily, K.D., Katz, J.S.: Evidence against integration of spatial maps in humans. Anim. Cogn. **9**(207), 207–217 (2006)
56. Taube, J.S., Valerio, S., Yoder, R.M.: Is navigation in virtual reality with fMRI really navigation? J. Cogn. Neurosci. **25**(7), 1008–1019 (2016)
57. Taylor II, R.M., Hudson, T.C., Seeger, A., Weber, H., Juliano, J., Helser, A.T.: VRPN: a device-independent, network-transparent VR peripheral system. In: Proceedings of the ACM Symposium on Virtual Reality Software and Technology, vol. 900, pp. 55–61 (2016)
58. Unity Technologies: Unity3D (2016). http://unity3d.com/
59. Usoh, M., Arthur, K., Whitton, M.C., Bastos, R., Steed, A., Slater, M., Brooks, F.P.: Walking > walking-in-place > flying, in virtual environments. In: Proceedings of the 26th Annual Conference on Computer Graphics and Interactive Techniques, pp. 359–364 (2016)
60. Vanoni, D., Ge, L., Kuester, F.: Intuitive visualization of reflectance transformation imaging for interactive analysis of cultural artifacts. In: International Conference on Augmented and Virtual Reality, vol. 8853, pp. 397–404 (2016)
61. Vass, L.K., Copara, M.S., Seyal, M., Shahlaie, K., Farias, S.T., Shen, P.Y., Ekstrom, A.D.: Oscillations go the distance: low-frequency human hippocampal oscillations code spatial distance in the absence of sensory cues during teleportation. Neuron **89**(6), 1180–1186 (2016)
62. VIS Games: Country landscape (2016). http://www.vis-games.de/
63. Wallet, G., Sauzeon, H., Pala, P.A., Larrue, F., Zheng, X.: Virtual/real transfer of spatial knowledge: benefit from visual fidelity provided in a virtual. Cyberpsychol. Behav. Soc. Networking **14**(7), 417–423 (2016)
64. Weisberg, S.M., Schinazi, V.R., Newcombe, N.S., Shipley, T.F., Epstein, R.A.: Variations in cognitive maps: understanding individual differences in navigation. J. Exp. Psychol. Learn. Mem. Cogn. **40**(3), 669–682 (2016)
65. Wickham, H.: ggplot2: Elegant Graphics for Data Analysis. Springer, New York (2016). http://ggplot2.org
66. Wickham, H., Francois, R.: dplyr: A grammar of data manipulation (2016). https://cran.r-project.org/package=dplyr
67. WorldViz LLC: Vizard (2016). http://www.worldviz.com/
68. Zatun: City development (2016). http://zatun.com/

Multimodal Semantic Simulations of Linguistically Underspecified Motion Events

Nikhil Krishnaswamy$^{(\boxtimes)}$ and James Pustejovsky

Department of Computer Science, Brandeis University,
415 South Street, Waltham, MA 02453, USA
{nkrishna,jamesp}@brandeis.edu
http://www.voxicon.net/

Abstract. This paper details the technical functionality of VoxSim, a system for generating three-dimensional visual simulations of natural language motion expressions. We use a rich formal model of events and their participants to generate simulations that satisfy the minimal constraints entailed by an utterance and its minimal model, relying on real-world semantic knowledge of physical objects and motion events. This paper outlines technical considerations of such a system, and discusses the implementation of the aforementioned semantic models as well as VoxSim's suitability as a platform for examining linguistic and spatial reasoning questions.

Keywords: Spatial cognition · Spatial reasoning · Spatial language · Event semantics · Simulation semantics · Spatial information representation · Spatial information processing · Underspecification

1 Introduction

Spatial expressions in natural language rely on a wealth of world knowledge and contextual information about the properties of objects and events discussed in order to arrive at a complete interpretation of the utterance in question, making them difficult to translate into visuals. Linguistic predicates encode a certain level of knowledge that affords using them for spatial reasoning, but the level of spatial information varies for each predicate, such that many expressions leave certain parameters underspecified.

Existing work in visualization from natural language has largely focused on object placement in static scenes [7,9,43]. We have recently introduced a focus on motion verbs, using a rich formal model of events, and relying on philosophical and cognitive science approaches to linguistic interpretation, to integrate dynamic semantics into our system of event visualization, in simulations of the associated actions [37,38].

In philosophy, "mental simulation" theory attempts to model everyday human psychological competence [29], providing a *process* driven theory of mind

© Springer International Publishing AG 2017
T. Barkowsky et al. (Eds.): KogWis/Spatial Cognition 2016, LNAI 10523, pp. 177–197, 2017.
https://doi.org/10.1007/978-3-319-68189-4_11

[22]. In cognitive linguistics, "simulation" has come to mean a mental instantiation of a linguistic utterance, playing a functional role in language understanding [4,14], based on the notion of an agent's *embodiment*, as also discussed by Narayanan and others [33]. This provides a shared semiotic structure exploitable by both a computer (as a minimal model [6,19]) and a human (via sensory interpretation). Finally, both Qualitiative Spatial Reasoning (QSR) and gaming-style AI approaches have been used to develop simulators for training driven by interactive narratives [10,16], which makes procedural simulation from language expressions a natural candidate for fast-prototyping of new scenarios.

In a dynamic semantics approach, verbs are treated as programs or processes [27] and so although the computational linguistics and cognitive linguistics communities do not often reference each other, in our opinion there is fertile ground for cross-pollination, starting with the approach of Pustejovsky and Moszkowicz [40], and for implementing language-based reasoning in a QSR framework, leveraging temporal and spatial calculi such as the Allen Temporal Relations [2] and the Region Connection Calculus (RCC) [17,18,42].

We previously presented a method for visualizing natural language expressions in a 3D environment built on the Unity game engine [37]. The goal of that work was to evaluate, through visualization, the semantic presuppositions inherent in differing lexical choices. Thus, we assert that the amount and nature of spatial information encoded in a predicate can be revealed through simulation, of which visualization is just one modality of expression. We developed VoxML [38], a modeling language which encodes object and event semantic information into *voxemes* or "visual object concepts," structured and stored in a *voxicon* (the "lexicon" of voxemes). This approach enables procedural simulation generation from semantic knowledge of an event and its participants. Using a notion of action verbs as programs [34,40], our system, given an utterance and scene containing all referenced nominals as 3D objects, enacts the verbal program over them.

This method of abstracting and composing objects and programs allows us to take a semantically complex natural language predicate, such as "lean" or "switch," enacted over arbitrary objects within the system's vocabulary, and immediately generate a visualization if such a verbal program can be executed over the mentioned objects (Fig. 1).

The remainder of this article describes the technical functionality of this system, **VoxSim**, and its utility as a platform for experimentation in linguistic and context-based reasoning (Fig. 2).

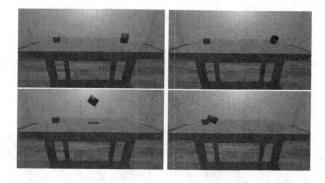

Fig. 1. Visualization of "lean the cup on the block"

Fig. 2. Visualization of "switch the blocks"

2   Architecture

VoxSim uses the Unity game engine [23] for graphics and I/O processing.[1] Input is a simple natural language sentence, which is part-of-speech tagged, dependency-parsed, and transformed into a simple predicate-logic format. These Natural Language Processing (NLP) tasks are currently handled by external applications networked to the simulator: we have interfaces for several parsers and resources, including the ClearNLP parser [8], SyntaxNet [3], and the TRIPS parser [15]. 3D assets and VoxML-modeled nominal objects and events (created with other Unity-based tools) are loaded externally, either locally or from a web server. Commands to the simulator may be input directly to the software UI, sent over a generic network connection, or selected within the **VoxSim Commander** application, a companion app for iOS. A diagram of the VoxSim architecture is shown in Fig. 3, and the front-end UI is shown in Fig. 4.

Objects from the library may be part of pre-built scenes made in the Unity Editor or may be placed in the scene by users at runtime using the "Add Object"

---

[1] The VoxSim Unity project and source may be found at https://github.com/VoxML/VoxSim/. The latest stable builds are posted at http://www.voxicon.net/.

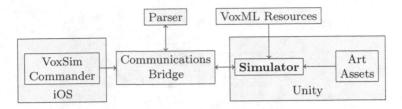

Fig. 3. VoxSim architecture schematic

Fig. 4. VoxSim UI with sample scene

menu. Users may enter input in the upper left or over network connection via VoxSim Commander. Output from VoxSim is printed in the upper right.

Given a tagged and dependency-parsed input sentence as shown in Fig. 5, we can transform it into predicate-logic format using the root of the parse as the VoxML PROGRAM, which accepts as many arguments as are specified in its type structure, and subsequently enqueuing any arguments that are either constants (i.e., instances of VoxML OBJECTs) or evaluate to constants at runtime (all other VoxML entity types, applied over OBJECTs). Other non-constant VoxML entity types are treated similarly to PROGRAMs, though they usually accept only one argument. Thus, the dependency arc CASE($plate, on$), for example, becomes $on(plate)$. The resulting predicate-logic formula is evaluated from the innermost first-order predicates outward until a single first-order representation is reached.

2.1 VoxML Overview

VoxML (Visual Object Concept Markup Language), is a modeling language for constructing 3D visualizations of natural language expressions [38]. It forms the scaffold used to link lexemes to their visual instantiations, or *voxemes*. There may be many-to-many correspondences between lexemes and their associated

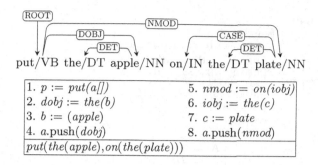

Fig. 5. Dependency parse for *Put the apple on the plate* and transformation to predicate-logic form.

voxemes. For example, the lexeme *plate* may be visualized as a square plate or a round plate, which would be different voxemes, and a single visual object may be referred to by multiple lexemes.

Each voxeme is linked to an object geometry (nouns are OBJECTs in VoxML), a dynamic logic program (verbs are VoxML PROGRAMs), an attribute set (VoxML ATTRIBUTEs), or a transformation algorithm (VoxML RELATIONs or FUNCTIONs). VoxML is used to specify the "episemantic" information beyond that which can be directly inferred from the linked geometry, Dynamic Intervsal Temporal Logic (DITL) program [40], or attribute properties.

An OBJECT voxeme's semantic structure provides *habitats*, or situational contexts or environments which condition the object's *affordances*, or attached behaviors describing what can be done to the object [36]. Habitats established by previous actions may activate or deactivate certain affordances, as when flipping a cup over prevents objects from going inside it.

3   Linguistic and Semantic Analysis

From tagged and parsed input text, all noun phrases are indexed to objects in the scene. A reference to *a ball* causes the simulator to attempt to locate a voxeme instance in the scene whose lexical predicate is "ball," while an occurrence of *a block* prompts an attempt to locate a voxeme with the lexical predicate "block".

Attributive adjectives impose a sortal scale on their heads [38], so *small block* and *big block* single out two separate blocks if they exist in the scene, and the VoxML-encoded semantics of "small" and "big" discriminates the blocks based on their relative size. *red block* vs. *green block* results in a distinction based on color, a nominal attribute, while *big red block* and *small red block* introduce scalar attribution, and can be used to disambiguate two distinct red blocks by iteratively evaluating each interior term of a formula such as *big(red(block))* until the reference can be resolved into a single object instance in the scene that has

$$\begin{bmatrix} \textbf{ball} \\ \text{LEX} = \begin{bmatrix} \text{PRED} = \textbf{ball} \\ \text{TYPE} = \textbf{physobj, artifact} \end{bmatrix} \\ \text{TYPE} = \begin{bmatrix} \text{HEAD} = \textbf{ellipsoid}[1] \\ \text{COMPONENTS} = \textbf{nil} \\ \text{CONCAVITY} = \textbf{convex} \\ \text{ROTATSYM} = \{X, Y, Z\} \\ \text{REFLECTSYM} = \{XY, XZ, YZ\} \end{bmatrix} \\ \text{HABITAT} = \begin{bmatrix} \text{INTR} = \dots \\ \text{EXTR} = \dots \end{bmatrix} \\ \text{AFFORD\_STR} = \begin{bmatrix} \text{A}_1 = H \rightarrow [grasp(x, [1])] hold(x, [1]) \\ \text{A}_2 = H \rightarrow [roll(x, [1])] \end{bmatrix} \\ \text{EMBODIMENT} = \begin{bmatrix} \text{SCALE} = \textbf{<agent} \\ \text{MOVABLE} = \textbf{true} \end{bmatrix} \end{bmatrix}$$

Fig. 6. *Ball* voxeme markup. VoxSim references voxemes by their lexical predicates.

all the signaled attributes[2]. The system may ask for clarification (e.g., *"Which block?"*) if the object reference is still ambiguous (Fig. 6).

We use a basic set of primitive programs to represent verbs, from which we build more complex programs. There have been many previous attempts to group verbs into distinct clusters, based on syntactic behavior [26], or to associate verbs with specific spatial semantic primitives [32]. Frameworks from the computer vision and AI communities include work on representing traffic configurations and behavior [20] and in human-robot communication [13, 44]. VoxML follows a similar model-theoretic approach, using an underlying semantics of a hybrid dynamic logic, Dynamic Interval Temporal Logic (DITL) [40]. Program content is then operationalized with the intent of decomposing the verbal and relational semantics while leaving object category labels intact, similar to approaches that seek to overcome descriptive constraints limited by robotic perception [31, 41].

In a 3D environment, any complex motion can be decomposed into series and compositions of translations and rotations, making those obvious verbal primitives in our visualization system. Other primitives include commonly-repeating subevents of other motions, such as "grasp," a fine-grained motion of the fingers that is difficult to decompose but appears as a subevent of nearly any human-object interaction. We can then assemble complex events out of primitive motions, as in "put" in Fig. 8, and then macro-complex events, such as "stack" as a sequence of "put" events.

3.1 Habitats and Affordances

We assume that every voxeme exists within an intrinsic "habitat" [30, 36], an encoding of the environment in which the object must exist simply to avoid violating any physical constraints, such as gravity, and conditions under which an object typically exists in the world.

---

[2] See [39] for details on discriminating and referencing objects through sortal and scalar descriptions.

An object's habitat introduces two parameters: it specifies how it is situated within a minimal embedding space (local embodiment); and by so doing this, it contextualizes the object, by making reference to the object's "affordances," i.e., the correlations between an agent who acts on an object and systematic or prototypical effects. For instance, a pencil at rest must be laying flat and not resting on its tip. While a table can be situated in almost any orientation, it has an intrinsic "top," its surface, as can be inferred from common utterances such as "the table is upside down". In a typical configuration, an object's inherent top will be aligned to the world's upward vector, so we denote this in VoxML with TOP $= top(+Y)$. Being able to identify this as a habitat allows VoxSim to then reason about what behaviors and resultant states are afforded by that object in that configuration.

A voxeme's semantic structure provides both "Gibsonian" and "telic" *affordances* [21, 35, 36], or attached behaviors, which the object either facilitates by its geometry (Gibsonian) [21], or purposes for which it is intended to be used (telic) [35]. For example, a Gibsonian affordance for a cup is "grasp," while a telic affordance is "drink from." Following from the convention that agents of a VoxML PROGRAM must be explicitly singled out in the associated implementation by belonging to certain entity classes (e.g., humans), affordances describe what *can be done to* the object, and not what actions it *itself* can perform. Thus an affordance is notated as HABITAT $\rightarrow$ [EVENT]RESULT, and an instance such as $H_{[2]} \rightarrow [put(x, on([1]))]support([1], x)$ can be paraphrased as "In habitat-2, an object x can be put on component-1, which results in component-1 supporting x." This procedural reasoning from habitats and affordances, executed in real time, allows VoxSim to infer the complete set of spatial relations between objects at each state and track changes in the shared context between human and computer. Thus, simulation becomes a way of tracing the consequences of linguistic spatial cues through a narrative.

3.2 Predicate-Argument Interaction

VoxML treats objects (NPs) and events (predicates) in terms of a dynamic event semantics, DITL [40]. The verbal semantics is based on a type system that encodes how a given formula ϕ and proposition π are executed/tested during the execution of a verbal program; programs can be a `state`, `process`, `transition`, `assignment`, or `test`, all of which are translated into DITL and operationalized differently.

This dynamic interpretation of events allows VoxSim's VoxML implementation to map linguistic expressions directly into simulations through an operational semantics that interprets predicates relative to their arguments' semantic encoding. Argument-sensitive distinctions in the operationalization of predicates themselves exploit the HEAD of the argument's type structure—a selected subset of geometric faces wholly or partially coterminous with the entire object geometry. This can be illustrated through the respective encodings for *on* and *in*. As shown in Fig. 7, both are configurational relations, but *on* requires the objects to be EC while *in* requires the figure object to be wholly or partially contained by the ground object. These relate directly to the affordances of an item. For instance, putting some object *on* a cup results in a support relation between the two, while putting an object *in* the cup results in a containment relation.

Additionally, the two relations specify different constraints. The spatial relation *on* requires the point of contact between the two objects to be located along the axis defined by a formula that will be found in the intrinsic habitat of the ground object and denoted with the notation *align*, subject to the full set of constraints that define that habitat. One such example would be the habitat constraints $\{align(Y, \mathcal{E}_Y), top(+Y)\}$ for a cup, where placing an object x $on(cup)$ requires contact between x and cup to be along the positive Y-axis (either of the cup or the world). Meanwhile, to put some object x on an object with an inherent orientation defined relative to a different surface, such as a wall with a facing surface or a TV with a screen, VoxSim exploits that object's habitat constraints $\{align(Y, \mathcal{E}_Y), front(+Z)\}$, and aligns x's Y-axis with the destination object's Y-axis, and x's front (if any defined), with the destination's front. However, the point of contact between the two objects in this situation is not concretely defined. The VoxML encoding leaves both faces along the +Y axis and faces along the ground object's +Z axis as viable candidates for contact points. That is, assuming regions respectively satisfying these mutually exclusive constraints are both unobstructed, an item such as a picture could be "on" a television or a wall in either configuration. Such an open question becomes a prime area for using simulation as an experimentation platform. This is discussed in Sect. 4.

Meanwhile, the spatial relation *in* enforces a constraint that requires a test against the current situational context before a value assignment can be made. An example is given in Fig. 9 of a knife in a cup. If the "placed object" is too large to fit inside the object it is to be placed in, VoxSim conducts a series of calculations to see if the object, when reoriented along any of its three orthogonal axes, will be situated in a configuration that allows it to fit inside the region bounded by the ground object's containing area. The containing area is situated relative to one of the ground object's orthogonal axes, and which axis and orientation this is is encoded in the ground object's VoxML type semantics. For example, a typical cup has some rotational symmetry around its Y-axis, as well as reflectional symmetry across its XY- and YZ-planes. These parameters compose with the cup's specification as a concave object to encode a concavity opening along the Y-axis, and the additional $top(+Y)$ habitat constraint further situates this opening along the object's *positive* Y-axis. Thus, as seen in Fig. 9, the knife must be reoriented so that its world-space bounding box aligning with the cup's Y-axis is smaller than the bounds of the cup's opening in that same configuration.

A typical wall with uniform surface topology affords no containment in either a Gibsonian or telic sense: however, something like a picture hanging on the wall may be interpreted as being contained by the bounds of the wall's surface, and this involves coercing the wall to its surface as a 2D region in order to satisfy one of the eight basic 2D relations in the Region Connection Calculus, whereas the wall voxeme taken as a whole is a 3D object. On the other hand, something

$$
\begin{bmatrix}
\textbf{on} \\
\text{LEX} = \begin{bmatrix} \text{PRED} = \textbf{on} \end{bmatrix} \\
\text{TYPE} = \begin{bmatrix}
\begin{array}{l} \text{CLASS} = \textbf{config} \\ \text{VALUE} = \textbf{EC} \end{array} \\
\text{ARGS} = \begin{bmatrix} \text{A}_1 = \textbf{x:3D} \\ \text{A}_2 = \textbf{y:3D} \end{bmatrix} \\
\text{CONSTR} = \textbf{y} {\rightarrow} \text{HABITAT} {\rightarrow} \\
\text{INTR}[align]
\end{bmatrix}
\end{bmatrix}
\qquad
\begin{bmatrix}
\textbf{in} \\
\text{LEX} = \begin{bmatrix} \text{PRED} = \textbf{in} \end{bmatrix} \\
\text{TYPE} = \begin{bmatrix}
\begin{array}{l} \text{CLASS} = \textbf{config} \\ \text{VALUE} = \textbf{PO} \parallel \textbf{TPP} \parallel \\ \qquad\quad \textbf{NTPP} \end{array} \\
\text{ARGS} = \begin{bmatrix} \text{A}_1 = \textbf{x:3D} \\ \text{A}_2 = \textbf{y:3D} \end{bmatrix} \\
\text{CONSTR} = \textbf{y} {\rightarrow} \text{HABITAT} {\rightarrow} \\
\text{INTR}[align]\textbf{?}
\end{bmatrix}
\end{bmatrix}
$$

Fig. 7. VoxML structures for "on" and "in," showing distinction in configurational value and constraints. The question mark in the typing of "in" denotes the test mentioned previously.

$$
\begin{bmatrix}
\textbf{put} \\
\text{LEX} = \begin{bmatrix} \text{PRED} = \textbf{put} \\ \text{TYPE} = \textbf{transition\_event} \end{bmatrix} \\
\text{TYPE} = \begin{bmatrix}
\text{HEAD} = \textbf{transition} \\
\text{ARGS} = \begin{bmatrix} \text{A}_1 = \textbf{agent} \\ \text{A}_2 = \textbf{obj1} \\ \text{A}_3 = \textbf{rel(obj2)} \end{bmatrix} \\
\text{BODY} = \begin{bmatrix} \text{E}_1 = grasp(A_1, A_2) \\ \text{E}_2 = [while(hold(A_1, A_2), move(A_2))] \\ \text{E}_3 = [at(A_2, A_3) \rightarrow ungrasp(A_1, A_2)] \end{bmatrix}
\end{bmatrix}
\end{bmatrix}
$$

Fig. 8. VoxML structure for "put"

interpenetrating the wall (perhaps by application of enough force), as in the left image of Fig. 10, would satisfy the *PO* configuration required by *in*.

In Fig. 8, "put" is given arguments `agent`, `obj1`, and `rel(obj2)`, where `rel` refers to the class of spatial functions including `on` and `in`. The typing of both "put" and "on" encode the calculation of such parameters as object trajectory and destination location (e.g., the position denoted by `on(block)` vs. `on(plate)` or `on(wall)`). As seen in BODY, object A_2 is moved to location A_3, calculated by operationalizing the specified relation over `obj2`. The results, depending on the arguments, may be configurations such as those shown in Figs. 9, 10 and 11.

In Figs. 9, 10 and 11 we can see the visualizations of the composition of these typing distinctions. The expression `on(wall)` selects for a vertical face of the object while in all other examples, `on` selects for the object's top. The location of "top" is computed based on the object's VoxML type structure. The top of a plate, a slightly concave object when situated in its default habitat, is located slightly lower on the Y-axis than the plate's highest overall point. The expression `in(cup)` selects the interior surface of the cup, an object with a telic affordance of containment, while `in(wall)` explicitly interpenetrates the wall, as "wall" lacks the containment telic role. The system attempts to maximally satisfy the constraints placed upon it by the NL expression. For instance, placing the knife object on(cup) lays the knife across the rim of the upright cup. In the same (horizontal) orientation, the knife cannot be placed at the location computed by in(cup), so the system must transform the knife so that the RCC representation of in(cup), $PO(knife, cup)$, can be satisfied without violating any of the physical or structural constraints of the cup or knife objects.

As events proceed, VoxSim maintains the current set of relations that exist between every pair of objects in the scene. The currently-implemented reasoning approach is built on top of RCC, particularly variants for relations in 3D space [1], but it can easily be extended to other QSR approaches, including the situation calculus [5], and the Intersection Calculus [25,28]. Where the spatial reasoning calculus may leave certain parameters underspecified, the object, relation, and event VoxML encodings allow additional parameters to inform VoxSim's reasoner in attempting to visualize a situation in accordance with the mental instantiation of the utterance provided, such as determining the angle of entry for an object into a cup, as in the example discussed in Sect. 3.2.

In some cases, even the combined force of spatial reasoning calculi and VoxML will not be enough to unambiguously supply all information missing from the linguistic utterance to create an adequate simulation: this is, of course, fertile ground for experimentation.

4   Underspecification

When constructing minimal models, it is common to leave certain parameters underspecified [19]. That is, it is permissible for a model to contain the proposition "the ball rolled" without providing information such as direction, speed, size of the ball, friction between the ball and the supporting surface, etc.; this information *can* be specified, but the model is still considered complete without it. On the other hand, when a ball rolls in the real world, these model-unspecified parameters all have values assigned to them, even if those values are not specifically measured. Likewise, a *simulation* of the same event requires that certain of these parameters be specified in order for the verbal program enacted over the arguments actually to be executed from frame to frame. Certain parameters, such as the precise location indicated by a relation over an object, can be calculated from the composition of the program and objects as discussed above

Fig. 9. "In the cup" vs. "on the cup"

Fig. 10. "In the wall" vs. "on the wall"

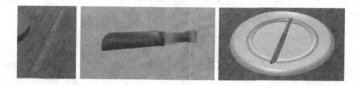

Fig. 11. "On the table" vs. "on the wall" vs. "on the plate"

in Sect. 3, while others are either not encoded in the semantics at all or the semantic composition leaves the value imprecise or ambiguous.

4.1 Current Results of Simulation Output

From the composition of VoxML and dynamic event semantics, we can achieve a model of an event that is "filled out" with information to an extent far greater than that provided by a minimal model. The kind of *forward composition* illustrated thus far can take a minimal model of an event and augment it with general-domain lexical world knowledge about the event predicate and its participants, which allows VoxSim to create a more extensive informational context than a minimal model provides, which it can then share with its human user. Visualization, an intuitively accessible modality for most humans, becomes a medium through which to share that context. From the minimal model, VoxSim's interpretation of encoded VoxML and dynamic semantic knowledge allows it to define the interpretation of the event predicate as a logic program with further specification than the logic program does in isolation, by drawing on and composing knowledge about the arguments, relations, and preconditions involved in the event. For example, in the simple utterance "roll the ball," we as language interpreters know that there must be a surface to roll the ball over, even though no such surface is mentioned in the utterance given. The VoxML type encoding for *roll* (Fig. 12) makes this explicit, representing the surface as A_3.

As mentioned above, in a minimal model, the nature of the surface (shape, consistency, etc.) can be left out completely. With forward composition and VoxML, VoxSim fills in some of these parameters by composing the event with the surface object. Object habitats and configurations therefore become *conditioning environments* that enforce constraints on the minimal model.

$$\begin{bmatrix} \textbf{roll} \\ \text{LEX} = ... \\ \\ \text{TYPE} = \begin{bmatrix} \text{HEAD} = \textbf{process} \\ \\ \text{ARGS} = \begin{bmatrix} A_1 = \textbf{x:agent} \\ A_2 = \textbf{y:physobj} \\ A_3 = \textbf{z:physobj} \end{bmatrix} \\ \\ \text{BODY} = ... \end{bmatrix} \end{bmatrix}$$

Fig. 12. Abbreviated VoxML type structure for "roll."

While the integration of context, spatially conditioning environments, and real-world knowledge may provide sufficient information to determine the *nature* of a spatial constraint or set of constraints, the precise *instantiated value*, down to the 3D coordinates and rotation of an object at each step of program execution, may still be left imprecise. For example, through forward composition, VoxSim may be able to determine the region within which an object must be placed to satisfy the completion of an event it is commanded to simulate, but the precise location within that region where the object should be by the end of the event is both left underspecified *and* there is no method from the lexical semantics to determine exactly what value that location should take. Nonetheless, in order for any platform such as VoxSim to execute the fully specified program at runtime, *all* required parameters must have a value assigned, including those that are potentially never mentioned in the linguistic utterance linked to the event and never raised in the additional encoding used by forward composition.

For instance, given a cup sitting upright (in the proper orientation), "put the lid on the cup" clearly describes an end state where the lid closes the cup's opening. However, if the cup is on its side, we find that, if the end location is chosen at random, such as by a Monte Carlo method, from possible configurations left available by the currently operating set of constraints and configurations, both a lid closing the opening of the cup, and one that is touching the cup on the positive Y-axis (i.e., explicitly "on top of" the cup independent of orientation) can be computed as satisfying the command "put the lid on the cup" (Fig. 13).

Fig. 13. Orientation-dependent visualizations of "put the lid on the cup"

Ambiguity of resultant configuration occurs even in default habitats. To say that something is "on the TV" can usually be interpreted specifically relative to the type of the object (e.g. using a type system such as Generative Lexicon [35]), where a physical object on the TV is *on top* of it while an image is on *the screen*, the TV's semantic head per VoxML.[3] However, in the case where the object on the TV is something, such as a sheet of paper, that could be placed on either surface, the ambiguity remains. When VoxSim must make a *simulation assignment* of values through random choice, either result may be generated as the end state of the event (as shown in Fig. 14), and a human is required to judge the appropriateness of either choice.

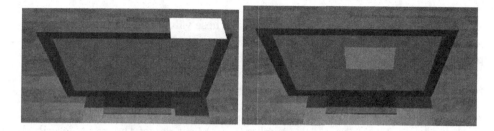

Fig. 14. Results from "put the paper on the TV"

Underspecification can thus arise in both post-conditions and in the action sequence of the event itself, such as when parameters like speed and direction of motion are left unknown. Additionally, depending on the motion predicate being simulated, the manner of motion itself may be left underspecified. "Move the cup to the center of the table" implies a path by the specification of the destination, but the manner by which the cup should be moved is not specified. Forward composition may narrow the search space—in this example, the table provides a surface to be moved over, which may make sliding or rolling (if the cup lacks a handle) preferable to other forms of motion—but ultimately the predicate itself contains unspecified parameters and so may be replaced in a simulation with another motion predicate that satisfies the same basic constraints and imposes others on top of them. Some examples are given below in Table 1, with *move* as the least specified motion predicate.

4.2   Experimentation and Early Results

Where a program's DITL formula says nothing about the nature of a parameter (e.g., it states that b_{n+1} is farther from b_0 than b_n is, but it does not state in which direction), we can use VoxSim to generate a set of visualizations of that event with randomly assigned values for the underspecified parameter, and have human judges evaluate the results of this Monte Carlo simulation generation to determine what, if any, "prototypical" values exist for that parameter.

---

[3] We ignore here the idiomatic non-spatial reading of *on TV*, denoting "the information content available through the medium 'TV'."

Table 1. Sample motion predicates and underspecified parameters

Program	Underspecified parameters
$put(y,z)$	Speed of motion
$slide(y)$	Speed, direction of translocation
$roll(y)$	Speed, direction of rotation
$turn(y)$	Speed, direction of rotation speed, direction of translocation
$move(y)$	Manner, speed, direction of motion

In order to better determine the nature of these values, we designed a series of experiments in which we asked human judges on the Amazon Mechanical Turk platform to make similarity judgements between a set of input sentences and simulations generated from them with randomly chosen values for parameters requiring value assignment.

1. From one input sentence, we generate three visualizations of the event and ask the judge to determine which visualization(s) best depict the event described by the input sentence. Multiple choices are allowed, and the judge may respond that none of the provided visualizations adequately depicts the event described.
2. From a single visualization of an event, we ask the judge to determine which of three sentences—one of which is the original input and two of which use different predicates in place of the original one—best describes the event depicted. Multiple choices are allowed, and the judge may respond that none of the provided sentences adequately describes the event depicted.

Table 2. Test set of verbal programs and objects

Programs		Objects	
move x	put x on y	block	grape
turn x	put x in y	ball	banana
roll x	lean x on y	plate	bowl
slide x	lean x against y	cup	knife
spin x	flip x on edge	disc	pencil
lift x	flip x at center	book	paper sheet
stack x	close x	blackboard	
put x near y	open x	bottle	
put x touching y		apple	

We captured a total of 3357 videos of individual events (3 each for 1119 input sentences generated from combining the objects and events in Table 2).

For each event generated, the underspecified parameters were logged to a SQL database to facilitate retrieval and evaluation. Videos were uploaded to Amazon Mechanical Turk to be evaluated by 8 workers for each individual task according to the guidelines listed above. We received a total of 8952 individual evaluations on the first task listed (8 evaluations per each of the 1119 input sentences), and a total of 26,856 individual evaluations on the second task (8 evaluations per each of 3357 videos). A full analysis of each predicate is currently in progress as of this writing, but we have completed evaluation on the input classes "put x near y" and "put x touching y."

"Touching" was randomly specified as one of the qualitative spatial relations "left," "right," "in front," "behind," or "on" with the addition of an RCC external connection (EC) constraint. Thus the acceptability judgment of the visualized event may be conditioned on the relation between the two objects at the end of the event, or on the motion of the moving object between configurations relative to the stationary object (Table 3).

Table 3. Results for visualizations of "put x touching y"

QSR	P(accept|QSR)
behind(y)	0.5474
in_front(y)	0.5816
left(y)	0.4995
right(y)	0.5560
on(y)	0.6683

Movement (M)	P(accept|M)	Movement (M)	P(accept|M)
behind→behind(y)	0.5347	left→behind(y)	0.5732
behind→in_front(y)	0.4758	left→in_front(y)	0.5853
behind→left(y)	0.5014	left→left(y)	0.5266
behind→right(y)	0.4888	left→right(y)	0.5211
behind→on(y)	0.7453	left→on(y)	0.6492
in_front→behind(y)	0.4523	right→behind(y)	0.5406
in_front→in_front(y)	0.6447	right→in_front(y)	0.5786
in_front→left(y)	0.4601	right→left(y)	0.4777
in_front→right(y)	0.5756	right→right(y)	0.5847
in_front→on(y)	0.6234	right→on(y)	0.7081

We observe a lower likelihood for visualizations to be judged acceptable when the moving object moves from behind the still object to in front of it, and vice versa. Visualizations where the moving object ends to the left of the still object are also less likely to be judged acceptable. This is a weaker correlation than the dispreference for behind-to-front/front-to-behind motion, but is still noticeable, falling about 1.16σ below the mean likelihood of acceptance. We also see a strong preference for the "on" specification of "touching." Like the apparent inclination against the left side, this seems to be independent of the moving object's starting location relative to the still object. These preferences may be factors of point of view or frame of reference, conjectures which will be the subject of further experimentation and evaluation.

Unlike "touching," specification for "near" must fall in a continuous range as it is difficult to define discrete relations that can further specify "near." The distribution of distances between the two objects at the end of the event was partitioned using quintiles (the interval from 0 to the first quintile being the least distance between the objects), which conditioned the acceptability judgement. QSR relations were also taken into account, but without the EC constraint implied by "touching."

Evaluators unsurprisingly preferred visualizations where the two objects ended up nearer relative to each other. In the first three distance intervals, we observe a slight preference for events where the moving object ends up behind the still object. This may be an effect of foreshortening caused by the point of view, as with some of the "touching" specifications. When conditioning on the joint distribution of the distance interval and the QSR relation, there is some apparent confusion in judgements of events in the fourth distance interval, where σ for the population of P(accept|QSR) is greater than .15, where in all other intervals σ for P(accept|QSR) falls between .019 and .051. This is possibly a factor of workers being unable to judge purely from the visuals whether an object that began its movement from a position in the fourth distance interval relative to the still object, actually ended the motion nearer than it began, whereas in preceding intervals, the resulting location was more likely to be unambiguously "near" regardless of starting location. These factors may be revealed by conditioning on starting location or distance (Table 4).

Evaluation for the remaining predicates is proceeding using similar qualitative and quantitative methods.

Table 4. Results for visualizations of "put x near y"

Interval	P(accept|QU)
First	0.7523
Second	0.6207
Third	0.3890
Fourth	0.3655
Fifth	0.1295

Interval	QSR	P(accept|QU,QSR)	Interval	QSR	P(accept|QU,QSR)
First	behind(y)	0.7730	Third	left(y)	0.3945
First	in_front(y)	0.7349	Third	right(y)	0.3825
First	left(y)	0.7338	Fourth	behind(y)	0.1713
First	right(y)	0.7712	Fourth	in_front(y)	0.4308
Second	behind(y)	0.6701	Fourth	left(y)	0.2093
Second	in(y)	0.5797	Fourth	right(y)	0.4699
Second	left(y)	0.6675	Fifth	behind(y)	0.0972
Second	right(y)	0.5819	Fifth	in_front(y)	0.1401
Third	behind(y)	0.4151	Fifth	left(y)	0.1250
Third	in_front(y)	0.3644	Fifth	right(y)	0.1348

4.3 Further Experimentation

While continuing to evaluate results of the above experiments, we are also augmenting them with with an automatic evaluation task intended to integrate VoxML and VoxSim with machine learning approaches.

o We are evaluating machine learning methods using the sparse feature vectors generated during the event capture process, training models to select the correct sentence originally used to generate the visualization in question from three candidates provided. As in the human evaluation tasks, it will be possible for the automatic evaluation to rate multiple sentences as equally correct, should the probabilities of multiple candidates come out equal in the model, or to rate none as correct, should no probability come out high enough. This evaluation is essentially a machine learning-based version of the evaluation done by humans in Task #2 discussed above and can be compared to those same results.

To date, we have established a baseline on this automatic evaluation task using a maximum entropy logistic regression classifier using generalized iterative scaling. Over a 10-fold cross-validation of the test set, the MaxEnt classifier achieves **48.50%** accuracy on selecting the correct event predicate alone, and **45.64%** when selecting the correct sentence in its entirety (Table 5).

Table 5. Accuracy tables for baseline automatic evaluation

Predicting predicate only			Predicting full sentence		
Total	Correct	Incorrect	Total	Correct	Incorrect
3357	1628	1729	3357	1532	1825
μ Accuracy	σ	σ^2	μ Accuracy	σ	o^2
48.50%	0.29066	0.08448	45.64%	0.02424	0.00059

The baseline results when selecting the predicate alone display a much higher variance than the results when selecting the entire sentence, pointing to the existence of some "confusing" features when judging the predicate by itself, or indicating some extra information provided by object features resulting in more consistent results across folds. Nevertheless, this baseline exhibits only 12–15% improvement over random chance in a three-way classification task and we expect more sophisticated machine learning methods will easily beat this baseline. We are exploring options available through Google's Tensor Flow framework, including the newly-released `tf-seq2seq` sequence-to-sequence model.

5 Discussion and Future Work

We have presented here a method for incorporating motion and dynamic spatial semantics into a visualization framework. We have shown the underlying processing pipeline from natural language input to minimal model to simulation to rendering, incorporating encodings of real-world semantic knowledge from DITL and VoxML to augment the minimal model. Resulting simulations show how composing knowledge of objects and events allows a computer system, VoxSim, to create visualizations that accord with human understanding of motion events, and we have presented some areas where the full level of compositional knowledge provided still leaves some ambiguity that prevents a single simulation from being generated until underspecified parameters are given values.

Following on this, we have outlined in Sect. 4.3 a further set of experiments to determine prototypical or "best" values for some of these commonly-occurring parameters. Preliminary results are presented above, and a full evaluation is forthcoming [24].

We are also developing methods for automatically composing complex behaviors from primitives, based on DITL, as well as building a corpus of linked simulations and event-annotated video in order to train algorithms to discriminate events based on their participants' motions [11,12].

Finally, we are planning on building links to lexical semantic resources such as VerbNet to allow us to leverage existing datasets for macro-program composition, and to expand the semantic processing to encompass event sequences, allowing us to generate single-input simulations of narratives beyond the sentence level.

VoxSim provides a method not only for generating 3D visualizations using an intuitive natural language interface instead of specialized skillsets (a primary goal of programs such as WordsEye [9]), but also a platform on which researchers may conduct experiments on the discrete observables of motion events while evaluating semantic theories, thus providing data to back up theoretical intuitions. We believe that visual simulation provides an intuitive way to trace the entailments that inhere in spatial expressions through a narrative, enabling a broader study of event and motion semantics.

Experiments such as those outlined above may be used by researchers to gather data on the semantic presuppositions humans hold regarding the prototypical realization of motion events, conditioned on variables like objects involved and point of view. Experiments of this kind can easily be segmented across population groups or across languages with the addition of appropriate vocabulary and NLP packages. We also believe that the automatic evaluation described can serve machine learning researchers in determining the salient features of motion events and object semantics from a computational and deep learning perspective, offering insight into the differences between human and artificial spatial cognition. A full description of those results will be forthcoming shortly.

Acknowledgements. We would like to thank the reviewers for their perceptive and helpful comments. This work is supported by a contract with the US Defense Advanced Research Projects Agency (DARPA), Contract W911NF-15-C-0238. Approved for Public Release, Distribution Unlimited. The views expressed are those of the authors and do not reflect the official policy or position of the Department of Defense or the U.S. Government. We would like to thank Scott Friedman, David McDonald, Marc Verhagen, and Mark Burstein for their discussion and input on this topic. All errors and mistakes are, of course, the responsibilities of the authors.

References

1. Albath, J., Leopold, J.L., Sabharwal, C.L., Maglia, A.M.: RCC-3D: qualitative spatial reasoning in 3D. In: CAINE, pp. 74–79 (2010)
2. Allen, J.: Towards a general theory of action and time. Artif. Intell. **23**, 123–154 (1984)
3. Andor, D., Alberti, C., Weiss, D., Severyn, A., Presta, A., Ganchev, K., Petrov, S., Collins, M.: Globally normalized transition-based neural networks. arXiv preprint arXiv:1603.06042 (2016)
4. Bergen, B.K.: Louder Than Words: The New Science of How the Mind Makes Meaning. Basic Books, New York (2012)
5. Bhatt, M., Loke, S.: Modelling dynamic spatial systems in the situation calculus. Spat. Cogn. Comput. **8**, 86–130 (2008)
6. Blackburn, P., Bos, J.: Computational semantics. THEORIA. Int. J. Theory Hist. Found. Sci. **18**(1) (2008)
7. Chang, A., Monroe, W., Savva, M., Potts, C., Manning, C.D.: Text to 3D scene generation with rich lexical grounding. arXiv preprint arXiv:1505.06289 (2015)
8. Choi, J.D., McCallum, A.: Transition-based dependency parsing with selectional branching. In: ACL (1), pp. 1052–1062 (2013)
9. Coyne, B., Sproat, R.: Wordseye: an automatic text-to-scene conversion system. In: Proceedings of the 28th Annual Conference on Computer Graphics and Interactive Techniques, pp. 487–496. ACM (2001)
10. Dill, K.: A game AI approach to autonomous control of virtual characters. In: Interservice/Industry Training, Simulation, and Education Conference (I/ITSEC) (2011)
11. Do, T., Krishnaswamy, N., Pustejovsky, J.: ECAT: event capture annotation tool. In: Proceedings of ISA-12: International Workshop on Semantic Annotation (2016)
12. Do, T., Pustejovsky, J.: Fine-grained event learning of human-object interaction with LSTM-CRF. In: Proceedings of European Symposium on Artificial Neural (ESANN 2017) (2017)
13. Dzifcak, J., Scheutz, M., Baral, C., Schermerhorn, P.: What to do and how to do it: translating natural language directives into temporal and dynamic logic representation for goal management and action execution. In: IEEE International Conference on Robotics and Automation, ICRA 2009, pp. 4163–4168. IEEE (2009)
14. Feldman, J.: From Molecule to Metaphor: A Neural Theory of Language. MIT Press, Cambridge (2006)
15. Ferguson, G., Allen, J.F., et al.: Trips: an integrated intelligent problem-solving assistant. In: AAAI/IAAI, pp. 567–572 (1998)
16. Forbus, K.D., Mahoney, J.V., Dill, K.: How qualitative spatial reasoning can improve strategy game AIs. IEEE Intell. Syst. **17**(4), 25–30 (2002)
17. Galton, A.: Towards an integrated logic of space, time, and motion. In: Bajcsy, R. (ed.) Proceedings of the Thirteenth International Joint Conference on Artificial Intelligence (IJCAI 1993), pp. 1550–1555. Morgan Kaufmann, San Mateo (1993)
18. Galton, A.: Qualitative Spatial Change. Oxford University Press, Oxford (2000)
19. Gelfond, M., Lifschitz, V.: The stable model semantics for logic programming. In: ICLP/SLP, vol. 88, pp. 1070–1080 (1988)
20. Gerber, R., Nagel, H.H.: Representation of occurrences for road vehicle traffic. Artif. Intell. **172**(4), 351–391 (2008)
21. Gibson, J.J., Reed, E.S., Jones, R.: Reasons for Realism: Selected Essays of James J. Gibson. Lawrence Erlbaum Associates, Hillsdale (1982)

22. Goldman, A.I.: Simulating Minds: The Philosophy, Psychology, and Neuroscience of Mindreading. Oxford University Press, Oxford (2006)
23. Goldstone, W.: Unity Game Development Essentials. Packt Publishing Ltd., Birmingham (2009)
24. Krishnaswamy, N.: Monte-Carlo Simulation Generation Through Operationalization of Spatial Primitives. Ph.D. thesis, Brandeis University (2017)
25. Kurata, Y., Egenhofer, M.: The 9+ intersection for topological relations between a directed line segment and a region. In: Gottfried, B. (ed.) Workshop on Behaviour and Monitoring Interpretation, Germany, pp. 62–76, September 2007
26. Levin, B.: English Verb Class and Alternations: A Preliminary Investigation. University of Chicago Press, Chicago (1993)
27. Mani, I., Pustejovsky, J.: Interpreting Motion: Grounded Representations for Spatial Language. Oxford University Press, Oxford (2012)
28. Mark, D., Egenhofer, M.: Topology of prototypical spatial relations between lines and regions in English and Spanish. In: Proceedings of the Twelfth International Symposium on Computer-Assisted Cartography, vol. 4, pp. 245–254 (1995)
29. Markman, K.D., Klein, W.M., Suhr, J.A.: Handbook of Imagination and Mental Simulation. Psychology, New York (2012)
30. McDonald, D., Pustejovsky, J.: On the representation of inferences and their lexicalization. In: Advances in Cognitive Systems, vol. 3 (2014)
31. Moratz, R., Fischer, K., Tenbrink, T.: Cognitive modeling of spatial reference for human-robot interaction. Int. J. Artif. Intell. Tools **10**(04), 589–611 (2001)
32. Muller, P.: A qualitative theory of motion based on spatio-temporal primitives. In: Cohn, A.G., Schubert, L., Shapiro, S.C. (eds.) KR 1998: Principles of Knowledge Representation and Reasoning, pp. 131–141. Morgan Kaufmann, San Francisco (1998)
33. Narayanan, S.S.: KARMA: Knowledge-Based Active Representations for Metaphor and Aspect. University of California, Berkeley (1997)
34. Naumann, R.: A dynamic approach to aspect: verbs as programs. Submitted to J. Semant. (1999). University of Düsseldorf
35. Pustejovsky, J.: The Generative Lexicon. MIT Press, Cambridge (1995)
36. Pustejovsky, J.: Dynamic event structure and habitat theory. In: Proceedings of the 6th International Conference on Generative Approaches to the Lexicon (GL 2013), pp. 1–10. ACL (2013)
37. Pustejovsky, J., Krishnaswamy, N.: Generating simulations of motion events from verbal descriptions. In: Lexical and Computational Semantics (*SEM 2014), p. 99 (2014)
38. Pustejovsky, J., Krishnaswamy, N.: VoxML: a visualization modeling language. In: Chair, N.C.C., Choukri, K., Declerck, T., Goggi, S., Grobelnik, M., Maegaard, B., Mariani, J., Mazo, H., Moreno, A., Odijk, J., Piperidis, S. (eds.) Proceedings of the Tenth International Conference on Language Resources and Evaluation (LREC 2016). European Language Resources Association (ELRA), Paris, May 2016
39. Pustejovsky, J., Krishnaswamy, N.: Envisioning language: The semantics of multimodal simulations (forthcoming)
40. Pustejovsky, J., Moszkowicz, J.: The qualitative spatial dynamics of motion. J. Spat. Cogn. Comput. **11**, 15–44 (2011)
41. Raman, V., Lignos, C., Finucane, C., Lee, K.C., Marcus, M.P., Kress-Gazit, H.: Sorry dave, i'm afraid i can't do that: Explaining unachievable robot tasks using natural language. In: Robotics: Science and Systems, vol. 2, pp. 2–1. IEEE (2013)

42. Randell, D., Cui, Z., Cohn, A.: A spatial logic based on regions and connections. In: Kaufmann, M. (ed.) Proceedings of the 3rd International Conference on Knowledge Representation and Reasoning, San Mateo, pp. 165–176 (1992)
43. Siskind, J.M.: Grounding the lexical semantics of verbs in visual perception using force dynamics and event logic. J. Artif. Intell. Res. (JAIR) **15**, 31–90 (2001)
44. Skubic, M., Perzanowski, D., Blisard, S., Schultz, A., Adams, W., Bugajska, M., Brock, D.: Spatial language for human-robot dialogs. IEEE Trans. Syst. Man Cybern. Part C: Appl. Rev. **34**(2), 154–167 (2004)

Author Index

Printed in the United States
By Bookmasters